The Politics of Attention and the Promise of Mindfulness

NEW HEIDEGGER RESEARCH

Series Editors:

Gregory Fried, Professor of Philosophy, Boston College

Richard Polt, Professor of Philosophy, Xavier University

The New Heidegger Research series promotes informed and critical dialogue that breaks new philosophical ground by taking into account the full range of Heidegger's thought, as well as the enduring questions raised by his work.

Titles in the Series

The Politics of Attention and the Promise of Mindfulness

Lawrence Berger

ROWMAN & LITTLEFIELD
Lanham • Boulder • New York • London

Published by Rowman & Littlefield
An imprint of The Rowman & Littlefield Publishing Group, Inc.
4501 Forbes Boulevard, Suite 200, Lanham, Maryland 20706
www.rowman.com

86-90 Paul Street, London EC2A 4NE

British Library Cataloguing in Publication Information Available

Library of Congress Cataloging-in-Publication Data

Names: Berger, Lawrence A., author.
  Title: The politics of attention and the promise of mindfulness / Lawrence
    Berger.
  Description: Lanham : Rowman & Littlefield, [2023] | Series: New Heidegger
    research | Includes bibliographical references and index.
  Identifiers: LCCN 2023023225 (print) | LCCN 2023023226 (ebook) | ISBN
    9781538177259 (cloth) | ISBN 9781538177266 (ebook)
  Subjects: LCSH: Attention. | Self (Philosophy) | Philosophy of mind. |
    Heidegger, Martin, 1889-1976.
  Classification: LCC BF321 .B47 2023 (print) | LCC BF321 (ebook) | DDC
    153.7/33--dc23/eng/20230707
  LC record available at https://lccn.loc.gov/2023023225
  LC ebook record available at https://lccn.loc.gov/2023023226

Contents

Preface

Although attention is a subject of interest in both philosophy and political science, there is need of a full-length study of its nature and role in the constitution of political realities. I intend to provide a rigorous analysis of the question, but fundamentally I argue that attention is something quite simple. It is human presence, or how we are presently engaged in the course of everyday activity. It brings with it whatever resources we have to bear on the current situation, which is how we are made manifest in relation to other individuals and the world at large. Despite its simplicity, however, traditional philosophical approaches cannot accommodate it because it is impervious to objectification. It is rather a holistic phenomenon that operates within a hermeneutical circle of attention, language, and bodily understanding, as I demonstrate in this book.

Attention is important in politics because it orients and shapes us in the course of worldly engagement. It is evident that its deployment is crucial in political outcomes, as was seen, for instance, in Donald Trump's domination of the media during the 2016 US presidential campaign. In fact, it has been argued that the Trump presidency came about due to realities that were produced by the media themselves, which depended in turn on the engagement of public attention. In particular, the instability and capriciousness associated with the movement of attention has important implications for the stability of the realities that are so produced. It is crucial that we understand its nature and how it can be gathered to promote the public good, as in, for instance, dealing with our present planetary emergency.

Attention is how we are made manifest, and under mutual attention it is how we do so in relation to one another. It also has the potential to unify us if we take responsibility for its movement. This means that the extent to which we are ontologically bonded is not determinate, but rather depends on the state of attention, or the extent of mindfulness that accompanies such engagement. In particular, the quality of discourse and action that issues from public spaces depends upon its state. Since worlds are literally built by way of action in these spheres, the implication is that the stability of the worlds in which we dwell, the extent to which activity is oriented to the common good, and the extent of human flourishing that is thereby enabled, all depend at least in part on the state of attention.

I draw on the thinking of Martin Heidegger in putting forward many of the claims in this book, but I limit most discussion of the specifics of his work to the final chapter to be more accessible to the general reader. However, any work on politics that involves Heidegger must at least mention his disastrous foray into Nazi politics. There is a vast literature on this subject, but my position is that Heidegger is not a political philosopher. He says as much in correspondence with Hannah Arendt, where he says that she is interested in political thought and he is not. He certainly has political opinions, and his illiberal orientation is consistent with many themes in his work, but Arendt also draws heavily on his thought and is much more inclined to liberal thinking. I have turned to Heidegger because I believe his philosophy provides a framework that enables us to better situate the phenomenon of attention and to comprehend its importance for politics. It offers an extraordinary vision of the place of the human being in the cosmos, which calls for the practice of acute and steadfast attentiveness, thus providing a standpoint that transcends traditional political oppositions.

Abbreviations

The following abbreviations for texts by Heidegger are used in this volume. When both a German text and a translation are cited, the German pagination is followed by a slash and the English pagination. When no translation is cited, any translation is the author's own. The abbreviation "tm" indicates that a translation has been modified, and "em" indicates that emphasis has been modified.

BEING AND TIME

SZ = *Sein und Zeit*. Tübingen: Niemeyer, 1953. Later editions share the same pagination, which is also provided in the English translations and in the *Gesamtausgabe* edition. The first edition was published in 1927. Trans. John Macquarrie and Edward Robinson. New York: Harper and Row, 1962.

GA = *GESAMTAUSGABE*

All volumes of Heidegger's *Gesamtausgabe* are published in Frankfurt am Main by Vittorio Klostermann. The date of publication, or dates if there is more than one edition, are followed by the date of original composition in parentheses. A translation is listed when available.

GA 5 = *Holzwege*. Ed. Friedrich-Wilhelm von Hermann. 1977 (1935–1946). *Off the Beaten Track*. Trans. Julian Young and Kenneth Haynes. Cambridge: Cambridge University Press, 2002.

GA 7 = *Vorträge und Aufsätze*. Ed. Friedrich-Wilhelm von Herrmann. 2000 (1936–1953).

GA 8 = *Was Heißt Denken?* Ed. Paola-Ludovika Coriando. 2002 (1951–
1952). *What Is Called Thinking?* Trans. J. Glenn Gray. New York:
Harper and Row, 1968.

GA 9 = *Wegmarken.* Ed. Friedrich-Wilhelm von Herrmann. 1976, 1996,
2004 (1919–1961). *Pathmarks.* Ed. William McNeill. Cambridge:
Cambridge University Press, 1998.

GA 11 = *Identität und Differenz.* Ed. Friedrich-Wilhelm von Herrmann.
2006 (1955–1963).

GA 14 = *Zur Sache des Denkens.* Ed. Friedrich-Wilhelm von Herrmann.
2007 (1927–1968). Partial translation: *On Time and Being.* Trans. Joan
Stambaugh. New York: Harper and Row, 1972.

GA 29/30 = *Die Grundbegriffe der Metaphysik. Welt—Endlichkeit—
Einsamkeit.* Ed. Friedrich-Wilhelm von Herrmann. 1983, 2004 (1929–
1930). *The Fundamental Concepts of Metaphysics: World, Finitude,
Solitude.* Trans. William McNeill and Nicholas Walker. Bloomington:
Indiana University Press, 1995.

GA 33 = *Aristoteles, Metaphysik Θ 1–3. Vom Wesen und Wirklichkeit der
Kraft.* Ed. Heinrich Hüni. 1981 (1931). *Aristotle's Metaphysics Θ 1–3:
On the Essence and Actuality of Force.* Trans. Walter Brogan and Peter
Warnek. Bloomington: Indiana University Press, 1995.

GA 40 = *Einführung in die Metaphysik.* Ed. Petra Jaeger. 1983 (1935).
Introduction to Metaphysics. Trans. Gregory Fried and Richard Polt.
Revised and expanded ed. New Haven, CT: Yale University Press, 2014.

GA 51: *Grundbegriffe.* Ed. Petra Jaeger, 1981. *Basic Concepts.* Trans. Gary
Aylesworth. Bloomington: Indiana University Press, 1993.

GA 65 = *Beiträge zur Philosophie (Vom Ereignis).* Ed. Friedrich-Wilhelm
von Herrmann. 1989, 1994, 2003 (1936–1938). *Contributions to
Philosophy (Of the Event).* Trans. Richard Rojcewicz and Daniela
Vallega-Neu. Bloomington: Indiana University Press, 2012.

GA 71 = *Das Ereignis.* Ed. Friedrich-Wilhelm von Herrmann. 2009 (1941–
1942). *The Event.* Trans. Richard Rojcewicz. Bloomington: Indiana
University Press, 2013.

GA 77 = *Feldweg-Gespräche.* Ed. Ingrid Schüßler, 1995, 2007 (1944–
1945). *Country Path Conversations.* Trans. Bret Davis. Bloomington:
Indiana University Press, 2010.

GA 79 = *Bremer und Freiburger Vorträge.* Ed. Petra Jaeger, 1994, 2005
(1949, 1957). *Bremen and Freiburg Lectures: Insight into That Which Is
and Basic Principles of Thinking.* Trans. Andrew Mitchell. Bloomington:
Indiana University Press, 2012.

GA 85 = *Vom Wesen der Sprache.* Ed. Ingrid Schüßler, 1999. *On the
Essence of Language.* Trans. Wanda Torres Gregory and Yvonne Unna.
Albany: State University of New York Press, 2004.

OTHER EDITIONS

EGT = *Early Greek Thinking*. Trans. David F. Krell and Frank A. Capuzzi. New York: Harper and Row, 1975.

ID = *Identity and Difference*. Trans. Joan Stambaugh. Chicago: University of Chicago Press, 1969.

PLT = *Poetry, Language, Thought*. Trans. Albert Hofstadter. New York: Harper and Row, 1971.

PM = *Pathmarks*. Ed. William McNeill. Cambridge: Cambridge University Press, 1998.

TB = *On Time and Being*. Trans. Joan Stambaugh. New York: Harper and Row, 1972.

WCT = *What Is Called Thinking?* Trans. J. Glenn Gray. New York: Harper and Row, 1968.

WP = *What Is Philosophy?* Trans. Jean T. Wilde and William Kluback. New Haven, CT: College and University Press, 1958.

Acknowledgments

This work had a long gestation, and many people helped along the way. In particular, I am grateful to Eugene Gendlin (†), Aaron Wildavsky (†), Deirdre McCloskey, David Klemm, Robert Shiller, and Herbert Simon (†) for the encouragement they provided early on.

I am grateful to have had the opportunity to study at the New School. Dmitri Nikulin was supportive of my thesis from day one, providing masterful guidance all along the way. Richard Bernstein (†) was the reason I came to the New School. We met at the University of Iowa, and his living exemplification of the spirit of humanism has been an ideal for me to live up to. I also owe much to James Dodd, Alice Crary, Zed Adams, Jay Bernstein, Simon Critchley, Bernard Flynn, and Dirk Setton for encouraging this work.

I wish to thank the Heidegger Circle, membership in which has been invaluable. I thank David Kleinberg-Levin, Richard Capobianco, and Thomas Sheehan for many helpful discussions. Michael Zimmerman, Lawrence Hatab, and Daniel Dahlstrom have also been most supportive and helpful, and thanks to Ed Berube for many friendly lunches and discussions. Of course, I owe much to the editors of this book series, Richard Polt and Gregory Fried, who have provided most valuable support and feedback.

I am particularly grateful to Robert Brugger for many years of guidance in and discussion of Focusing. And I owe the most to my wife, Teddi, for being my reader, muse, and life partner for thirty years of the journey.

Thanks also to Indiana University Press and Vittorio Klostermann GmbH for permission to cite from GA 33, *Aristoteles, Metaphysik Θ 1–3. Vom Wesen und Wirklichkeit der Kraft*, translated as *Aristotle's Metaphysics Θ 1–3: On the Essence and Actuality of Force*.

†: Deceased.

Introduction

Everyone knows what attention is (James [1890] 1983, 381)—and I would add that everyone knows it is important in politics, for it is central to who and what we are as human beings, both as individuals and in collectives. I take this to be the case literally, that as human presence, attention lies at the center of our relations to the people, things, and events of this world. This is not to say that we are harmoniously unified by way of that centering; that is hardly the case, as a cursory look at our political situation will show. But the extent to which we have any presence at all, the extent to which we are made manifest as encounterable by self and others, depends on attention. It may be the case that one is distracted and dispersed, which will be evident to others if they are present, but at any moment there is typically some central manner in which one is engaged, perhaps in what one is thinking or worrying about. That, I argue, is the presence of attention, and it is how we come across to people depending on how they relate to us in turn. It is a precious thing, especially in political affairs, because it is essential for the formation of any bonds that may hold between us.

James says that we know what attention is, but cognitive science finds it to be anything but a simple matter due in part to an implicit commitment to physicalism. An example is Chun, Golomb, and Turk-Browne (2011), who say that "attention has become a catch-all term for how the brain controls its own information processing" (74) and discuss the consensus finding that it is not a unitary phenomenon. The following is illustrative of the metaphysical assumptions that are operative in this literature:

> Attention is not unitary. Rather, attention should be considered as a property of multiple, different perceptual and cognitive operations. Hence, to the extent that these mechanisms are specialized and decentralized, attention mirrors this organization. These mechanisms are in extensive communication with each other, and executive control processes help set priorities for the system overall.

However, such priority setting is still independent of the actual nuts and bolts of selection and modulation within the multiple mechanisms. (76)

Thus, on the scientific view, attention is a feature of multiple mechanisms that communicate with one another and where a central mechanism coordinates activities among the processes. But the reliance on a metaphysics of mechanisms (metaphorical or not) is problematic for this approach, because a machine, by definition, proceeds with minimal human intervention. If the executive decision maker is a mechanism itself, it would appear that the essence of the human being has been reduced to a mechanical process. These processes support the presence of the self in the course of worldly activity, but we are certainly not reducible to them, or so I argue.

It is difficult to reconcile the primacy of the mechanical with attention when the latter is conceived as human presence, as it is here. Thinking in terms of mechanisms may be useful for sub-personal processes that work in the background, but attention itself is the very foreground in which we find ourselves, how we are presently engaged in any manner whatsoever. There are many ways in which we can be so engaged, which can be described as speaking, touching, reading, walking, staring, moving, reflecting, etc., where in each case we are made manifest in a particular manner depending on who we are and how we understand the situation at hand. Moreover, in the course of any of these activities we can be more or less gathered or collected. If we are scattered, dispersed, or distracted, that is how we are as a whole, how we come into presence, and likewise if we are gathered and focused. I argue that this understanding of the nature of attention is incongruous with reduction to a mechanical system.

James's view is that we know what attention is in a pragmatic sense, in that, for instance, when someone asks for our attention we know what to do. We can sense whether or not others are paying attention to us, and we know our performance will suffer if we don't attend to the task at hand. We also know that we are capable of gathering our attention and therefore ourselves, for we can "gather ourselves together" (James [1890] 1983, 382) and focus on matters of essential import when the situation calls for it. That is, in stark contrast to the view from cognitive science, *attention is a unifying phenomenon*, as I argue over the course of this book.[1] This understanding of ourselves cannot be dismissed as illusory or epiphenomenal, for it is the essential ground for engaged activity of any type. But it is not a fixed ground; rather, it presents itself in the form of potential ways of being in the world.

There are two interrelated dimensions of attention:

- *The emergence of entities*: Attention is typically studied from the point of view of selection, which I argue is an aspect of the more general orienting and centering in relation to the presence of worldly entities, as we come into presence at the same time. It is the manifestation of the self, which is where we speak from or how we show ourselves in the course of worldly engagement. It is the center from which action arises, and the public space is where we are centered as a community, where we are made manifest as a people.
- *Effort of attention*: Efforts of concentration or vigilance are also associated with the phenomenon, but I focus on the possibility that such effort can go above and beyond the ordinary, which enables one to be more gathered and open in relation to the presence of worldly entities. This will be considered below as *active attention*, in contrast to the *passive attention* that typically holds. In the latter case we can be gathered by affect, for instance, but this is not active attention in the sense put forward here. Active attention (closely related to mindfulness) is characterized by an acute and sustained attentiveness that enables explicit self-awareness, integration, and more profound relations with others.[2]

Attention is how we collect ourselves, both as individuals and collectives. We can gather ourselves for the sake of openness, in particular for openness to others, which is essential to our humanity. Moreover, we know what attention is because it is where we are centered, how we come into presence as engaged in the everyday. This is why James says that everyone knows what it is, for it is the essence of the first-person perspective, which cannot be understood assuming a world that can be apprehended only by way of distanced observation and theoretics. Indeed, cognitive science finds attention to be mysterious because it is itself the basis for any such objectivating activity.[3]

KEY CLAIMS

Two central claims are put forward over the course of this book: (1) attention is human presence, or how we are made manifest in the course of engagement, and (2) it moves according to a hermeneutical circle of attention, language, and bodily understanding. These claims owe much to the thought of Martin Heidegger, as I show in chapter 9, which can be seen in brief as follows:

1. Attention can be understood as human being, or human presencing. Heidegger's notion of the ecstatic nature of human existence is put here in terms of attention as an extended presence (see chapter 1).
2. Since presencing is also a speaking for the later Heidegger, the relation between attention/being and language is crucial for the hermeneutical

circle I put forward in terms of attention, language, and understanding. This triad appears in the discussion around the circle in *Being and Time* (SZ), with understanding and the hermeneutical circle put forward in §32, and discourse and hearing in §34.[4]

Attention as Human Presence

Attention is how the self is made manifest in the course of worldly activity, how embodied resources and sensibilities (e.g., thought, feeling, emotion, skills, energies) are brought to bear in various modes of engagement. Rather than being ensconced in a private mental realm, attention is our extended presence in relation to people and things as they are made manifest in relation to us, and it is thus the basis for the intersubjective bonds that lie at the heart of political realities. It is centrally important in human existence because it is literally how and where we are centered, where embodied resources and sensibilities are brought to bear in the course of everyday engagement.[5] I refer to embodied resources instead of the more commonly employed cognitive or processing resources because attention, as a holistic phenomenon, commands all the resources that make up the human being. Thinking in terms of cognition is consistent with the detached view of mind in which humans are cast as "knowers" rather than incorporating other dimensions such as the affective and somatic (e.g., Lerman, Rudich, and Shahar 2010; Kupper, Widdershoven, and Pedersen 2012). Attention brings the potential of integrating the human being as a whole, which can lead to transformed ways of being in the world. This is the claim to be pursued here.

Attention as my presence means that I cannot be there without it; if it is elsewhere, so am I. This theme appears in Heidegger's *Fundamental Concepts of Metaphysics* (GA 29/30: 95/63): "How often it happens, in a conversation among a group of people, that we are 'not there,' how often we find that we were *absent*, albeit without having fallen asleep. . . . In such being absent we are precisely concerned with ourselves, or with something else. Yet this not-being-there is a *being-away*" (29/30: 95/63). Thus although we are not "there," our attention is still engaged in some manner, in that we are oriented to entities that are not associated with the present goings-on. In such a case, I myself appear to others as absent in the conversation, as being otherwise engaged. Therefore, attention as presence is how I am made manifest in the world, engaged with the things themselves. It is how I am occupied, how the self engages with worldly entities.

It is important to note that a peripheral awareness is associated with attention. Gurwitsch (1964), for example, distinguishes between theme (focal center), context (periphery of objects relevant to the theme), and margin (ultimate horizon).[6] The claim here is that attention is how the self is made manifest. The engagement of the self with worldly entities can be characterized as peripheral or central depending on the deployment of attention, while there is little or no engagement with entities on the margin. That is, an entity that is peripheral to the central focus is made manifest as such and is recalled as such.[7] It is intimately related to Husserlian intentionality in that it is how the ego directs itself toward its thematic objects, as discussed in chapter 1.

Attention must be approached as a first-person phenomenon, and as such is resistant to the detached approaches of the natural sciences. Given its role in experiential contexts, this means in particular that any associated vocabulary must also be taken into consideration. The understanding of attention that appears in the language is of particular import given the intimate relation between the two that is constitutive of the hermeneutical circle. For it is by way of attention that we come to understandings that are preserved in language (chapter 2), and when we are aware of the movement of attention itself that reflexive understanding is preserved in its associated terms. Therefore, it is essential to take these terms seriously in the study of attention.

For instance, we talk about ourselves as distracted, scattered, or dispersed, which describes our state in the course of engagement. Otherwise we say that attention is captured or taken by something other than the task at hand. These expressions are in the language, reflecting a common understanding that does not represent a "folk psychology" (in a pejorative sense) but rather a first-person phenomenon that lies at the heart of our worldly existence. We talk about being immersed or absorbed in various activities; we can be "carried away" by emotion. This should be taken literally, that attention is very much affected by powerful emotions, as can be seen in expressions such as "she's the apple of my eye" or "my heart goes out to you." We may realize that attention has been absorbed in worrying about how things are going and not paying attention to loved ones. Such things matter when we reflect upon what our lives amount to. All this and more must be considered in coming to an understanding of the nature of attention.

My claim is that the understanding of attention as human presence is implicit in the language, in the very meaning of the term. It would be nonsensical, for instance, to say that although I am fully engaged in a particular activity, my attention is engaged not in this but in some other activity. Only when attention shifts to an activity can one say, "I am" to engagement in that modality, that one is explicitly aware of being engaged in such a fashion. In fact, saying "I am . . . " attentively results in the deployment of attention in a corresponding manner. For instance, if I say, "I am speaking" or "I am walking," attention attests to the truth of the matter by being directed accordingly. That is, when I say, "I am speaking," attention is directed to the very act of speaking itself. If, on the other hand, I say, "I am walking" while seated on the couch, I know it to be false because attention is directed in accordance with what I understand walking to be, and I see that I am not walking. There is a relation in the language between me in the first person and my attention, which must be taken seriously in any account of attention.

We also understand as a matter of course that attention is required for full engagement, for full presence in the course of an activity.[8] It is common, for instance, for students' minds to be elsewhere, which means that they do not hear all that the professor has to say, or, at a minimum, they do not take in all of the nuances of the presentation. We understand that we can be more or less present, more or less collected or dispersed. If attention is scattered and dispersed, so are we; likewise if it is focused and collected. This means that a more gathered attention brings more of oneself to bear in the course of engagement, as one sees and hears in a more profound manner.

Of course, it is typically the case that such a full or active presence is not exercised. For instance, Varela, Thompson, and Rosch (2017) point out that the mind tends to wander incessantly and that we are unaware of it until we are called on to attend to a specific task. This means that attention is typically passive in that we are immersed in various matters, so that it is still operative but proceeds unawares. This is the distinction that I make between active and passive attention.

Attention and the Lived Body

Attention is our presence in the world, which, importantly, includes our own bodies. It is an extended presence in that it can move from the sensation of the lived body (interoception) to external objects (exteroception), and thus across what is referred to as the *lived body-environment*. In referring to the lived body I am following Husserl's distinction between the lived body (*Leib*) and the physical body (*Korper*), where the former refers to how the body is experienced as we live within it while the latter is how it is viewed as a physical object. I am also employing the notion of the body-environment, which recognizes the intricate relation between the body and its environment that shows itself in the freedom of attention to extend from one to the other.

Any modality in which we are engaged (including thought, reflection, imagination, etc.) occurs by way of such a placement in the lived body-environment, but we are typically unaware of it and its movement. It is possible, however, to place it intentionally in any manner whatsoever, and from there to stay with its movement in the body-environment—either as the situation demands or simply because we are free to move it at will, collecting ourselves as we do so. This is the essence of what I am referring to as active attention.[9] When we stay with that embodied movement there is a stabilization and opening which is required for the long-term efficacy of the public space, or the space of appearances in Hannah Arendt. I show that the effort to stay with that opening, to hold and sustain it so we can be made manifest together as ontologically bonded, is essential for what Arendt refers to as power, as contrasted with violence (see chapter 8).

What is key for human relations is that we can sense bodily how the attention of others is deployed and who they are in that presence, especially when we are face-to-face in mutual attention. We know when people are attending to us and when they are not; children, for instance, certainly know when attention is not being paid to them. This is an important aspect of our relations with others that must be understood, which argues against the notion of "the mental" that stands in the way of a more profound understanding of the nature of attention. Rather than being restricted to an inner realm, attention extends into the world as the gateway to relations with all things, including our fellow human beings. In this sense it is fundamentally an intersubjective phenomenon.

In proceeding I draw on enactivist thought, which has developed in response to conceptions of the mental that show themselves in theories such as computational theory of mind and representationalism. The idea is that rather than being passive processors of information in a world that is stripped of meaning, we participate in the production of meaning: we *enact* it. Enactivism focuses on phenomena such as self-organizational systems and sensorimotor cycles, assuming the lived body-environment to be the field of action, and it draws on phenomenological thought, especially Edmund Husserl and Maurice Merleau-Ponty. Rather than assuming the mediation of mental representations in engagement with others, it argues for a direct understanding of the minds and acts of others, in contrast to the currently predominant theory-theory and simulation-theory.

This literature has developed in response to the Cartesian notion of the mind as a private, isolated entity, emphasizing instead the embodied and situated nature of cognition. Rather than abstract intellection, the emphasis is on practical reason, or attention to the specifics of each situation. Ideas are not mental entities in the head, but are rather socially situated and include gestures, speech acts, and motor action. The implication is that context is crucial in inquiring into the nature of physical reality, especially in quantum physics, in that the embodied physicist cannot be separated from the reality that is under investigation (see chapter 3).

The Hermeneutical Circle

Attention moves within a hermeneutical circle of attention, language, and understanding, which is a holistic phenomenon that is operative soon after birth. This means that attention is not a form of "mere awareness," for it always operates within a context. Its deliverances serve as the basis for the formation of the self in its possibilities for further manifestation, and as the basis for the formation and dissolution of political realities. I show that the circle is operative as soon as we enter this world, for it is well recognized that children develop the capacity to jointly attend to objects in conjunction with others at around nine months of age, where they not only attend to the same objects but are aware that the others are also doing so. There is a large literature on joint attention (e.g., Eilan et al. 2005, Seemann 2011b), which generally considers attention in infancy and its role in the acquisition of language. But what is also crucial is that prior to joint attention there is mutual attention beginning at birth, where infants recognize faces, in particular the face of the mother, and shortly thereafter engage in protoconversations with caregivers. Indeed, Trevarthen (2002) argues that the ability to recognize the mother's face lies in experience gained in relation to the mother in the womb.

The implication is that attention is first operative in face-to-face interactions, which are essential to who we are as human beings over the course of our lives. I am arguing that it is essentially the same from birth until death, where the movement of attention within the circle is a holistic matter that depends on the whole of who we are at any moment. Rather than subsuming that movement to posited mechanisms or structures, this approach fully respects the human by arguing that it is determined not by independent structures but rather by who we are as whole human beings within the various contexts we inhabit. As intelligent, meaning-seeking beings, the way we understand ourselves and the world in which we dwell shows itself in this, the very movement of ourselves, in how we are made manifest in the course of worldly engagement. This is my essential thesis.

Attention is how we are made manifest in relation to entities that show themselves, where aspects of ourselves are made manifest according to our embodied understanding, which is itself formed in interaction with others by way of attention and language. It is directed by the confluence of language and understanding, and language is forged in the interaction of attention and understanding. This intricate relation between attention, language, and understanding determines how things are made manifest to us, and it is the basic framework within which any ontological determinations can be made. This puts significant limits on the sorts of claims that can be made regarding the status of categories such as the mental and the physical, as discussed in chapter 3.

Relational Holism

Attention is a holistic phenomenon that cannot be accommodated within traditional metaphysical schemes. Limited conceptions of its nature arise due to the assumptions that are typically employed, such as physicalism and representationalism. The assumption of the primacy of the physical, which is implicit in most scientific inquiries into attention, is insufficient for insight into its nature, as in the work of Chun, Golomb, and Turk-Browne (2011), discussed above. I also consider the work of philosophers such as Jennings (2020) and Mole (2011), who provide relatively narrow views of the phenomenon. In general, theorists rely on conceptions of the mental as separated from physical reality, assuming a derivative status relative to a physical underpinning, as in theories that argue for supervenience on the physical. I argue in chapter 3, however, that attention is neither mental nor physical, for it enables us to relate to both kinds of entities, such as the theories of physics and their referents.

This suggests the need for another ontology, for attention is how we relate to all that is. We cannot gain any distance from it because it is where we dwell, and it is only by way of active attention that it is possible to become aware of its action from the first-person perspective. I therefore advocate for a relational holism in which attention plays a major role, as it is how we come into presence and thereby relate to anything at all. In this approach, relations enjoy a primacy over any particular entities, and the whole enjoys a primacy over any particular relations. This means that independent entities cannot serve as the ontological ground, but rather that any such entities are made manifest only in relation to one another and the whole, which implies that the movement of attention itself, as the basis for human relations, cannot be directed by any such ontic entities.

In considering this approach I rely on enactivist thought and phenomenology (largely Husserl, Dan Zahavi, and Heidegger), emphasizing the importance of first- and second-person perspectives rather than the third-person perspectives that are derivative of the former.[10] I also note that relational ontologies have been put forward in physics (Teller 1986, Esfeld 1999, Rovelli 1996, discussed in chapter 3), feminist thought (Stoljar 2018, Mackenzie 2019), enactivism (Gallagher 2017), Eastern thought (Bitbol 2019), analytic metaphysics (Benovsky 2010, Paolini Paoletti 2018, Santos 2015), social science (Gergen 2009), joint attention (Seemann 2011a, Campbell 2011), political thought (Steiner and Helminski 1998, Sturm 1998), theology (Polkinghorne 2010), and the work of scholars such as Benjamin (2015) and Topolski (2015), who apply the notion to the work of Arendt (discussed in chapter 8), among others. In conjunction with these metaphysical assumptions, I favor ordinary language philosophy and natural life contexts for the study of attention. In general, I take a holistic approach and examine the implicit presuppositions that are employed in competing visions.

THE POLITICS OF ATTENTION

Attention is typically conceived in economics and political science as a limited capacity resource, and the politics of attention refers to the effort to attract attention to promote various candidates and positions. On the view put forward here, however, attention is our presence in the world and how we are formed as individuals and collectives. It is often assumed to be passive and subject to manipulation, but I argue that while it is indeed ordinarily passive, it is possible at least in principle to take charge of its movement by simply staying with it as it occurs. This is our ultimate responsibility for ourselves and others, to take charge of this, our very ontological movement, which is the path to freedom, autonomy, and resistance against oppression. This would appear to be an impossible task given the paradox of control of attention, of control of one's own movement, but the support of a community intent on enabling such efforts can render it more feasible.

Attention is how we are made manifest, and under mutual attention it is how we are made manifest together in public spaces. This means that the very spaces that are essential for the exploration of who we are and how we should live together are constituted by way of attention to matters of shared concern. For what would make a space public if not our mutual presence, a presence that is achieved by way of attention? Any forum that lacks the attention of its members is hardly a meeting of the minds. But any sort of presence is not sufficient; what is required is active attention, effort above the ordinary solely for the purpose of being open and responsive to what may present itself. Passive attention, on the other hand, which is far more prevalent, means absorption in everyday affairs with no cognizance of its movement. There are considerable political implications to such passivity, in that we see the fragmentation of public spaces and subjection to techniques of diversion and distraction away from the substantive matters that concern us all, given the flitting about that enables, for instance, rapid news cycles and reduced ability to focus on matters of importance. We need to be able to stand our ground in the face of tyranny, for example. While passive attention is subject to capture and hence the possibility of the nefarious use of the power that is so acquired, active attention enables power to stay with the people.

We know that a unified public attention is capable of achieving many things, while a divided and dispersed attention can lead to widespread misery.[11] Passivity means that instead of coming together we turn away from one another into private realities that are de facto, not de jure.[12] For attention, language, and understanding work together in constituting the worlds in which we dwell, so when attention is dispersed we end up with the divergent understandings that characterize public life today. Fragmentation of the media in particular entails political conflict as different views of reality are promulgated. In this case we are subject to manipulation that can only be avoided by efforts of active attention and the associated ontological bonding that enables us to take hold of our movement together.

I turn now to a review of works that are related to the general approach that is taken in this book, followed by a review of more traditional approaches to attention that support the claim that attention is how the self is made manifest in the course of engagement in the world.

LITERATURE REVIEW

The work that corresponds most closely to the approach put forward here is Ganeri's (2017) *Attention, Not Self*. In this text Ganeri draws on the Indian Buddhist tradition, largely focusing on the work of Buddhaghosa, a monk who lived in Sri Lanka in the fifth century CE. At the same time, he is in conversation with a wide range of other literatures, such as phenomenology, cognitive science, enactivism, and philosophy of mind. He thus aspires to a cross-cultural philosophy that draws on theories from a variety of milieus to incorporate more of the perspectives that make up the human condition.

Ganeri puts attention at the center of human activity and argues that when it is given priority in this manner there is a resulting reorientation in the philosophical analysis of mind: "[Attention] has a central role in explaining the structure of the phenomenal and of cognitive access, the concept of the intentionality or directedness of the mental, the unity of consciousness and the epistemology of perception" (2017, 1). When applied specifically to the treatment of attention in the present book, I argue for a reorientation of the notions of activity and passivity and the associated notion of control that is so important in political thought. In particular, the notion of top-down attention as being under the control of the subject will be brought into question. In addition, as discussed above, the primacy of the physical comes into question when attention is recognized as the center of worldly engagement rather than being restricted to an inner realm.

Most important is the intimate relation that Ganeri puts forward between attention and the self. He argues that many of the functions that are typically associated with selfhood come about by way of attention. For instance, Ganeri sees attention as "the ongoing structuring of human experience and action" (2017, 12). The self is understood as a complex of interacting parts whose operation is centered at the center of attention (19); otherwise he sees no underlying entity that serves as its basis. He rather posits an empirical, functioning self that consists of those aspects that have been made more central in the course of attending (331). It is not "a mere collection," but is rather "those specific elements which attention centralized."[13] I argue in chapter 6 that such a role for attention is essential for any conception of a "minimal self," as in the formulation that Zahavi (e.g., 2019a) has put forward.

The implications are crucial for how selfhood is understood, for while it is ordinarily conceived in terms of structures of consciousness, when attention is understood to be the basis for its manifestation the implication is that any such structures depend on the deployment of attention itself. On this view, the consideration of questions of such as freedom, autonomy, and intersubjective bonds must take account of attention. Thus the deployment of attention bears on questions regarding both the nature of the individual and the intersubjective relations which are crucial for political thought.

Jennings puts forward a theory of attention where the self (specifically, top-down attention) is responsible for controlling or directing it. She argues that this corresponds to the everyday notion of attention (2020, 34) and that it should be understood as such. Although Jennings sees attention as central for perception, she argues that is not the case for consciousness and action, so there is an unusual conception of the self at work here. Jennings also seeks to incorporate our contribution to the production of meaning in her theoretical edifice, but there is little flesh that is put on a self that is posited to unify experience and produce significance, other than being a higher order phenomenon of the brain. In what follows I review Jennings's work as an example that embodies the sort of metaphysics and hence conception of attention that I contest. Jennings's approach has been inspired in part by Husserl's conception of attention as being directed by a transcendental ego, which I also consider in part II.

Ben Berger's (2011) *Attention Deficit Democracy* argues that attention (and the energy and action that follow) is essential for the effective functioning of democratic systems, and he critiques Arendt's argument for the intrinsic value of political engagement as idealistic and inconsistent, preferring Alexis de Tocqueville's instrumental approach. I respond to this critique in chapter 8, noting in particular that it is important to recognize that the public space is itself grounded in mutual attention to one another.

Other Literature

I now turn to works in the cognitive science literature that touch on various features that correspond with my conception of attention as how the self shows itself, where the latter is understood to be the basis for human agency and thus the control, direction, and organization of the human being. Although to my knowledge this conception of attention has not appeared in cognitive science or philosophy of mind, there are many approaches that are consistent with aspects of it. I consider those that focus on the relation between attention and (1) aspects of the self, (2) human presence, and (3) the integration of the human being. While I develop metaphysical assumptions that vary from those that are typically deployed in such studies, this congruence shows that aspects of the underlying matter come to the fore regardless of the background assumptions that are employed.[14]

Attention and the Self

Many themes associated with the notion of selfhood are related to attention in the literature. For instance, it is difficult to conceive of a self without emotion, for emotion speaks to what matters to us as human beings. The relation between emotion and attention has been of considerable interest (e.g., Eysenck 1982, Barrett et al., 2007), and emotion is particularly important in enactivist thought. The relation between the self and memory is also essential for any reasonable notion of self, and the relation between attention and memory is studied extensively (e.g., Pashler 1998, Cowan 2008). The mark of attention is the enhanced processing and memory that occurs with its presence, which we see in spotlight theories where entities at the center of attention appear more clearly and vividly.[15] Enhanced processing (e.g., Wright and Ward 2008) means that more resources are brought to bear in relation to any entities that present themselves. This is how the self is made manifest in a given situation.

Attention is associated with action in Wu's (2014) work, which argues that it enables a solution to the "many-many" problem of matching perceptual inputs with behavioral outputs. Related to this is the problem of control, which is typically handled in the literature by way of the distinction between top-down (endogenous) and bottom-up (exogenous) attention, where the former is voluntary control of attention while the latter is control by forces external to the agent. I argue, however, that both of these modes of attention are typically passive, rather than being under the control of the subject, and that only active attention represents true "control" where (paradoxically) the self is made manifest in the very act itself.

Posner and Petersen's (1990) attention system theory posits alerting, orienting, and executive control as three essential networks in the brain that form the attention system. Under my metaphysical assumptions and conception of attention, alerting corresponds to ontological effort, orienting to one's presence as oriented to the entities with which one relates, and executive control to the integration that can come about by way of ontological effort. I argue that executive control as presented in the literature is not first-person control but rather proceeds at the sub-personal level, for the movement of attention usually proceeds unawares and is therefore not under the control of the subject. Self-control and freedom are possible only when one stays with the movement of attention itself.

Effort and will are also essential dimensions of any notion of selfhood, and they have also been associated with attention. Kahneman's (1973) *Attention and Effort* finds no difference between human effort and attention, and James ([1890] 1983) sees attention as the essence of volition. Thus we see that many of the essential concepts associated with the self are also present in the literature on attention. My proposal, however, is to relate attention and the self in a new manner, as I argue that attention is how the self is made manifest in the course of worldly activity, how it comes into presence.[16]

Attention as Human Presence

Many theorists today seek to avoid a notion of self that is a mere part of the human being, invoking the notion of homunculus to point to the incongruity of a self within a self that remains as mysterious as ever. Jennings seeks to avoid this difficulty, although I argue that she is not successful in this regard. Ganeri argues that attention fulfills many of the functions ordinarily imputed to a self, as noted above. The approach here is to conceive of attention as human presence, as *my* presence, how and where the self is made manifest, with some aspects more prominent than others, depending on the circumstances.

In this regard I go beyond the notion of selection that is central for the treatment of attention in the cognitive science literature. It is conceived there as the filtering of stimuli that present themselves to the senses, but this requires my presence, for I must be there for the selected object to appear to me. We participate in how things show themselves in a way that is profoundly different from the mere selection of some features over others in what is assumed to be a physical environment that is mind independent. Rather than being information processors, as presumed in the notion of selection, the placement of attention in the lived body-environment has significant implications for how entities are made manifest, as I show in chapter 1.

Although attention is typically not thought in terms of presence in the technical psychology literature, we do see the relation between the subject and presence put forward in the phenomenology literature and between attention and presence in the mindfulness literature.[17] We see the latter relation, for instance, in the work of Depraz, Varela, and Vermersch, where mindfulness is equated with attentive presence (2003, 16). In the practice of becoming aware, they discuss the cultivation of a quality of presence by way of mindfulness and say that the effort is to pay attention to the process of manifestation of the entities that arise and subside, not their contents (33). This is crucial for understanding the sense in which presence is meant in the conception of attention that I put forward here. The idea is that all experience in which we participate, in which we are present in a first-person sense (not in the sense of being physically present), occurs in what Depraz, Varela, and Vermersch refer to as the "attentive space," and what Ganeri refers to as the window of attention. This is the site where we are made manifest in relation to all that presents itself to us by way of a variety of possible modes of engagement, which includes our fellows in political discourse. The effort Depraz, Varela, and Vermersch aspire to is to stay with that process without being absorbed in the content that arises, which can occur only by way of acute and sustained attentiveness. This is how to become aware of the movement of attention in which we are always already engaged but so immersed in its contents that we miss the very process of manifestation itself. We can also see it in the work of Brown and Ryan (2003), who consider the benefits of "being present," and in Parker and colleagues (2015), who discuss the science of presence.

The relation between the subject and presence is also prominent in the phenomenology literature, as in Merleau-Ponty, who refers to "the subject's vital area: that opening upon the world which has the effect of making objects at present out of reach . . . exist for him as touchable things. . . . " ([1945] 2002, 135):

> The question is always how I can be open to phenomena which transcend me, and which nevertheless exist only to the extent that I take them up and live them; *how the presence to myself which establishes my own limits and conditions every alien presence is at the same time depresentation and throws me outside myself.* (423)

Merleau-Ponty is laying out what can be understood as a relation of identity and difference, in which we come into relation to other entities by way of extending ourselves to them. We still relate to them as other, but at the same time, that extended presence enables a common space for mutual manifestation. We shall see more from Merleau-Ponty in what follows, in particular with respect to the notion of attention as extended presence (chapter 1).[18]

Attention and Integration

Several themes of unification and integration appear in the attention literature. For instance, Treisman's (1988) feature-integration theory finds that attention enables the accurate combination of features of objects. While this occurs on the sub-personal level, Mole's (2011) theory of cognitive unison defines attention as a state where all relevant cognitive resources are deployed for the task at hand. I argue below, however, that this is better characterized as a state of full attention, for attention is still deployed when one is not fully engaged or when one is not fully present, when the mind tends to wander. For in this case there is still an orientation toward a central focus of engagement at any moment, be it daydreaming or worrying, that may be later recalled as what one was doing at the time. Mole's characterization, which focuses on human beings as cognizers, also misses the full breadth of human engagement, including the affective and somatic dimensions, as discussed above and in what follows.

There are also references in the literature to the role of attention in organizing consciousness (e.g., Watzl 2017), where some objects and activities are more centrally located, whereas others are on the periphery.[19] In this regard there are considerable commonalities with Husserl, whose work will be discussed in parts I and II.[20] Self-organization is also a key concept in enactivist thought, which features in Ellis's (2005) theory of attention.

Other literature points to attention as a holistic phenomenon. Allport (2011) sees attention as a state or relation that emerges from the action of the whole organism. While it is typically conceived in terms of control or processing constraints, Allport argues that any such observable processes are themselves the manifestation of attention as a whole-organism state. This is similar to my position that various dimensions of the human being are made more prominent than others in the course of engaged activity. I consider this further in chapter 2 when discussing Fuch's (2018) *Ecology of the Brain*, which offers a similar view on the relation between brain, body, and environment.[21]

A final holistic dimension lies in the possibility of gathering ourselves by way of sustained attentiveness, or mindfulness (e.g., Brown, Creswell, and Ryan 2016). This I claim is the highest form of self-organization to which we can aspire. We can be more or less gathered, organized, or harmonized in relation to others, which shows itself in our personal, professional, and political lives. See also Kuravsky (2022) on the role of attentiveness in Heidegger.

PLAN OF THE BOOK

The book consists of three parts of three chapters each. Part I critiques the metaphysics that are typically assumed in the study of attention and puts forward an alternative that is based on enactivist and phenomenological thought. In chapter 1, I show that the center of attention is an extended presence that goes beyond the bounds of the neural as typically posited in physicalist ontologies. Rather than being ensconced in a private realm, that presence is the basis for our relation to all things, including our fellow humans.

Chapter 2 lays out the hermeneutical circle of attention, language, and understanding that forms the framework for the movement of attention, which, as my presence in the world, is the condition for experience and action. These three dimensions are each essential for life experience, and each is holistic in themselves. In their conjunction they interact seamlessly in producing the circle as a whole, which can itself be more or less integrated and open depending on the state of attention. Of particular importance is the joint attention that can open a space in which we enter into communion with one another, enabling the formation of the shared understanding that is the basis for language. Charles Taylor's notion of hermeneutical truth is also discussed, which is important for the political (see chapter 8).

Chapter 3 argues that the predominant view that assumes the primacy of the physical cannot accommodate the phenomenon of attention. I show that attention is neither mental nor physical, so it transcends any such dichotomy. I rather show that a relational ontology can accommodate it, for attention plays an essential role in our relations with all things. This will be the basis for the claim in chapter 9 that attention is how we participate in the manifestation and relation of all that is, which Heidegger refers to as being.

Part II considers the relation between attention and the self. Chapter 4 puts forward the central claim of attention as human presence, how the self is made manifest in relation to manifesting entities in the course of worldly engagement. The self is made manifest as bodily modes of engagement are brought to the foreground, at the center of attention, to meet worldly demands. They are oriented to the center as called for in the present circumstances, directed to the thematic object that is the organizing focus for the activity.

Chapter 5 considers the relation between phenomenological reflection, introspection, and mindfulness. It finds that attention is essential for all three, which has implications for how they are conceived. Chapter 6 considers Zahavi's notion of the minimal self and argues that attention is essential for any such conception. Moreover, its movement is spatiotemporal in that it is always placed in the lived body-environment, meaning that attention is our unfolding and potentially deepening presence and openness. This spatiotemporal movement, with its inherent possibilities, is how the self is made manifest as engaged in worldly activity.

Part III considers the relation between attention and the political. Chapter 7 looks at the relation between self and community as put forward by Zahavi, who sees joint attention as a supplement to the minimal self which enables communal relations. I argue, however, that the conjunction of attention and language is the basis for the constitution of self, community, and world. I also argue that relying solely on face-to-face interaction for communal bonding is insufficient. Active attention is necessary for ontological bonding that can produce stable and responsive institutions for the promotion of the common good in the long term.

Chapter 8 argues for the intrinsic value of mindfulness and mindful political engagement, where the latter enables the community to engage the whole human being in articulating and achieving hermeneutical visions of the common good. It recommends the widespread engagement of mindful citizen councils for this purpose. Chapter 9 turns to Heidegger's corpus in support of many of the claims that are put forward in the book.[22] It argues that we belong in this cosmos because we are related to all that is by way of attention, and when being is itself made manifest it appears in more appropriate ways in which we can go about living together in the world.

The ultimate question considered herein is the role and potential of attention in political affairs. Given the challenges we face on a planetary scale, how are we to act in unison to promote the common good? My claim is that attention is our center as we engage the world; it is our worldly presence. As the site of human action, it is how we ourselves are made manifest, as gathered or dispersed. We can be more integrated, more harmoniously gathered, both as individuals and as members of collectives, by engaging in the practice of active attention. This means that attention offers the possibility of acting in unison, which may enable more effective approaches to the dangers that we face as a human race.

PART I

The Metaphysics of Attention

Chapter 1

Attention as Extended Presence

It is widely accepted in the psychology literature that processing resources are oriented to the focus of attention in the course of perceptual and other forms of experience. The key question is whether (1) the entire process is physical except for the possibility of transmutation into mental representations, in which case experience occurs in isolation from the physical reality, or (2) the self is made manifest at the center of attention wherever it is placed in the lived body-environment, as resources are oriented to the center of engagement.[1] On the latter view, we are not isolated at all, but rather inhabit our bodies and the world with our presence, a presence that is centered in attention. It should be noted, however, that under passive attention we are typically absorbed in activity and unaware of that embodied presence. This means there is a de facto detached realm in which experience takes place, which can lead in turn to the untenable assumption that the realm is de jure. I show below, however, that the deployment of attention determines the relation between subject and object, which may or may not be detached based on its state.

I put forward this conception in contrast to the widely held assumption of the primacy of the physical, where it is assumed that stimuli impinge upon the senses and make their way to the brain after filtering by attentional mechanisms, which then leads to output in the form of bodily action. This input-output system is consistent with the emphasis on detached observation and theoretics because we are indeed assumed to be detached from the object of study. As an alternative, I put forward a holistic conception where attention is an extended, worldly presence that is supported by neurophysiological processes. In this respect it is in concert with the notion of the extended mind (Clark and Chalmers, 1998), which posits that cognitive operations extend beyond the confines of the brain, a thesis that is in part a reaction to the ever-expanding encroachment of the physical on any space for human existence.

The ontological status of the physical indeed goes unquestioned in much contemporary philosophy, whereas that of the mental is much more problematic. Oddly, by making such assumptions we are left with the question of how we ourselves fit in what is essentially a physical cosmos. Along these lines, Nagel (2012) argues that the success of this world view has come at the cost of excluding the mind itself. He critiques what he refers to as the "dominant scientific consensus," which posits the formation of physical systems that are capable of evolution from dead matter, leading implausibly to developments such as the genetic code, consciousness, meaning, cognition, reason, and value. Although it is far from a well-confirmed hypothesis, it is often put forward as the scientific worldview by philosophers and scientists and is widely accepted by many individuals in Western secular societies. Nagel says that this has come about due to advances in physics and biology that were made possible by excluding mind from the physical world, but the difficulty now is to reincorporate it in a meaningful manner. He attributes the staying power of such a thin theory to the lack of a comprehensive alternative that enjoys the authority of scientific rigor.[2]

The problem is that we are the theorists; we have developed the physics and biology that have been so successful, yet the tendency is to posit the dichotomy that renders our presence derivative of the physical and thereby denies the commonly experienced intimate contact and relation with the things of this world. But the fact that we are able to develop such theories renders that ontological assumption questionable, for what can be the basis for these capacities when we ourselves are cut off from the object of study? If we consider the possibility that we are indeed exquisitely related to the things of this world, it may be the case that there is much more to human potential than distanced observation and theoretics, to which the humanities may be better able to speak.

This question has crucial implications for how we understand ourselves and our relations with others, for the predominant view implicitly assumes that we are cut off from one another as well. Indeed, if the physical is what is ultimately real, it follows that people are essentially physical and therefore related extrinsically, and we are left with a Hobbesian world and a social contract view of the bonds that hold between us. The fear is that when physicalism becomes the common sense of a nation, the possibility of doing harm to entities who are little more than "matter in motion" becomes all too real. I argue, however, that consideration of attention brings such metaphysical schemes into question, opening the possibility of bonds whose strength depends on the extent to which we reach out to one another by way of attention.

ATTENTION AND PHENOMENOLOGY

I now show that attention is essential for the practice of phenomenology and the associated veracity of intuition. I demonstrate this by way of attentional explorations that seek to test the claim that the center of attention extends into the lived body-environment. The approach is thus to address the question by way of attention itself, or more precisely, active attention as discussed in the introduction. For attention is the essence of the first-person perspective, and an important form of reflexivity (termed here *immanent reflexivity*) can be achieved by staying with its movement in the course of engagement.[3] That is, it is possible for attention itself to be experienced by attending to this very movement, by either directing it intentionally or staying with it as it follows its own inclinations.[4] When we do so, we gather ourselves, because that is where we are bodily, as we are made manifest as centered in attention and holding that stance. As such, we know with certainty that we are present in that manner, to the extent to which we are able to sustain it. The ability to do so is essential in adjudicating any claims regarding the nature of attention, because in this manner we are explicitly and directly related to the matter of inquiry itself.

For this purpose I turn to the thought of Edmund Husserl, who originated the modern practice of phenomenology. In *Ideas I* Husserl (2014, §35) associates attention with the apprehension of intuitions at the foreground (which I refer to as the center of attention) relative to a background of intuitions that have the potential to come to the fore at any time. For Husserl, intuition is a bodily, "in person" actuality, which is given in an originary way and hence indubitable. Intuitions can be particulars or essences (categorial intuitions), and attention can shift from one to the other at any time. This movement actualizes intuitions at the foreground, the central focus that can serve to orient the entire intentional structure for further action. In this manner, Husserl sees attention as essential for agency and egoic acts in general.

Attention is intimately related to the Husserlian notion of intentionality ("consciousness *of* something"; 2014, 162), where, in a section entitled "Intentionality as the Main Theme of Phenomenology," he says, "In every currently actual cogito, a 'focus' radiating from the pure ego is directed at the 'object' of the respective correlate of consciousness . . . , achieving the quite diverse sorts of consciousness *of* it" (162). Husserl also says that the focus of attention is what it is because of the background, which is the context for its intelligibility. Intuitions are "lifted" out of the background, thereby enabling their apprehension. He sees this as a modification of consciousness from potential to actual or from implicit to explicit. It enables clarity of apprehension of entities from out of the "halo" of background intuitions.[5] I follow

Husserl in distinguishing between attention and consciousness along these lines, assuming that attention is the foreground or center of the field of all possible intuitions.[6]

Husserl notes that attention enables the exploration of all aspects of lived experience,[7] for one is free to direct it in any manner whatsoever:

> I can let my attention wander out . . . to all the objects I directly "know" as being here and there in my surroundings, of which I am immediately co-conscious—a knowing that has nothing of conceptual thinking in it and only changes into a clear intuiting when attention is turned toward [it], and even then only partially and mostly in a very imperfect manner. . . . In the free activity of experiencing that brings what is on hand into what I intuit, I can pursue these connections of the actuality immediately surrounding me. (2014, 48–49)[8]

He shows how the focus can move from objects of perception such as trees, and then, "suddenly, our focus turns to an object of memory 'occurring' to us. . . . Our focus passes through a noesis of remembering into a world of memory; our focus wanders in this world" (2014, 182). This sort of movement is essential for the practice of phenomenology, for it enables us to explore aspects of the lived body-environment and associated dimensions such as memory and thought in order to address a variety of questions regarding the structures of lived experience. Examples of Husserl's explorations are considered in chapter 4, which, importantly, include the lived body itself, as I demonstrate in what follows.

EXTENDED PRESENCE

A well-known objection to the extended mind thesis is that of Adams and Aizawa (2001), who argue that any posited extended cognitive operations are ultimately derived from neural processes. A response has been taken up by enactivist theorists such as Gallagher (2017), who distinguishes between mental and operative intentionality, where the latter as motoric and bodily enjoys a primacy over neural activity. Gallagher cites Merleau-Ponty ([1945] 2002, 162):

> The body's motoric experience is not a particular case of knowledge; rather, it offers us a manner of reaching the world and the object, a "praktognosia," that must be recognized as original, and perhaps as originary. My body has its world, or understands its world without having to go through "representations," or without being subordinated to a "symbolic" or "objectifying function." (Gallagher 2017, 79)

The idea is that we inhabit our bodies, which in turn are intimately related to the worlds in which we live. This means that any representational systems that are posited to replicate perceptual and other objects are derivative of that more primordial relation, so that operative intentionality is ontologically prior to neural activity and its associated representations. Our relation to the body can also be seen in the role of attention in intentionality, as its freedom of movement means it can shift to operative intentional objects by way of attending to the lived body itself. Since Husserl assumes that attention is directed by the transcendental ego, and indeed that it is part of the latter's structure, the implication is that bodily intentionality can be related to the ego/self in this manner; for egoic attention determines which intentional objects are thematic, while all others are peripheral to that central activity (Husserl 2001).

In chapter 4 I discuss how this leads to the claim that attention is how the self is made manifest, without regard to any assumption as to direction by a transcendental ego. With the ego excised, it follows that the only center of experience is that of attention itself, whose presence extends into and moves within the lived body-environment as the basis for relation to all things, either by way of mental or operational intentionality, rather than being ensconced in a private realm. Moreover, I argue below that any mental intentionality is also rooted in the body and experienceable as such, which means that all intentionality is ultimately operative and therefore ontologically prior to neural activity and any associated representations.

There are many examples of this sort of extended presence.[9] For example, Fuchs and De Jaegher argue that the lived body extends to whatever object it is interacting with, which they refer to as "incorporation" (2009, 478).[10] They provide an example of jumping over a creek, which is possible only if the gaze and "whole-body intention" is directed to the other bank (473). In this case, attention must extend to the other bank if the jump is to be successful and if peripheral activities such as anticipation of the trajectory are to be appropriately oriented to the task. They also discuss a tennis player who feels the ball approaching, which, as an incorporated target, immediately evokes the corresponding movement of the arm. In this case, attention has extended to the ball and the appropriate response follows.[11]

Fuchs and De Jaegher argue that incorporation does not require the object to be near or on the body. They say the tennis player "actually moves with the ball from where it starts and *feels* it approaching" (2009, 473). The extent to which attention actually extends to the ball, thereby relegating other modes of engagement such as thought and rumination to the background, determines the extent of relation to the thing itself as it approaches. That is, the extent of such contact is an empirical matter, since it is a question of how attention is actually deployed. For instance, if one is worried about how the game is going or focused on an aching back, the ball will receive little or no attention, and thus little or no contact will be achieved; but if one attends acutely to the ball, one's presence extends to the entity itself. The contact achieved by way of attention determines the success or failure to hit the ball with the racket, for it determines how the self is made manifest and thus how the body is deployed in the engagement.

It may be argued that it is impossible for mental entities like attention to penetrate into physical realities, but we know that a connection is posited in cognitive science between the tennis player and the ball in the form of stimuli that are filtered by attention, resulting in the perception of the ball. The question is whether this process is properly considered to be physical, or whether our presence in the world may be admitted by way of the relational ontology that is put forward herein. Indeed, in chapter 3 I argue that attention is neither mental nor physical and therefore transcends the distinction, which will argue for the latter ontology.

Gallagher discusses similarly how baseball fielders chase down fly balls, and after critiquing representationalist explanations argues that what is essential is simply "seeing the ball that is 'out there' in the world, and directly acting in the world" (2017, 13–14). The intuition is that fielders must pay attention to the ball all the way into the glove. They stay with it as it moves toward them, and that centering is most prominent because they focus on it unwaveringly. This means that the presence of attention must be "out there" in the world, staying with the ball while it is in flight, which orients the peripheral capacities that support bodily movement and presence.

It may be argued that the fielder attending to the ball can be explained by the representationalist model, where attention determines which stimuli are selected for representation within the brain, which in turn enables output that guides embodied action toward catching the ball. This, however, ignores the fact that when attention is paid in this manner the necessary peripheral capacities are also oriented toward the ball in an action of the whole human being. The task requires online presence rather than offline representations (Gallagher 2017, 14), which, in my terms, is the presence of attention and its associated embodied resources at the site of action. The center of attention enables this coordination of the whole human being, and one must stay with it to accomplish the task.

The fact that the fielder can experience direct contact with the ball, which is the basis for any representational activity, trumps the physicalist explanation. He sees that the slightest deviation of attention from the flight of the ball means failure to catch it. He knows that his presence is called for and knows when he is distracted and loses contact with the ball. That presence is real, and he knows it. I am with the ball, and I know it as it comes into my glove, indubitably, because I am present to it, where this "I" has formed as my resources are fully engaged at the center of attention. I am present to the ball, not in an inner realm; that is certain. Any neural processes that support that presence are only part of the whole human being, who is made manifest as present to the ball.

FUCHS ON THE LIVED BODY AND EXTENDED PRESENCE

I am following Husserl's distinction between the lived and physical bodies, where the former is the body as experienced from the first-person perspective, while the latter is experienced as an object. Attention is first and foremost a phenomenon of the lived body, which I refer to simply as the center of attention or the center of the lived body. Other aspects are peripheral to activity in the center and will be oriented according to the readiness that comes about by way of attentiveness. The central claim is that the self is made manifest as centered in attention together with supporting elements from the periphery.

Fuchs (2018) argues that the lived and physical bodies are dual aspects of the same underlying referent, the organism as a whole, in contrast to the mental and physical (as typically conceived), which have no such common referent. Since the lived body is the body as experienced from the first person, the key question is where the experience occurs: in the brain or in the world. Fuchs argues that the brain is obviously an important part of the organism but that consciousness is the "integral" of the whole organism, or how it presents itself as a whole, how it is made manifest. Fuchs sees conscious experience as an integrated and intensified life process, as I argue for attention. Thematic consideration of attention is beyond the scope of Fuchs's text, but for our purposes it is closely related to his conception of consciousness.[12]

Fuchs argues that while the lived body is largely coextensive with the physical organism, it can extend beyond its confines in support of functional demands. As we have seen, we need to be present to support activities such as playing tennis and baseball with the appropriate peripheral resources. Fuchs also says that the objective space of the organism and the subjective space of bodily experience are intertwined and mutual modify one another (2018, 16). He provides as examples the tip of the blind person's cane, the driver who feels the street under the car tires, and an amputee adapting to a prosthesis. Consciousness for Fuchs exists primarily in interactions with the environment, not in the brain. Although such events are cognitively registered in the brain, the latter is not capable of thought, reflection, and other capacities associated with personhood, which require the lived body. All that is present in the brain is neuronal activity, which is necessary but not sufficient for consciousness, for this is exactly the explanatory gap that continues to plague philosophy of mind.

The question now is whether attending to the lived body itself (interoceptively) takes place within the brain by way of mental representations, or whether we are present to the sensations of the body themselves. I argue that we inhabit our own bodies, which is the basis for any bodily representations that we do have. Once this is established the extended attention thesis follows, as I show below. Fuchs (2018, 13) provides an example of a patient telling a doctor that she feels pain in her foot. If she relies solely on mental representations and not the actual site of the pain, it is difficult to understand how she communicates with the doctor, for if experience occurs within the brain it would seem that the pain should also be located there.[13] The fact that she does so successfully shows that the lived body is not purely subjective and that "the subjective space of my pain and the objective space of my foot do not belong to two separate worlds which are only connected with one another in a causal way (namely via physiological processes in the brain)" (17). It rather shows that we have intersubjective validation of the pain's location in the physical body, which argues for the coextension of the lived and physical bodies. Fuchs also points to Husserl's explorations in which the body manifests as a unity with two different aspects, subjective and objective, which similarly argues for the co-apprehension of subject and object (see the section entitled "The Subject-Object Relation" below), and he cites the precritical Kant in this regard:

> I would, therefore, *keep to common experience*, and would say, provisionally, where I sense, there I am. I am just as immediately in the tips of my fingers, as in my head. It is myself who suffers in the heel and whose heart beats in affection. I feel the most painful impression when my corn torments me, not in a cerebral nerve, but at the end of my toes. No experience teaches me to believe some parts of my sensation to be removed from myself, to shut up my Ego in a microscopically small place in my brain from whence it may move the levers of my body-machine, and cause me to be thereby affected. Thus I should demand a strong proof to make inconsistent what the schoolmasters say: my soul is a whole in my whole body, and wholly in each part. (17–18; Kant [1766] 1990, 49, em)

Kant says it is common experience to be present in the body, although he does not distinguish here between attention and consciousness. To see how this refers to attention it would be necessary to distinguish between cases where I am more fully centered in these activities rather than peripherally engaged, where in the latter case we would say that I am only present peripherally.

Fuchs's argument is that the brain in itself cannot experience anything. He discusses the example of the potter whose feeling is in the touching hand.

Mere central processing cannot achieve what the immediate presence in his hand makes possible: the linking of perception, movement, and objects in a *common intermodal action space*.[14] This is what Fuchs refers to as the extended or ecological subject, who is actually in the world as a bodily being; it is not an illusion that we inhabit our own bodies. The gathering that occurs at the center of attention (as I refer to it) enables the coherence of various sensory and kinesthetic modalities established within this space, with the extent of such coherence depending on the quality of attention, or so I argue.[15] This can be conceived in my terms as the relation between attention and its embodied resources and sensibilities, where the self is made manifest by way of their action at the center of attention. There is no need for central processing in this case because the body is already integrated in the environment, biologically connected to it; hence Gallagher's argument that bodily intentionality enjoys a primacy over the neural. It is true that representations in the brain can play an important role, especially in higher-order cognition, but attention is how my presence as a whole is brought to bear in response to environmental demands above and beyond that which any representations may afford.

THE EXPERIENCE OF THOUGHT

I now consider how thought itself occurs within the lived body-environment. The notion of thought occurring in the head is taken for granted, but there is little in the way of phenomenological studies that address the question systematically. For this purpose I turn to the cognitive phenomenology literature (e.g., Bayne and Montague 2011), which seeks to describe what it is like to think or cognize in various forms. In particular the question of "inner speech" is addressed, where this sort of thought is often assumed to occur in the vicinity of the head (Langland-Hassan and Vicente 2018). Although it is considered to be a common, everyday experience (Perrone-Bertolottia et al., 2014), its achievement by way of introspection can render it suspect in the eyes of many scholars. However, given that the latter is typically understood as "turning attention inward" (e.g., Roessler 1999), it can be argued that the quality of attention determines the viability of the notion that thought occurs "in the head," for when attention is directed to explore the lived body-environment in this manner, there is little else besides its quality to evaluate the veracity of what is seen.[16] Turning attention inward can itself be seen as directing attention to the sensation of the head from within, which is fully consistent with the notion of attention being deployed in the lived body-environment, given that the head is part of the lived body. It is considered to be inward because attention is more typically oriented to perception or other modes of engagement, not in sensing the body in this manner.

Thus, the extent to which thought occurs in the head can be verified by staying with (attending to) its sensation while in the course of thought. This can be quite difficult given that attention is typically absorbed in thought, depending on the demands of the task at hand and/or any associated emotional arousal, where the term "absorbed" means that one is unaware of one's bodily presence in the course of an activity. But it is at least possible in principle to gather oneself while thinking and in so doing widen and deepen the "window on the world" discussed in the introduction, which I encourage the reader to verify. This enables one to recognize that one is embodied, as always, which means that any such mental activity—including imagination, reflection, and the like—occurs within the lived body and is as such a bodily phenomenon. The implication is that all such intentionality is ultimately operative and that it can be experienced as such by appropriately deploying attention. For if the activity occurs at the personal level, it must be experienceable, and given the relation between attention and experience, that can occur only by way of attention. Given our ever-present embodiment, the ability to widen the attentional window immediately leads to the realization of thought's embodiment.

Staying with the sensation of the head is thus a phenomenological experiment to verify the extent to which certain types of thought occur in the vicinity of the head, or if they are accessible to phenomenological investigation at all. (Of course, sayings such as "That's using your head" and "I calculated it in my head" suggest that the relation between thought and the head is preserved in ordinary language and should thus be taken seriously.) The act calls for directing attention to the sensation of the head, which can be done more or less acutely and steadfastly. Although we habitually tend to be immersed in the action of the various capacities, it is possible to direct attention actively in this manner, which, as indicated above, is the essence of the phenomenological method. Readers can verify for themselves the possibility of directing and sustaining attention in this manner, by actively attending to the sense of the head simply for the sake of seeing if a widening and/or deepening indeed occurs and if thought can be seen in this manner.

When one takes hold of attention in this way, it is possible to move it to any other region, such as the sensation of one's feet, for instance. One can place attention there, moving from the head so the center of experience now extends to the feet, as long as the effort is present. That does take considerable effort, for one's attention is typically passive, with habit determining the paths it takes, say in intellection, emotional rumination, monitoring the road when driving, or attending to one's cell phone. But it is possible to persist in attending to one's feet as long as the impulse to do so remains operative, as we see indubitably that one's center extends to the feet in this manner.

Similarly, one may extend to the sensation of the floor and beyond, and we see that it can be intentionally extended beyond the limits of the physical body, for attention knows no bounds.

It is interesting that when Adams and Aizawa refer to the mind as being "in the head," they mean that it is in neural activity and thus the physical body, but when we attend to activities such as inner speech, the head is considered in the sense of experience, which means the reference is to the lived body. which is centered in attention focused on the head. There will be correlations, of course, between neural and experienced activity, given that the lived and physical bodies both have the organism as a whole as their underlying referent. But the center of the lived body can extend beyond the brain when we undertake to widen the window of attention, as in the phenomenological experiment. Thus, in this case the perturbation of ordinary experience by way of the experimental intervention makes the case itself that attention can extend beyond the brain into the broader lived body-environment. Therefore, when thought is understood to be something that can be experienced by way of attention, the implication is that it can extend beyond the neural. The extension does not refer to the content of thought but rather to the actual event of thought within the lived body-environment as supported by attention. Therefore, once the distinction is made between the lived and physical bodies, we have the basis for the extension of attention beyond neural activity, for the latter does not exist in isolation from the lived body-environment in which the brain is housed.

THE SUBJECT-OBJECT RELATION

I now wish to show that there is no de jure subject-object relation, only de facto deployment of attention in relation to worldly entities. For this purpose I inquire into whether the body manifests as a unity with two different aspects, as indicated in the discussion of Fuchs above. Consider Merleau-Ponty's reversibility thesis (inspired by Husserl's explorations), where one hand is the subject and the other is the object. He says that "the two hands are never simultaneously in the relationship of touched and touching to each other" ([1945] 2002, 106). My contention is that attentive presence in one's hands determines which is subject and which is object, and indeed Merleau-Ponty recognizes this when he says, "The physical thing becomes animate. Or, more precisely, it remains what it was (the event does not enrich it), but an exploratory power comes to rest upon or dwell in it. Thus I touch myself touching; my body accomplishes 'a sort of reflection'" (1964, 166). To see this for oneself, one may perform an experiment as follows:

1. Begin with both hands clasped together. If one attends to the sensation of the right hand, that hand becomes the subject. The center of attention has moved to the right hand as a result of the indication to do so. If one stays with the sensation in an effort of one's whole being, one experiences oneself as centered there. The hypothesis is that one is made manifest in that manner when this condition is satisfied, where one is bodily related to oneself in this manner.

2. If one extends attention subtly to the sensation of the right hand at its point of contact with the left, the right hand becomes the touching hand and the left hand is touched. The center remains in the right hand, which is now experienced as touching the left. The right hand is the subject and the left hand is the object, which may be experienced as having various properties.

3. Shift attention to the sensation of the left hand. It moves there covertly and the subject follows. If one extends attention to the point of contact with the right hand, the left hand is now touching the right hand as long as attention remains centered in the left. Reversibility is thus effected by way of the movement of attention, the center of extended presence.

4. Shift attention to the sensation of both hands clasped at the same time. The center is now in both hands. That is where one is centered, where one has come into presence. The two hands are now one, as the center has expanded to include both. There is no subject-object relation here, but rather another form of bodily self-relation. This shows that any subject-object distinction depends upon the deployment of attention.

We see how this supports Fuchs's coextension thesis in that the lived and physical bodies can reverse positions based on the deployment of attention, which determines how the lived body is centered and thus how the subject is made manifest.

Although there is no physical movement in the course of the experiment, the movement of attention is essential in corporeal movement of all sorts. For instance, when one wishes to move one's arm, it shifts to the sensation of the arm prior to the movement. The thought to move the arm arises and the center shifts to support the movement. The same holds when one begins to speak, for the center shifts to the parts that are engaged in the act when it occurs with awareness. The self follows attention, as its manifestation follows the movement of attention.[17] This supporting presence is the font of speech and action, versus being ensconced "in the head."

This relation between attention and subjectivity can be seen in the language itself. As discussed in the introduction, attention must be correspondingly deployed to be able to say, "I am seeing" or "I am touching." It may be true that one's feet are touching the ground, but only when attention shifts to the sensation can one say "I" to that, can one say, "I feel my feet touching the ground."[18] Consider an example provided by Merleau-Ponty, where he is leaning on his desk with both hands: "It is not that I am unaware of the whereabouts of my shoulders or back, but these are simply swallowed up in the position of my hands" ([1945] 2002, 115). The assumption is thus that attention is in the hands—that is where one is centered—and that one is therefore touching the desk. That is the center of attention, and the shoulders and back are in the background. But one may take the same posture and intentionally move attention to the shoulders and back. Phenomenologically, one is no longer touching the desk (although the hands have not moved), for the center has moved to the shoulders and back while the desk has faded into the background. One can then say, "I was only peripherally in contact with the desk," and indeed actually saying so would direct attention back to the desk, in which case one can say, "I am now touching the desk (and speaking at the same time)." This illustrates the intricacy of the movement of attention in its relation to language.

The same applies to other modalities, such as thought and imagination. It is implicit that attention is the basis for the activity, and it can thus be said that I am thinking, imagining, and so on. One cannot say that although one is presently thinking about a particular matter, one's attention is engaged not in this but in some other activity. In general, one cannot say that one is engaged in any bodily activity without attention. An observer may note that one is walking, but if one is deep in thought while doing so, then that is how the "I" is engaged. Only when attention shifts to the activity of walking itself does the focus of engagement shift. For instance, if one is walking while deep in thought, the center is in the vicinity of the head. In this case, little attention is paid to the act of walking itself, which proceeds by way of background processes unless attention is called by some imperative that presents itself. If attention shifts to walking due to unanticipated terrain, for instance, the center shifts. One is then literally in the terrain as it engages the body, focusing on environmental contours and how one negotiates its perils, as a different set of resources is called to the fore and the self comes into presence in a new manner. One's skills in managing difficult terrain suddenly come to the fore, and the thoughts in which one was previously immersed recede to the background. Attention may shift back and forth between thought and bodily engagement, thoughts can be about the environment and other topics, and the center can be more or less diffuse, but there is always some form to the center of attention within the body-environment—there is some manner in which I come into presence that corresponds to the demands of the moment. This is the window on the world that can take any shape based on how one understands (broadly construed) what the situation calls for.

Thus, while it can be said that walking and thinking are both operative modalities, attention refers to the center of engagement itself, where the self is made manifest at any moment. It is *my* field of activity, what I am aware of and can remember. Self-manifestation means that when one is lost in thought one may be able to recall only what one was thinking about, whereas the details of the terrain will be inaccessible. All else is peripheral to the center of attention; one is not there, not engaged in negotiating the terrain, but rather in thought. The self comes into presence at the foreground, at the center of embodied engagement.

The Subject of Pain

Let us return to the question of pain in the foot discussed above. I am arguing that we inhabit the body and can experience the pain directly by way of the presence of attention in the foot itself. There are, however, sophisticated arguments in philosophy of mind that contest this claim. Consider, for instance, the work of Crane, who, in the course of a discussion of the experience of ankle pain, argues that "consciousness need not reside in the intentional objects of awareness in order for the state of awareness to be conscious" (2014, 143). Although not all intentional objects are physical for Crane, he sees consciousness in effect as a separate realm that is cut off from the physical, for the subject does not stand in relation to such objects in the same way that it does to the intentional content of an experience. He cites Dretske in this regard, who says that pain is an experience of a physical state, and that "the experiences are conscious, yes, but not because we are conscious of them, but because they make us conscious of the relevant states of our bodies" (1995, 102–103). Thus, Crane assumes that although the ankle is the intentional object to which the mind is directed, we are aware of it only by way of neurophysiological processes, thereby ruling out the possibility of inhabiting the body in the way that I propose.

There are, however, problems with Crane's account, in particular when it comes to the role of attention. In the course of arguing that pain is a mental state ("a state of consciousness, or an event in consciousness" [2014, 124]), he puts forward a theory of intentionality where the mind (or an intentional state) is directed to the part of the body where the sensation is felt. This is referred to as an intentional object, which is "that at which one's mind is directed" (129). He also considers the "aspectual shape," which is the point of view from which the object is encountered. Intentional objects are "always presented under a certain aspect, or in a certain way" (129). In particular, "bodily sensations exhibit aspectual shape: their objects are presented in certain ways, to the exclusion of other ways" (136).[19] This means that the object manifests itself in a particular way irrespective of the subject, whose influence comes about by way of what Crane calls the intentional mode (what I refer to as a mode of engagement).

Crane distinguishes between the intentional object and its content, which is how we describe what the object is like (2014, 129), or how it appears to us, including the aspectual shape. Together with a specification of the intentional mode, which may be a believing or wishing, or the like, we have an intentional state where the subject is related to a content by a mode (130). These relations all occur within consciousness, but Crane says the subject is not related to the intentional object itself because it may not exist, pointing to the example of phantom limbs. Thus, although he wishes to think of this as a work in phenomenology, "the idea of how things seem to the subject" (146), there are still metaphysical presuppositions in play, as indicated above. For the subject is cut off from the intentional object, which means that the former exists in an ensconced realm that is isolated from the body itself, in this case. Indeed, why is it necessary for the object to exist? Phenomenology in the Husserlian tradition suspends belief in the existence of its objects and focuses only on how they manifest themselves. Crane seems to be abiding by this stricture, pointing out that he is concerned with how things appear, what the phenomenological facts are (133), not what entities are in themselves. So when one feels that a phantom limb hurts, that is how it manifests, which must be considered to be an intentional relation between the subject and the phantom limb. For otherwise, what could be the basis for the content that is ascribed to it? It is certainly described as pain from a phantom limb. When we in fact assume that the intentional object *is* related to the subject, the implication is that the subject is related to the pain in the ankle, not just the content. And in fact, Crane himself says that the pain in the ankle "seems to be a part of me, and it seems to be the *ankle* which is hurting me" (138–39).

We always relate to objects as they are made manifest, not as they are in some absolute sense, but this does not mean we only relate to intentional content. We relate to intentional objects as they are made manifest to us—that is, in relation to us, whether or not they enjoy a physical existence. We relate to fictional and historical characters, for instance, by way of the various media in which they are made manifest, and can say that we feel something about them. That is, they *mean something* to us, and are made manifest in multiple ways, with some aspects more prominent than others. This sort of relation is conceived more appropriately in a relational ontology, where entities do not exist in and of themselves but only in relation to other entities, which in the present case means that the subject is what it is in relation to its intentional objects. This points again to a physicalist bias in Crane's thinking, in that he requires the relation between subject and object to be mediated by representational content even when referring to one's own body, let alone for other entities which are more removed.

What is odd about Crane's exposition is that he does not tell us anything about the nature of the subject. It just appears on the scene after he introduces the notions of intentional object, mode, and content, and then claims that the subject is related to the content by way of the mode. He notes the limited scope of the project at the end of the essay, which is to provide "a systematic account . . . of what it is like to have a certain kind of experience" (2014, 148), but a specification of the nature of the subject cannot be avoided. For what sort of subject is not related to its intentional object, which in this case is one's body? Is it the brain? That would appear to be intimately related to the body if the subject is ultimately physical. If it is not then we are faced with the explanatory gap, which is beyond the scope of the paper (148), and we remain puzzled about why there is no relation. For the subject itself can also have an effect on the intentional content, as the latter is not based solely on the properties and manifestation of the intentional object. For instance, perception can sometimes be blurry, which would appear to be due to the subject's visual capabilities assuming a minimal sort of embodiment. Of course, bodily orientation will also matter, and in fact the relation between sensorimotor capacities and perception is a major theme in enactivist thought (e.g., O'Regan and Nöe 2001). Indeed, another theme in this literature is that the meaning of the entities themselves depends on the contribution of the subject, for meaning is *enacted*; the subject is engaged in more than mere information processing. Crane seeks to deal with this by way of the notion of modes, but that refers more to detached cognition of objects rather than participation in how the entities are made manifest, which would fall under the "aspectual shape" notion for Crane. And this brings us to a major theme, which is that it is not only the intentional object that presents itself in a variety of ways, *but also the subject*. Self-manifestation is in fact is a key question in phenomenology (e.g., Zahavi 1999), which is much related to my claim that the subject is made manifest by way of attention. Before I turn to this, however, I wish to discuss how attention is employed in Crane's text.

Attention is quite prominent here, but as in the case of the subject, it appears with no explanation. Perhaps this is because it is merely considered to be "bare awareness" (Crane 2014, 135) and not worthy of serious theoretical resources. But Crane does talk about how the mind is directed to the intentional object, and he also talks similarly about how attention can be so directed. For instance, he says that "[p]ains and other sensations feel to be located in parts of the body. To attend to a sensation is to attend to the (apparent) part or region of the body where the sensation feels to be" (133). It would thus appear that Crane takes attention to be *how the mind is directed to the body*. He does not make this explicit, but it would be difficult to deny, given that both are directed to the intentional object, and we see that attention and the mind/subject are very much related in this exposition. Indeed, it would not make sense to say, "My mind is directed to the body, but my attention is directed elsewhere," and in fact Husserl refers to the "ray of attention" in discussing its role in intentionality. Crane does indicate that there can be more than one intentional object that is represented in the intentional content, but prior to any representational activity there will objects that are more prominent than others based on the deployment of attention.

Crane also recognizes the role of attention when discussing the transparency of experience, where we seek to inspect our experience and end up simply attending to the objects themselves. As he puts it, "When we attend to our pains . . . we attend to the part of the body in which we feel the pain. This is analogous to part of what is meant by the 'transparency' of visual experience: if we want to attend to our visual experiences, what we normally do is to inspect the objects of experience" (2014, 144). Thus Crane takes attention to be how the mind is directed to the body and how we inspect our own experience, which is central to the phenomenology that he seeks to practice. It is a small further step to my claim that attention is how the self is made manifest in relation to entities that are themselves being made manifest in relation to us. In this context it means that the subject's relation to the intentional object depends on the placement (the window) of attention and the mode of engagement. We are thus treating the subject and its manifestation in the same manner as Crane has treated the intentional object and its aspectual shape, or how it is made manifest.

Consider further the example of the patient telling the doctor about the pain in her foot. Crane says that the intentional content has to do with ways of talking about the object of an intentional state (2014, 129–30). Suppose the doctor asks the patient to say what the pain feels like or what it's like to have that pain. The patient understands what the doctor is asking, and her attention shifts to the painful foot, enabling her to say that it feels like a sharp, high-pitched pain. This is consistent with Crane's account, as we have noted that he says, "To attend to a sensation is to attend to the (apparent) part or region of the body where the sensation feels to be" (133). Then the doctor starts to feel the foot and asks, "Is this where it hurts?" The patient, now attending to the foot and the doctor's touch, says, "No, it's a little lower than that." Thus the content is not static, but rather unfolds in the context of the exchange with the doctor and the movement of attention to ascertain what the pain feels like and where it is located. This is the movement of attention that is described in the hermeneutical circle (see chapter 2). There is an intricate relation between attention to the intentional object and the content that emerges in the course of the interaction, which is referred to as "participatory sense making" in the enactivism literature (e.g., Fuchs and De Jaegher 2009). The subject is very much related to the intentional object in this manner.

I am arguing that the nature of the relation between subject, content, and object depends on the deployment of attention. This is not mere awareness, for it determines how attention is placed in support of its embodied resources and sensibilities in a coordinated response of the whole organism, and hence how pain is experienced by the subject. For we have seen that the presence of attention is essential in performance of all sorts, as in baseball and tennis, which holds more generally as the basis for the deployment of all modes of engagement, including modes that Crane refers to, such as feeling that the ankle hurts me.

It is essential to note in this regard that the deployment of attention is an empirical matter. This has been recognized by Kant ([1787] 1965, A54/ B78–79), who distinguishes between pure and empirical apperception, associating attention with the latter.[20] Steinbock provides an interesting example that is applicable in the current context: While he is reading a newspaper, there is a sense of irritation that nags at him. (He notes here that although the source of irritation is not prominent, it can still affect one by its presence in the background, which suggests why subliminal advertising can be effective.) The irritation makes it difficult to concentrate, and he becomes aware that he is annoyed, though he does not know why. He finally realizes what the source is when attention is redeployed: "Only when a certain threshold is crossed, either, e.g., by a sound becoming progressively louder, by a sudden loud bang, by the pattern of the noise changing . . . does it dawn on me that there is an obnoxious buzzing from the fluorescent lights. . . . This can only happen at a certain point when it is made an explicit theme by turning toward it attentively" (2004, 31). The same could be said of a nagging pain. One realizes what the source is when one turns to the site of the pain and therefore experiences it differently, for it is now the center of attention as more resources are oriented to it, which forms a relation between the subject and the disturbed area that manifests painfully. The subject is made manifest at the center of attention, which has moved from reading to the source of pain in the body.[21]

Crane says that pain is not a relation to a body part. What his theory is trying to capture is how things seem to the subject, not what causes the pain (2014, 146). But on my account attention has shifted to the pain, and it hurts. It is not the intentional content (representation including aspectual shape) that hurts, but the ankle. This does not mean, however, that the ankle has become conscious, as noted above.[22] It is rather the case that the center of the lived body has moved to the ankle, so that the associated resources and sensibilities are deployed in feeling pain there. This can lead to a variety of responses that can be emotional, discursive, or bodily, which in turn call for new deployments of attention in support, and so on.

What is key is that the relation to pain varies according to how attention (and hence the subject) is deployed. For instance, if one is otherwise engaged, the pain may be peripheral and less distressing. One may be deep in thought and less preoccupied with it. Alternatively, if one is upset and concerned that it indicates a potential illness, then those emotions will manifest bodily and be associated with rumination on the possible implications. In this case attention may move between the pain in the ankle, emotion, and rumination in a vicious cycle where each feeds on the other. Another possibility is that one may simply choose to attend directly to the sensation of the pain in the ankle and stay with it, resisting the temptation to ruminate. In this case, if one stays with it and allows the window of attention to widen to include more of the surrounding body, a new perspective may arise. These are some of the ways in which attention can be deployed in producing varied experiences of pain.[23]

Another example is physical exercise. If I am thinking about my plan for the day while exercising, then if muscle pain begins to arise I may thoughtlessly stop and go on to another exercise, or quit altogether. Alternatively, if I attend to the body while exercising, I can more easily withstand the impulse to give up and can continue the activity. There are a variety of ways in which this can play out, a variety of ways in which attention can move in response to thoughts and other perceptions that arise in the course of such an activity, which ordinarily proceeds unawares. In general, when there is no awareness of that movement, we are subject to influences such as social media, which can affect us subliminally, as Steinbock (2004) has noted. If one stays with the movement, on the other hand, that is the way to freedom, both metaphysical and political, as we are more able to withstand influences that pervade the background and thus come to awareness in the act of resistance. This is the immanent reflexivity that has the potential to free us from unconscious influences, as discussed in part III.

Thus the movement of attention is an empirical matter, and I claim that any posited structures of consciousness are contingent upon that deployment. I argue in chapter 4 that this movement cannot be determined by any particular entity, but only the whole organism in relation to all that is as specified in the hermeneutical circle. Therefore, rather than passively processing information, the subject as made manifest by attention exerts a large influence on how we come into relation with the intentional objects that are simultaneously being made manifest in relation to us.

Crane's position also has implications when the intentional object is another person. What do I relate to, the person or the content, when the content is how I describe what it is like to be with the person? If I give her my full attention, I do not impose myself on who she is but rather allow her to manifest freely and be heard. We can bond ontologically when we are open to one another in this way, which is of essential import for the ethical and political realities in which we dwell.

Suppose, for instance, that I am comforting a friend who is in personal distress. I understand that I will be most supportive if I am simply able to listen; that is what she needs, the connection with a fully present human being to help lift the distress out into the open. What determines how attention is paid in this circumstance? What will stabilize my presence to enable the deepest, most profound listening? Powerful feelings are in place that hold the attention, given the affection I feel and how I understand myself as a friend and human being, but that is not enough. For as she pours her heart out, attention can wander. Something comes up that reminds me of my failed marriage, and I am suddenly no longer present. I am back in my own distress, in a part of my life that has not healed. Then I notice (i.e., my attention is drawn to the fact) that my friend's countenance has changed in light of my absence, for she has noticed my lack of attention, which in turn brings me back to her.

These passive movements arise from my embodied understanding (including affect), which would suggest that something else is called for if there is to be freedom in this most fundamental movement of myself. Such fleeting freedom that may come about is possible only when I hold on for the sake of being present. I hold on, staying with my embodied presence regardless of any influences that may take attention away, resisting the impulses to be absorbed or immersed in whatever distracts from the task at hand. I see the human being in front of me who needs attention and stay with her in her distress. This grounds me in the situation and gives her the attention she needs. I must eventually fall from this stance, but this is the sort of effort that is called for, to stay grounded rather than absorbed in the entities that arise in the process. I must be gathered and collected in the face-to-face encounter and thereby open to the possibility of freedom from the influences that typically predominate. Thus, rather than merely being "bare" awareness, attention is crucial in interpersonal relations as we relate to one another in the flesh, not by way of simulations or inferences, as is widely held in contemporary philosophical thought.

I argue, however, that the reason we do not experience ourselves as extended is that the movement of attention proceeds unawares. My claim is that attention is always extended, but we are unaware of being embedded in a body-environment as described above. Only when attention is brought under direct, conscious control is one aware of the movement of attention and its extension in the world. Thus the extended mind thesis must ultimately be tested phenomenologically.

Chapter 2

The Hermeneutical Circle

As human presence, attention comes before thought, rationality, emotion, will, transcendental ego, or anything else that may be posited as the seat of human action. When it is captured by the political process, our freedom is at risk, but as an action of the whole human being it cannot be controlled by any of the above. We can only seek to stay with that movement, the very movement of ourselves. In this chapter, I show that this movement emanates out of something greater than ourselves, which is a hermeneutical circle of attention, language, and bodily understanding. One implication is that no individual entity can determine its movement, because any such entities are themselves made manifest by way of the movement of the circle. Thus, the only way that something can affect my attention is by way of understanding and language, and I can attend to its bodily action and transcend its effects. It must be understood either implicitly or explicitly, which means that it can be focused on and made explicit because it affects *me*, it moves my presence. Thus, it must be made manifest in some manner at the site of my own coming into presence, which is the center of attention itself. But I can be *grounded* at that very site by way of active attention, in which case I can withstand its effects and in so doing gain insight into its nature, which is the path to transcendence. This is one aspect of the claim for the primacy of attention that is put forward herein.

The hermeneutical circle can be viewed as the understanding directing the movement of attention, the deliverances of which revise the understanding and its associated terms, leading to further movement, and so on. Attention is how we focus on particulars, where the guiding understanding is performative, in that it shows itself in what we take to be most important or interesting in a situation, explicitly or implicitly. I begin with the lived body, which is presumed to be a body of understanding (including the brain) which extends into the lived body-environment by way of attention. The body of understanding is also known as a bodily intelligence or sentience, which is associated with a felt intuition or sense, as discussed below. Understanding is conceived here quite broadly as the full panoply of what we bring to bear in worldly engagement, our thrown understanding or *factical being* in Heidegger's terms, or dimensions such as affect, intellect, instinct, and sensorimotor abilities more traditionally. Thus, I assume that understanding is bodily, and the intricate relation between body and environment entails its manifestation within the lived body-environment. Language is also conceived broadly to include discourse, gestures, the arts, and so on, as the vehicle of shared understanding, where each understands a common matter from a particular point of view, which is ultimately where attention is placed. The circle is thus the basis for the action of the whole human being, centered as it is in attention.

Attention is itself a holistic phenomenon, in that it can gather us as a whole and relate us to all that is, as are the other two dimensions. Language consists of a web of meanings where the meaning of a particular term depends on the rest of the web, and the body consists of a set of processes that are related by what Eugene Gendlin refers to as "crossing," as discussed below. Thus, all three are holistic in themselves, but in their conjunction they interact seamlessly in producing the circle as a whole, which can itself be more or less integrated and open depending on the state of attention.

In particular, the understanding of language itself determines how attention moves when encountering its signs. For instance, the understanding of a linguistic utterance is demonstrated by the resultant deployment of attention, as when I say "I am speaking" (see discussion above in the introduction). Attention and language also work together in further articulating the understanding, which directs attention, and so on.

The three elements consist of very different media that work together in producing our presence and relation to the world. Each can be conceived independently but does not appear in the absence of the other two. Understanding considered in itself (abstracted from the hermeneutical circle) is implicit, becoming explicit when it works together with attention in producing language. Attention is how we are placed in the body-environment, where the signs that constitute language appear. These, in turn, in conjunction with attention, disclose and constitute the array of human worlds.

The three dimensions are essential for life experience:

1. Attention, for instance, is a most concrete part the everyday. It is crucially important in relating to others and being successful in life. James ([1890] 1983, 381, cited above) tells us that everyone knows what it is and can sense when they are and are not getting it. In this regard, I have argued that attention is an extended presence, extending into the lived body-environment, and it is thus how we relate to anything at all.

2. The lived body-environment is where life occurs, and attention is how we inhabit it. It is also the site of implicit understanding, as I show in discussing Gendlin's work below.
3. Language opens the variety of meaningful worlds for us. And everyone knows what language and understanding are, too, for we know what it is to speak and understand, which implies that the triad consists of absolute essentials for human presence in the world.

The relations between the elements are intricate. Attention is how we are made manifest in relation to entities that show themselves, where aspects of ourselves are brought to bear, being made manifest according to our embodied understanding, which is itself formed in interaction with others by way of attention and language. Attention is directed by the confluence of language and understanding, and language is forged in the interaction of attention and understanding. Language as shared understanding is an intersubjective phenomenon, while bodily understanding is particular to the individual, which means that the movement of attention is guided by both intersubjective and idiosyncratic influences (see figure 2.1). This intricate relation between attention, language, and understanding determines how things are made manifest as we come into presence ourselves.[1] The circle can be more or less open, depending on the action of attention, which enables a more profound participation in the cosmos in which we dwell.

In terms of the embodied resources and sensibilities with which we are endowed, understanding is made manifest as they are deployed, for we show how we understand something in the course of worldly engagement. That is how understanding is demonstrated. At the same time, understanding comes about by way of engagement with worldly entities and states of affairs: that

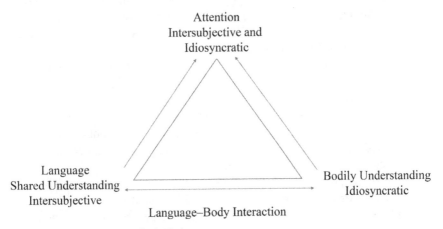

Attention
Intersubjective and
Idiosyncratic

Language
Shared Understanding
Intersubjective

Bodily Understanding
Idiosyncratic

Language–Body Interaction

Figure 2.1. The Hermeneutical Circle

is, by way of attention. Thus attention is directed by the understanding that is made manifest in the action of these modalities, which in turn are constituted by the access that is provided by attention itself, leading to the further deployment of attention, and so on.[2] This sort of circular movement is well known in more limited contexts, such as the cycle of perception (Neisser 1976), the gestalt cycle (Weizsäcker 1940), and the sensorimotor cycles that are considered in enactivist thought (e.g., O'Regan and Noë 2001).

Below I discuss in more detail the relations between the elements of the circle. They will all be operative in any given instance, but some of the analyses will focus on only two at a time. I consider the foreground-background relation and the relations between attention and understanding, language and understanding, and attention and language. I conclude that given the possibility of active attention, there is a *primacy of attention* that holds with respect to the other two dimensions. Understanding and language only point, they indicate, but attention is our placement in the lived body-environment itself, where life happens.[3] The implication is that the quality of that placement determines the quality and stability of the worlds that are produced in the action of the circle. My claim is that this action of the whole human being is required to be able to meaningfully change the webs of relations that make up human worlds, for it acts on the very basis for the relations themselves.

There are six steps to the argument:

1. Attention as human presence can be viewed as the foreground of engaged activity, whereas language and understanding work in the background unless called to the fore. This is how our presence can act on language and understanding, and in this manner the world, for it brings them to bear in the course of worldly engagement.
2. Attention is always placed in the lived body-environment. It can mobilize, command, or prime the body for action, harmonizing the deployment of resources as the self is made manifest as more or less gathered and open in relation to others.
3. The bodily understanding and language are intimately related. The effect of attention on the body shows itself in the language by way of this linkage.
4. Language emerges out of the placement of attention as the understanding is articulated. Its origin, acquisition, and development are intimately related to that placement. Attention and language together enable the disclosure and constitution of the meaningful worlds in which we dwell.
5. Given the possibility of active attention, this means that the quality and stability of these worlds depends on the grounding of attention in its placement. In particular, the state of attention enables the emergence of

more appropriate ways of being together in the situations in which we find ourselves engaged.

6. Hermeneutical truth emerges in the interaction of the elements of the circle, where the deliverances of attention have primacy, but it can always be challenged by the narratives that are enabled by language and understanding in a dialectical process. The communal unification that can come about by way of the public gathering of attention is essential for the ability to speak truth to power, as discussed in chapter 8.

TAYLOR AND GENDLIN ON LANGUAGE AND IMPLICIT UNDERSTANDING

In making the argument I draw on works of Charles Taylor and Eugene Gendlin, which, although nominally focused on language and implicit understanding, respectively, actually incorporate all three dimensions in some detail. I begin with some background on these works, where I show how the circle functions in each of them. Taylor sees attention and bodily understanding as essential for the acquisition and development of language, and Gendlin sees attention and language as intimately bound up with the functioning of implicit bodily understanding.

Taylor on Language

I examine Taylor's (2016) *The Language Animal: The Full Shape of the Human Linguistic Capacity* and show how attention and understanding are operative there. It is not difficult to see the presence of attention in the text, for Taylor argues that joint attention is an essential dimension of the language faculty. It forms a social space in which we enter into communion with one another, enabling the establishment of the shared understanding that is the basis for language. I show below that attention plays an even larger role in the text than Taylor indicates, serving as the basis for the openness, clarity, contact, and felt intuition that are also important in this work. In addition, bodily understanding plays a key role, and I conclude from this that attention and the body of understanding are essential for the acquisition and development of language. At the same time, attention and language serve as the basis for the ongoing articulation of bodily understanding, thereby completing the circle.

In this text Taylor distinguishes between designative and constitutive theories of language. The designative theory is part of the standard metaphysical position that I am contesting. Associated with Thomas Hobbes, John Locke, and Étienne Bonnot de Condillac (HLC), this theory assumes that words are assigned arbitrarily to entities that are already made manifest. Taylor says that while this may be appropriate in limited realms where distanced observation is appropriate, it is insufficient for the majority of human worlds of meaning that we occupy. He rather argues for a constitutive theory following Johann Gottfried Herder, Johann Georg Hamann, and Wilhelm von Humboldt (HHH), where hermeneutical reasoning and dialectic are operative in a never-ending exploration of the depths of human being, in the abundance of worlds we inhabit by way of language and attention.

For HLC, language develops one word at a time, with no relation to the existing web of terms. These are merely conventional descriptions of given realities, in contrast to a hermeneutical circle, where attention enables the engagement with manifesting entities within a web of relations and terms that are constitutive of those relations. The understanding of those terms shows up as a bodily sentience or felt intuition of our situations, as discussed below.

HLC assumes that language plays a neutral role in naming independent objects, where the entities are not affected in the naming. Taylor argues, however, that any such activity assumes a preexisting point of view from which such entities are encountered, which is the basis for any purported "neutral" act of description. The formation of this perspective occurs, in my terms, by way of the hermeneutical circle of attention, language, and understanding, thereby enabling the entities to show up in relation to us. This is an inherently meaningful process, given that self-understanding (which is about what matters to me) is key for the deployment of attention. For the understanding that guides attention is brought to bear in worldly engagement and made manifest as my presence, as the self that shows itself in relation to others and the world (see chapter 4).

This means that things don't just come to our notice, they are not given as brute facts to be described. We must be present for the things to appear to us, which occurs by way of the circle. This is the difference between HLC and HHH, that attention is not simply directed by an "ego" or other mechanism to preexisting entities, but rather the movement of attention in conjunction with the action of language and the body of understanding both discloses (makes manifest) and constitutes manifesting entities themselves (their meaning, how they are understood), including ourselves. My contention is that this applies to all the worlds we inhabit, including the world of physics (see chapter 3). Moreover, attention is our presence as mediated by language and understanding, but it can be intentionally gathered to go deeper, arriving at felt intuitions that go beyond the present understanding and language.

The difference in metaphysical assumptions in the two positions is evident. On the designative view, we are cut off from the worlds in which we dwell, viewing an objective reality by way of distanced observation and description. On the constitutive view, we are immersed in meaningful worlds that matter to us. Even scientific investigators are so immersed; they understand themselves as such and their studies engage them in a most meaningful manner. While the former view can lead to nihilism, the latter allows for intrinsic meaning.

Gendlin on Implicit Understanding

Gendlin produced a large corpus in both philosophy and psychotherapy, beginning with *Experiencing and the Creation of Meaning* ([1962] 1997).[4] He developed a psychotherapeutic technique known as Focusing, which is now part of the universe of tools that are available for therapists, along with establishing the Focusing Institute,[5] which as of 2020 had seventeen hundred members in fifty-eight countries. The prominence of the term "focusing" indicates the importance of attention in both the therapeutic process and his philosophy. Fundamental for him (as it is for the enactivist thinkers) is the notion of body-environment, where he details the intimate relation between the two. Of course, the body is made up of environmental materials, but there is also an ongoing exchange of substances and reciprocal constitution of body and environment. On the one hand, Gendlin refers to us as *Homo faber*, fundamentally engaged in producing objects and otherwise shaping the world, but at the same time the body itself is continually incorporating environmental materials. He discusses how a plant takes in water and how lungs take in air. In the latter process, for instance, air comes into the lungs and blood cells, and there is no dividing line between body and environment. For Gendlin, the body *is* the lungs expanding; the air coming in and the lungs expanding cannot be separated. Processes such as these are what Gendlin refers to as *body-constituting*. Gendlin (2017b, 116) discusses three such "generative" processes: (1) body-constituting, (2) behavior, and (3) patterning (gestures, art, language, and culture), which are associated with all living things, animals, and humans, respectively.[6] Gendlin claims that these three intricately related processes are fundamental in the constitution of body, environment, and world. The implicit understanding Gendlin puts forward is operative in the conjunction of the three processes.

Gendlin's three generative processes determine how the world is differentiated and also how objects are produced in the course of worldly interaction, where an object is defined as a part of the environment to which the body responds with a specific process. Three types of objects are produced that correspond to these processes: (1) in body-constituting, we respond to particular aspects of the environment, such as food and daylight; (2) in behavior space, objects exist as behavior possibilities; and (3) patterning (or language broadly conceived) produces the world of human situations (clusters of behavior possibilities), which are the most important objects in our lives.

The notion of the body developed here is much more than muscles, flesh, and organs; it is rather the body of lived experience. The sensation from within can be attended directly, but regardless of whether one does so or not, it is an ever-present dimension of our lives. It enables access to what Gendlin (2009) refers to as our bodily sentience, or the implicit understanding that can become a *felt sense* when attention is directly placed in it.[7] For Gendlin, consciousness is an embodied phenomenon, and the vast majority of conscious life takes place implicitly.

Gendlin says that bodily knowing is an indispensable feature of daily getting along in the world. If it were absent, we would not know how to function. He provides many examples of how implicit understanding functions in our lives, with explicit thought playing little or no role in the process, such as the following (2009, 334).

1. From just a few words we can grasp a complex situation. Someone reports: "Jim said no." The single statement of a single fact brings a new understanding of the whole situation.
2. In the opening scene of Henrik Ibsen's *Hedda Gabler*, a man comes to deliver a telegram. From how she treats him, we suddenly understand the kind of person she is.
3. The coming of a new thought can also reorganize a situation. "Oh, he's afraid of George!" we think, and immediately a great deal has changed.

Of particular interest is the sophistication of the implicit understanding, which incorporates a wide variety of possible behaviors and the effect of each on the other in any given situation. For instance, Gendlin (2017b, 128) discusses how we know implicitly that if we kick a ball we can no longer pick it up and throw it, and that if we kick someone we can no longer fondle them, or the fondling will now be a comforting. In addition, after any behavior, we are implicitly aware of many things that we couldn't do before. The claim is that this sort of knowledge functions in every situation.[8]

This leads to two interrelated concepts, those of (1) implying and occurring and (2) crossing. Implying and occurring are closely related to the relation between attention and understanding that is being put forward here. The implicit understanding implies that a certain event will occur at the center of attention, but whether that indeed occurs depends on the suitability of body-environmental conditions. There is an uncountable number of processes that make up the implicit understanding, which Gendlin (2017a) refers to as a coordinated or unseparated multiplicity because they "cross" with one another due to how each process affects the others, depending on the relevance of the occurrence to each. We have seen this, for instance, in the above example of kicking a ball, where related processes are affected by that event. This means that there is a dense web of interrelations between the processes, but Gendlin claims that at any moment all these implicit processes as a whole point to only one occurrence, in what he calls "focaling" or "relevanting."[9] Attention is, in this manner, the gateway between the implicit understanding and occurrences, which are how things are made manifest within the lived body-environment. It is important to note that these references to attention are not separable from the web of implicit processes, for we are not considering a linear process in which implying is followed by occurring, and so on; rather, Gendlin (2017a) develops a theory of space and time that is consistent with this setup.

I indicate below how, using this framework, Gendlin is able to explain the emergence of linguistic symbols that are independent of specific bodily processes but are nevertheless able to generate the web of language that emerges out of this dynamic of implying and occurring within the context of the three generative processes.

FOREGROUND AND BACKGROUND

The circle can be fruitfully thought in terms of foreground and background. Attention as our extended presence is the foreground for engaged activity, while language and the body of understanding form the background for such activity. The background guides and supports the movement of attention, which in turn brings aspects of that background, the confluence of language and understanding, to bear in the course of engagement. Thus the two background dimensions are brought to the foreground and made manifest in that manner, and the deliverances of attention shape them for further interaction.

Attention as foreground is our presence, which is essential for entities to be made manifest in relation to us. It is the site of experience, where we are brought to the fore in relation to such entities. For instance, chewing one's food typically occurs in the background, while attention is elsewhere. But when one must be aware of how one is chewing—for instance, after a tooth extraction—then attention focuses directly on the actual action in the body. It should be noted, however, that even when chewing is in the background, attention is placed somewhere else in the lived body-environment as support for whatever other activity one is engaged in. Although one is often not aware of one's placement therein, that presence is the basis for the engagement and orientation of the body of understanding in activities that are often considered to be "mental."

There is thus a relation of mutual support between foreground and background, between the explicit and the implicit (see figure 2.2). The body of understanding (shaped as it is by language) includes sub-personal processes (e.g., brain, nervous system) that support and direct the engagement of attention, which reciprocates in supporting the deployment of background

Chapter 2

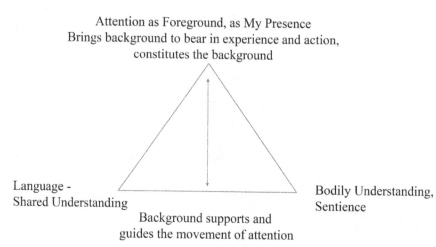

Attention as Foreground, as My Presence
Brings background to bear in experience and action,
constitutes the background

Language -
Shared Understanding

Background supports and
guides the movement of attention

Bodily Understanding,
Sentience

Figure 2.2. Mutual Support

resources in engaged activity at the personal level. The brain and physiological systems support action at the center, but it is the action at the site of our presence itself that is key for the possibility of autonomous life activity.

The question for philosophy is, which ultimately determines human action, foreground or background? The typical assumption is that action is self-conscious, in which case it is reasonable to assume that the foreground guides activity. But there is a long tradition, going back at least to Baruch Spinoza, which emphasizes the role of affect in determining action. My contention is that thinking in terms of attention as foreground renders the active/passive dichotomy that is associated with it crucial for this question, together with the question of autonomy and selfhood.[10] The claim (to be pursued in chapters 6 and 8) is that when attention is passive, the background determines its movement, but the possibility of active attention is the ultimate basis for the primacy of attention as the foreground for human activity. The hallmark of active attention is explicit self-awareness, of knowing directly that we are embodied in the present moment when we gather ourselves by way of the intentional placement of attention in the course of engaged activity. We must be self-aware in such an action, for that placement is the site in which our very presence is made manifest.

This is to be contrasted with the endogenous-exogenous distinction that is made in the attention literature regarding its movement. There it is assumed that any internal goals and intentions that lead to shifts in attention are endogenous (top-down) and thus under the control of the subject, whereas external stimuli that lead to shifts are exogenous (bottom-up).[11] But from the perspective of the hermeneutical circle, any such dichotomy ignores the fact that the movement of attention emanates from the understanding of the human being as a whole, deployed as it is in a given context and more or less integrated depending on the state of attention. Therefore, whether or not the preceding objects of attention were external stimuli or internal processes is hardly a criterion for determining whether or not attention is under the control of the "subject." In fact, the very notion of the subject is in question from this perspective, for, as I argue in chapter 4, the self itself is made manifest in the course of the movement of attention, as bodily resources and sensibilities are brought to bear in the course of engagement at the center of attention.

It is true that goals and intentions are part of the understanding, but so is the reaction to the stimuli. How are we to distinguish the two? The latter may be implicit, but in this case the understanding still guides attention. Why would control exist only in the former case? If we were to replace the endogenous/exogenous distinction with the explicit/implicit distinction, this would highlight the fact that there is no firm boundary between the two because what is implicit becomes explicit when attention is paid to it, which renders the explanandum determinative of the distinction itself. This also is indicative of the larger point, that there is no entity that controls attention, for its movement emerges out of the understanding of the human being as a whole, which should be respected as such and not be reduced to posited structures, for these would also have to be made manifest via the action of the circle if they were determinative of its movement.

THE PLACEMENT OF ATTENTION

Attention moves according to the understanding, which is constituted by way of the interaction of attention and language. That understanding *places* attention in the lived body-environment, which is how the former is brought to bear in the course of engagement, that is, it is how we ourselves are made manifest in relation to worldly entities (see chapter 4). We can see this in the case of the baseball player considered in chapter 1, where the placement of attention is crucial in determining whether or not the ball is caught. The understanding guides attention, in this case, the self-understanding that the fielder enjoys. She understands herself as a fielder and has experience playing the position, which has resulted in the body's musculature being formed in accordance with its demands, all of which is part of the body of understanding. Her attention focuses on various aspects of the game as it proceeds, based on what she understands. She focuses on the pitcher and the runners, and as the ball is pitched, she focuses intently on the batter. The sharper her focus, the more readily she responds if the ball is hit in her direction. That focus results in the body responding immediately in going after it, and split seconds are precious in this regard. Her attention stays with the flight of the ball, and the body responds in moving toward the projected site of the catch. It is the placed focus that commands the body in its movement. If it is distracted in any way, the body is similarly driven off course, which can be the difference between catching the ball and missing it.

Similarly, distraction from the habitual seat of action plays a key role in the well-known case of Chuck Knoblauch, the second baseman for the Mets who suddenly lost the ability to throw the ball to first base. Dreyfus (2005) blames it on the role of attention, which he equates with reflection, distracting from the task at hand. But I am arguing that attention is the seat of human action for all modes of worldly engagement, including reflection. In the present case, Knoblauch was habitually configured in a particular way when throwing to first base, where attention successfully supported the activity, but something arose to disrupt it. It could have been an anxiety, illness, or injury that led to the change and resulting failure, then leading to further disruption in a self-defeating cycle. The key here is that it was not necessarily reflection interfering with a well-established habitual task, as Dreyfus sees it, but it could have been any event that reconfigured the foreground-background relation that held previously. Dreyfus has too narrow a conception when he equates attention with reflection.[12]

This means that attention plays the role of a command center, as it were, in that the body follows the commands that emerge (implicitly or explicitly) from the center of attention. That is, rather than there being an entity that determines attention in its movement, it is rather the case that attention itself, as placed in the body-environment, "controls" how the body and its resources are engaged in worldly activity. There is no entity whose thoughts direct the action; rather, thought is itself just one aspect of the whole human being, which is also made manifest by way of the movement of attention. Of course, attention is itself guided by the extant understanding, as we indeed have a hermeneutical circle here. But attention as our very presence in the world is how the self manifests itself, how we control anything at all, as attention brings that understanding to bear in its placement in the body-environment. The argument is that the effectiveness of that control lies in the state of attention, the extent to which attention is intentionally gathered, from which the harmonization of the body in action follows. Attention enables the priming of the body for action, which activates and readies the deployment of its resources and sensibilities.

Heidegger provides an example that makes this point. He considers a sprinter preparing to race when arguing for the actuality of potentiality (*dunamis*) against the Megarians:

> Let us consider a sprinter who, for example, has (as we say) taken his or her mark in a hundred meter race just before the start. What do we see? A human

who is not in movement; a crouched stance; yet this could be said just as well or even more appropriately about an old peasant woman who is kneeling before a crucifix on a pathway; more appropriately, because with the sprinter we do not simply see a kneeling human not in movement; what we call "kneeling" here is not kneeling in the sense of having set oneself down; on the contrary, this pose is much more that of being already "off and running." The particularly relaxed positioning of the hands, with fingertips touching the ground, is almost already the thrust and the leaving behind of the place still held. Face and glance do not fall dreamily to the ground, nor do they wander from one thing to another; rather, they are tensely focused [*sind gespannt gehalten*] on the track ahead, so that it looks as though the entire stance is stretched taut toward what lies before it. No, it not only looks this way, it is so, and we see this immediately; it is decisive that this be attended to [*bedenken*] as well. What limps along afterwards and is attempted inadequately . . . is the suitable clarification of the essence of the actuality of this being which is actual in this way.

What exhibits itself to us is not a human being standing still, but rather a human poised for the start; the runner is poised in this way and is this utterly and totally [*er ist im Stand dazu, und er ist das ganz und gar*]. Thus we say—because we see it without looking any further—that he is poised for the start. The only thing needed is the call "go." Just this call and he is already off running, hitting his stride, that is, in enactment. But what does this say? Now everything of which he is capable is present [*anwesend*]; he runs and holds nothing back of which he would be capable; running, he executes his capability. . . . The one who enacts is just that one who leaves nothing undone in relation to his capability, for whom there is now in the running actually nothing more of which he is capable. This, of course, is then the case only if the one who is capable comes to the running in full readiness, if in this readiness he extends himself fully. But this implies that he is then genuinely in a position to run only if he is in good condition, completely poised, in full readiness. (GA 33: 217–18/187–88)

Attention activates the bodily resources, leaving nothing undone, as it commands them accordingly, in full readiness. In my terms, the potential becomes actual by way of acute attention. The resources are poised for action, and all are present. The sprinter is fully ready, as all resources are prepared for the start.[13] The face and glance are *tensely held* on the track ahead; they are at the ready. All is stretched taut toward what lies ahead. The runner is *poised* (*im Stand*), and *is* this utterly and totally. Everything of which he is capable is present; this is an ontological effort, an effort of his whole being. He comes to the running in full readiness, he extends himself fully, he is resolved. Thus, as Heidegger goes on to say, the actuality of potentiality is a matter of *holding* (*Halten*) *oneself in readiness*. This *being held* is its actual presence.[14]

This is an example of active attention, but regardless of how active or passive it is, attention is always placed in the lived body-environment, thereby bringing language and understanding to bear in support of engaged activity (see figure 2.3). This is the fundamental choice we have, which sets the tone for the whole circle and the resulting human realities, for as our presence, it is the only site in which we can act on the understanding and thus the shared language. It offers the possibility of grounding ourselves within the circle and providing some stability above and beyond the reign of impulses, which lack our presence by way of attention and are therefore blind. Although this is always a potential choice, the placement of attention in the lived body-environment is typically passive and therefore driven by the extant understanding, which means that one is not aware of that placement, of being placed in, or inhabiting, a body-environment. Only when one intentionally gathers oneself in this manner is an actual choice being made.

The impulse to move attention may come from an external source, such as the suggestion to attend to the foot and floor, but it still has to be understood as such, interpreted in such a manner to lead one to act, if one so chooses, in the stipulated manner. This means that when one confronts a threat of violence, even at the point of a gun, the response comes about by way of the understanding. Therefore, the movement of attention cannot be determined by a given entity, because it depends solely on the given understanding. The key question is whether attention is active or passive, where in the latter case the understanding itself takes over without the benefit of the enhanced presence and relation that can come about when we are intentionally present. When attention is active, on the other hand, the understanding as a whole is more integrated, as more of oneself is brought to bear in a harmonized fashion on the matter of engagement. This is how the circle is grounded, in that the state of attention determines the extent to which the understanding is

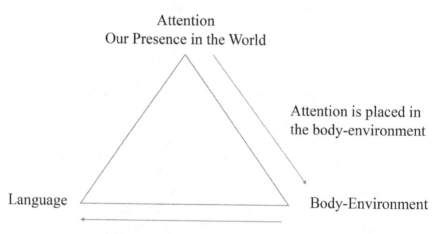

Figure 2.3. The Placement of Attention

integrated and more consistent with the reality that is brought by attention, which determines, in turn, the possibility of stabilization and transformation. This is a groundless, abyssal ground, for there is nothing outside of the circle that determines the state of attention itself.

In the above case of the doctor and patient, for instance, the patient's attention moves passively in response to the doctor's queries. The doctor asks where the pain is and attention moves in response, as the understanding of the statement is made manifest in that very movement. We also saw the possibility of a transformed quality of experience when attention is intentionally placed, in the case of the pain in the ankle and pain due to exercise, and saw in the case of listening to the friend that even when we bring an understanding of the need for acute attention, that placement is sustained only as long as a more powerful impulse does not arise. This is a key difficulty in sustaining active attention: that it is possible only to the extent that the supporting understanding enables it, which in turn is subject to reorientation in the course of the effort.

In this regard, we considered in the last chapter an example of consciously placing attention, where the reader was asked to place attention in the sensation of one's feet and then let it move to the floor. We have direct access to the body of understanding by way of attention, and by way of the body to the entities engaged with in the environment. Since the body of understanding guides attention in its movement, the body itself and the terms of its engagement (which come about by way of prior engagement and articulation) guide attention in its placement in the body-environment. That is, the impulse to move in such a manner comes, as always, from the body, formed as it is by language and previous deployments of attention. The movement is guided as such, but it can always go beyond the given language and understanding as it is placed in relation and we are made manifest as engaged in varied manners.

Attention is placed in the lived body-environment, that is the key move, and it is the basis for Gendlin's practice of Focusing. That placement is what we speak from, the site of engaged resources and sensibilities (see again figure 2.3). It produces a resonance (a bodily sentience or intelligence) that guides us as we navigate the world, and we speak from that resonance. That is what makes the words we speak fit the situations we find ourselves in, to the extent that the understanding is appropriate. When one directs attention to the bodily sentience, the implicit understanding can become a more palpable felt sense. Gendlin often discusses the role it plays in the creative process, where one is searching for the right phrase or gesture to carry a work forward. We feel that all the typical words or gestures do not work and keep open in searching for what will. What is immensely intelligent is the sense of knowing that one does not know, that nothing in one's current repertoire seems to meet the demands of the moment. One can stay with the bodily felt sense until a thought arises that works, and one knows it immediately because it resonates with the implicit bodily knowing (rightness). This is one instance of the felt sense at work.

Applying this to Focusing, the truth of a statement (typically about a personal situation) can be checked against the felt sense by way of intentional and sustained placement of attention directly in the body of understanding. With attention rooted in that manner, the meaning of any utterances can be checked by way of their resonance with the bodily felt sense and modified to better fit it. Moreover, the utterances can be further modified in response to any changes that come about in the felt sense due to the articulation itself. Thus we see an intricate relation between attention, language, and understanding that serves as the foundation for this technique, which has been practiced in therapeutic contexts for many years.[15]

The thesis put forward in the next two sections is that language and shared understanding develop as we attend to one another and the world. Understanding operates in the lived body-environment, which is the site of manifestation of entities and linguistic symbols. Attention is placed there, in relation to all that is, thereby enabling language to open us to worlds of meaning. Language is thus the vehicle of shared understanding, connecting us to humanity at large, together with realms such as the visual arts, music, and the sacred. It enables the communal understanding and movement of attention that is the condition of the possibility of shared worlds.[16] But at the same time, attention is essential for this, given that it is the open ground for the connections. We shall also see joint attention as the basis for the acquisition and development of language and shared understanding, which argues again for the primacy of attention.

THE LANGUAGE-UNDERSTANDING RELATION

We discussed above Gendlin's notion of generative processes, where body-constituting processes interact with the other two processes: behavior and patterning. We can see the constitution of the body, for instance, when muscles develop in sports or in the course of an occupation. Action and speech affect body-constituting, as muscles and nerves respond and are formed. The rules of a game exist in the muscles, determining how they grow and exist in a patterned world, which is the basis for the coping activity that figures such as Dreyfus (2005) emphasize.

Gendlin (2017a) describes how each generative process emerges from lower ones. Behavior is a "special kind" of body constitution, where bodily sentience interacts with perception. The body is formed for behavior, which structures are passed along from generation to generation. Patterning arises when gestures replace behavior sequences, which is like talking about a sequence instead of actually going through it. Gendlin (2017b, 119–20) gives the example of hierarchical monkey societies in which getting ready for a fight causes huge changes over their whole bodies, and where males turn their backs at the end of a fight. Instead of fighting, just making the turn in deference to a superior substitutes for going through the whole fighting sequence, so they don't have to get ready for it. The large bodily shifts take place only if the turn does not occur. Thus, the gesture replaces the behavior, and we are on the way to patterning and language.

Patterning results in a vast expansion of behavior possibilities as the human world develops.[17] Linguistic actions in situations become behaviors too, which is another aspect of the relation between the generative processes. What we do with patterns is part of the behavior context. There is a wide variety of possible behavioral patterns given the understanding of the situation, which implicitly considers all the possible effects of other possibilities. As discussed above, Gendlin calls this "crossing." Sequences cross with each other and eventually lose all onomatopoeic characteristics, resulting in the (in the English case) twenty-six letters of the alphabet. Thus we see the intimate relation between the lived body and linguistic activity.

The Right Fit between Words and Situations

Another aspect of the relation between the bodily understanding and language lies in the body's ability to speak and arrange words in ways that fit the situation. This is the rightness that Taylor (2016) talks about, which he puts in terms of a felt intuition, and which Gendlin speaks of as a felt sense of our situations. This is the key assumption the HLC position makes, that the words fit their referents.[18] It is true that bodily resonance guides us through life as we encounter various situations, but the relation is not given, depending as it does on the state of attention (see figure 2.4). So words can be more or less appropriate for their situations, which depends on the quality of our presence.

For Taylor (2016), bodily understanding appears in the form of bodily know-how, which translates into the metaphors that are so important in language development, and in the question of the rightness of the fit between a word and its referent. In the latter case Taylor discusses a bodily sentience, a "felt intuition" that is the basis for knowing if a word is right. We know how to get around in the environment, we know up and down, back and forth, all of which serves as the basis for the formation of metaphors and other vehicles that are essential in the development of language. Taylor also discusses how language possessors have an ongoing need for further articulation of the meanings that come about in language use, where there are two dimensions, felt intuition and articulation in words, which he refers to as direct and

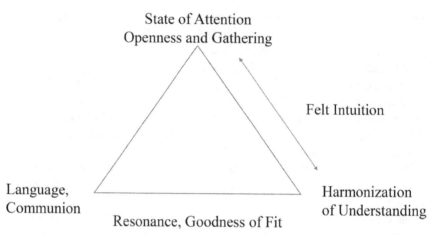

State of Attention
Openness and Gathering

Felt Intuition

Language,
Communion   Harmonization
                    Resonance, Goodness of Fit   of Understanding

Figure 2.4. The Right Fit

indirect pathways. Felt intuition comes about by way of direct experience of the matters at hand, which requires attention, while such meanings also require clarification and defense when engaged with others in worldly affairs. Taylor refers to this dialectic as hermeneutical reasoning (2016, 221), and sees the ultimate basis for ratification in felt intuition, where we know by way of direct experience that something is true (253). This theme is discussed further in the section entitled "Hermeneutical Truth" below.

It would appear to be obvious that the clarity attention brings enables one to come up with words that are appropriate for what one is currently experiencing. But we must ask, how does such a focus enable one to know that the words fit the experience? One cannot arbitrarily assign any words one likes, for they must be capable of being understood by others. What can be the basis for the assignment? I have been arguing that presence to the thing itself, always within the hermeneutical circle, provides the grip that enables one to know which words are appropriate, depending on how sustained the attention is. As Gendlin puts it, "The words come directly from my living bodily in the situation. The words come already arranged in phrases. They come arranged both grammatically and pragmatically. Of course always both, since they would not have their situational meaning without their grammatical patterning" (2017b, 121). Thus, the words arise by way of the implicit understanding that is brought to bear by way of attention, coming formed in sentences with no explicit consideration of the rules of grammar.[19] The words fit the situation depending on the quality of the presence that is brought to bear on it.

Taylor considers this question with regard to the expressive stances we take in worldly activity. For instance, he often refers to a biker who acts in a manner that could be referred to as "machismo," even if that manner of expression is not initially associated with the term. But at some point a space opens that only a word can fill (2016, 230), when we need to better understand the point of the behavior. We know the word fits when our bodily sentience resonates with the word when it is invoked. It brings the matter into focus; as we see the point of the behavior more clearly, it is made more explicit and we have a better grip on what it is about. We understand the import, where it fits in the web of practices within the context of one's life and that of the community at large, and the associated feeling and its complex of emotions changes along with the behavior. All this depends on the quality of the attention that enables the stances to come into focus for further articulation.

Shared Understanding Is Preserved in Language

There is an understanding that is preserved in the language we all share as members of communities. The manner in which the body presents itself in the course of engagement is part of the process of manifestation. For instance, when we hear the expression "my heart goes out to you," this reflects the action of the body itself in interpersonal relations when we feel empathy for the circumstances of another. This is the sort of exploration that phenomenology is meant to uncover. One must be acutely attentive in the course of such interaction, opened up to what is occurring in the body of understanding. The claim here is that it is possible to see the sort of bodily dynamics that underlie such an expression. An expression like this gains currency when it resonates with enough of the population, which means that the wisdom of the body supports what it is saying.

Taylor discusses the various ways in which "heart" appears in the language (2016, 231–33). We experience certain feelings in proximity to certain organs, and the intricacy of these relations shows itself in how the feelings are expressed. This can be seen, for instance, in expressions such as "you have my heart," indicating a love interest, or "have a heart," calling for compassion. Courage is seen in "stout hearts" and "hearts of oak." The fact of emotional experience in the vicinity of the heart is seen in "it warms my heart," "my heart is all aflutter, now that I hear her voice," "she broke my heart," and "my heart bleeds." This is not a fixed, natural state of affairs, for the relations will vary by culture due to the intricacies of the relations between elements of the circle. Taylor concludes,

> There is a kind of reciprocal relation here. We learn to distinguish the emotions by the way we feel them in our bodies, and communicate them through our bodies. But we also learn to identify our bodily feelings and their "seats" through the language of the emotions. This process of mutual definition yields the corporeal geography of the emotions, which have their "seats" in certain

"organs." These bodily verbal interchanges end up opening a field of the sayable and giving shape to it. (233)[20]

Thus, the meaning is felt in the body, and sustained presence by way of attention to that feeling is the path to self-understanding. Other terms show how the presence or absence of attention makes itself known. For instance, there are terms such as "being absorbed" rather than "collected," "immersed" rather than "awake." From the perspective of our embodied being in the world, absorption and immersion mean that we are literally absent from the present bodily goings-on, where body-environmental processes take over and we literally disappear in them. We saw this in chapter 1, where we considered being habitually lost in thought, but it is possible to bring attention to bear out of that absorption to our bodily presence while the thought continues, which enables us to see the event as it occurs. These bodily events make their way into the language because of the intimate relation between speech and our being in the world. That is, the very shape of our bodily presence shows itself in the language that emerges from it.

I turn now to a discussion of the relation between attention and language, specifically in the origin of language and its acquisition in childhood, followed by a consideration of how attention figures in its ongoing development.

THE ORIGIN, ACQUISITION, AND DEVELOPMENT OF LANGUAGE

In terms of the triangle, language develops when entities manifest at the center of attention, as it is directed by the understanding, which includes the present understanding of language itself (or at least protolinguistic capacities in early childhood).[21] That is, something presents itself for a potential encounter, and the attention is directed in a manner that depends on the extant understanding. If the attention is *held* during the encounter, if I remain present to it, that enables the manifestation of the entity in a new way. I can speak from that presence, and the new understanding and its associated terms is shared when I am in the presence of others who attend to the same thing (see figure 2.5).

I discuss below how we are born with the capacity to engage in imitation and protoconversations, which eventually leads to the acquisition of language by way of joint attention to the same entity. So, when a potential entity presents itself, it takes a shape depending on the bodily capacities that are in place. Any such emergence is contingent upon the manner in which the entities present themselves, so the direction by the understanding is not determinative. But the conjunction of the deliverances of attention and the preunderstanding produces a shape, a pattern in the manifestation that enables

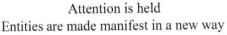
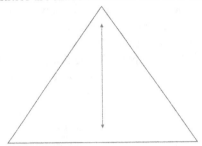

Attention is held
Entities are made manifest in a new way

Language   Bodily Understanding

Understanding directs attention
and is modified by its deliverances

Figure 2.5. Development of Language

a new articulation and associated terms. At the same time, the understanding is itself articulated by way of the new deliverances, which means that understanding also develops in the process. Language thus develops out the bodily understanding, including that of the language itself, by way of the deliverances of attention as guided by the understanding; there is a circularity here, in that language contributes to its own development, in conjunction with attention and understanding. We turn now to treat the questions of the origin and acquisition of language from this perspective, followed by further discussion of its development.

The Origin of Language

Taylor spends most of chapter 2 of *The Language Animal* (2016) on the question of how language grows, focusing on the phenomenon of joint attention, which is essential in early childhood development for the acquisition of language, as well as in the ongoing development of language. He also considers Herder's theory of the genesis of language, where a space of attention transcending ordinary immersion in worldly engagement opens, in which a distinguishing mark appears that leads to the creation of the associated sign. Taylor refers to such spaces, which he also associates with Heidegger's clearing, as enabling communion when we attend to one another. This means that we are made manifest together, thereby enabling deeper connections between individuals by way of mutual attention. This has obvious implications for the politics of public spaces, as discussed further in chapter 8.

Taylor often points to Herder's critique of Condillac as the first move in the debate between the HLC and HHH positions regarding the origin of language. In his approach, Condillac assumes there are prelinguistic objects such as mental content or representational "ideas" and their associated natural signs, such as cries of fear. Language comes about when an "instituted sign" enables one to *focus* on the ideas and thereby direct the play of one's imagination. Notice that attention appears as central in this account, enabling access to the content and control of mental activity. It is also central for Herder, which points to the essential role attention plays in the linguistic dimension.

Herder argues that Condillac has assumed the existence of ideas, signs, and their associations, but, as discussed above, the fit between a sign and its referent is in question. To approach it Herder develops a notion of "reflection (*Besonnenheit*)," where a new space of attention (*Aufmerksamkeit*) enables the recognition of objects *as* the entities that they are, rather than reacting to a signal for task effectiveness. This rather calls for signs which are attuned to that recognition.

Taylor notes this relation between attention and language in an earlier discussion of Herder, where the capacity of reflection, defined as the capacity to focus on objects by recognizing them, is inseparable from language: "Instead of being overcome by the ocean of sensations as they rush by us, we are able to distinguish one wave, and hold it in clear, calm attention. It is this new space of attention, of distance from the immediate instinctual significance of things, which Herder wants to call reflection" (1995, 88). Language is born when we see something as more than how it figures in a world of nonlinguistic creatures. For instance, a lamb can be prey or a sexual partner, but as an object of attention for a language user, "[i]t is recognized as a being of a certain type through a distinguishing mark (*Merkmal*). This mark in Herder's story is its bleating. . . . In other words, in the reflective stance the lamb is first recognized *as* a lamb; it is first recognized as an object rightly classed as 'the bleating one.' An issue of rightness arises, which cannot be reduced to success in some life task" (1995, 88).

The Acquisition of Language

Attention and language work together in disclosing and constituting the world. Language guides attention, opening up realms of disclosure, while attention develops and articulates language and understanding. Joint attention, in particular, is well known to be essential in the acquisition of language (see figure 2.6). We share experience and understanding by attending to the same objects and events, and language enables the coordination and develops as we jointly attend—as it must in order for the understanding of language to be shared, and there being no private languages.

The process begins from birth, as has been detailed in the joint attention literature. The most common definition of joint attention is that two or more individuals attend to the same object, and each is aware that the other's

Joint Attention

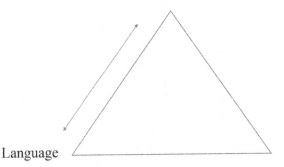

Language   Shared Understanding

Body-Language interaction

Figure 2.6. Origin and Development of Language

attention is so directed. The interest in this started in developmental psychology, where it was observed that at about age one infants learn to follow the gaze of the mother at it moves to external objects, from which develop linguistic and conceptual capabilities. More recently philosophers have become interested in the subject, addressing questions such as the nature of other minds and common knowledge (Eilan et al., 2005).

The mother (assuming she is present) is recognized shortly after birth based on experience during gestation, which indicates the initial presence of attention and understanding. Soon thereafter the child starts to imitate the caregiver's gestures and speech, thereby beginning the process of language acquisition. Therefore, understanding and a protolanguage are present soon after birth. The next few months of life are characterized by mutual (or dyadic) attention between infant and caregiver, which leads to joint attention, the emergence of pointing, and the transition from pointing to gestures and the production of basic sentences. We are born with the capacity for imitation and an implicit understanding of the difference between self and others. The interaction between child and caregiver has been described in terms of protoconversations by Trevarthen (1979, 1993).[22] Protoconversations eventually lead to the acquisition of language as child and caretaker attend to the same objects and processes in the course of interaction.

While primary intersubjectivity is characterized by mutual attention between child and caretaker (Reddy 2005), joint attention is key in secondary intersubjectivity, for now infants and adults attend to shared situations in which the infants learn what things mean and what they are for. They begin to understand movements and expressions within pragmatic contexts, which is the basis for the development of such understanding over the course of a lifetime. What is crucial is that the understanding developed in primary and secondary intersubjectivity does not disappear as the child matures but rather serves as the basis for the further development of understanding. Of course, at any particular time much of the understanding will be implicit, but it will still be operative in determining how we respond to a particular situation.

Thus, we begin life with an understanding of self and other, a preconceptual ability to focus on others and imitate them, and the ability to engage those others in protoconversations. We begin in the circle of attention, understanding, and language, and never leave it. Although attention and language enable a distancing from absorption in the immediate, there is no way out of the circle. Of course, there is no need to leave the circle, for attention is the basis for relation to anything at all, and understanding is ecstatically open to its deliverances. The extent to which a given understanding is transcended depends upon the state of attention.

The Ongoing Development of Language—Taylor on Joint Attention

Taylor devotes chapter 2 of *The Language Animal* (2016) to the role that joint attention plays in the ontogenesis of the linguistic capacity, as indicated above. New words are learned for a salient common focus (53), the referent. He refers to joint attention as a mutual manifestation, much in line with my focus on attention as human presence, as how the self is made manifest and how we are made manifest together. He refers to it as an interspace, a shared presence, where each perspective is brought to bear in this open region. It enables us to know things together, which forms the common ground that is the basis for communication (58).

Language comes about when child and caregiver share an intense common focus which enables an emotional bonding. Joint attention is a "more intense and conscious mode of being together" (2016, 90), a condition for language. Language is normatively shared, as children reproduce the words that are addressed to them (59). One is in a social space, a site of recurrent communion with our fellows. This is where emotional bonding with others occurs, where we focus together on matters of mutual concern.

The common focus enables the associated words to be shared, even though the child and caregiver have different perspectives, which the child senses as richer on the side of the adult. This is the primary locus where language is maintained and developed. In this way, children learn proper ways of acting in the world that embody a sort of expressive or descriptive rightness in contrast to the task rightness, which all animals are capable of, that is paradigmatic for the HLC position.

The implication is that attention and language together enable the disclosure and constitution of the worlds we live in. Language opens up spaces for the expansion of human meanings. It enables us to relate to things in new ways, and it constitutes the worlds of our involvements by establishing new emotions, goals, and relations. To make the case, Taylor describes how language enables the formation of what he refers to as the "meanings and footings" that make up human realities. Meanings have significance and relevance in our lives. They are not given, independent entities, but are rather articulated in an ongoing process of worldly engagement and discourse, and footings are the more or less established modes of relation that are constitutive of the worlds in which we dwell. Thus, linguistic expression is such that it makes its own meaningful content rather than encountering given entities. We find terms for objects that are not independent of their designations, such as feelings and emotions, which change with new articulations. We are engaged in an ongoing process of extending the range of articulation at the center of engagement where such meanings are expressed and footings are negotiated.

HERMENEUTICAL TRUTH

The quality of attention is essential to come to more appropriate ways of being together in the world, for it enables insight into human meanings, or hermeneutic, historically situated, truth. I focus now on Taylor's (2016, chap. 6) approach to hermeneutical reasoning, where we seek understanding in a dialectical approach where any accounts that are provided for our values are tested by experience, which can in turn be challenged by further such accounts. I argue that all else being equal, more insight will be correlated with higher quality attention.

Attention and Articulation

We have seen Taylor and Gendlin emphasize the importance of bodily intelligence. They focus on notions such as felt intuition/sense as the basis for navigating worlds of meaning, where attention is essential for the quality and validity of such intuitions. This is how we can come to more insight, better ways of understanding ourselves and ways to live, and more appropriate ways of living together with others when these matters are considered in public spaces. But the insights can always be challenged relative to the global web of meanings and associated accounts, which leads to Taylor's (221) notion of hermeneutical reasoning (see figure 2.7).

In this regard, Taylor discusses how language users have an ongoing sense of a need for further articulation of the meanings that come about in language use. Felt intuition comes about by way of direct experience of the matters at hand, which requires attention, while such meanings also require clarification

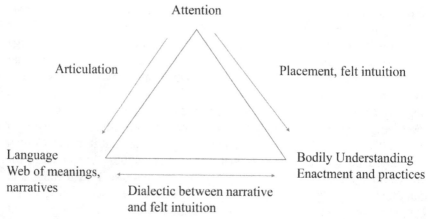

Figure 2.7. **Hermeneutical Reasoning**

and defense when engaged with others by way of etiological or philosophical accounts. Taylor sees the ultimate basis for ratification in felt intuition, where we know by way of direct experience that something is true (2016, 253). And we have seen how Gendlin's Focusing technique allows one to focus attention directly on the felt intuitions as they are experienced bodily and thus gain deeper insight into what they are about, which can lead to their transformation. This can be experienced in therapeutic settings or in engagement in the public sphere, where the latter can lead to communal insight into the nature of the common good in a shared atmosphere where the truth of the intuition is made evident, although never closed as the dialectical process proceeds unabated.[23] For there is infinite depth to the articulation of the meanings and their associated expression in language, as this process is embedded in the lived body-environment whose depths can always be further plunged by way of acute and sustained presence.

Power and Strong Sources

Hermeneutics, as advanced by Taylor, is open to ultimate questions regarding our place in the cosmos. We approach these domains in the same manner, by way of felt intuition with a quality that depends on the extent of mindfulness. The question of the validity of any potential insights is always at issue, especially in public spheres, and he addresses it by arguing that we can get it wrong here, that we see we can improve our understanding, gaining insight, and that we can respond to queries regarding the reasons for our beliefs in public realms. He calls the basis for such insights "independent sources of value," which are subject to intersubjective validation.

Chapter 3

The Ontological Status of Attention

I am arguing that the predominant view that assumes the ontological primacy of the physical cannot accommodate the phenomenon of attention. I rather propose that a relational ontology can accommodate it, for it plays an essential role in our relations with all things. To pursue the theme, I now argue that attention is neither mental nor physical, so that it transcends any such dichotomy. I proposed in chapter 1 that the placement of attention can extend beyond the confines of the skull, which argues for this claim. I indicated that thought itself can be experienced as being accompanied by the lived sensation of the head in an expanded intermodal space of attention, which would be a center of attention where both mental and physical properties manifest, for the sensations would be characterized as physical and the thought would be mental. I also showed that the subject-object dichotomy depends on the deployment of attention. I continue to argue along these lines while providing more justification for the approach. I show that attention is the basis for the identification of something as mental or physical, public or private, theoretical or real/physical, and so on. Any such categorization must occur at the focus of attention as placed in the lived body-environment.

ATTENTION AND MANIFESTATION

Attention is how properties that are considered to be either mental or physical are made manifest in the first place, for it is how we relate to all that is. That is the starting point from which any scientific activity and third-person point of view must proceed. Moreover, any such relations are not static, given attention as their basis, for we can be more or less present, more or less related to any particular entities and the whole. This points to the primacy of attention, not the primacy of the physical.

The meanings of terms such as "mental" and "physical" show themselves in the way they guide us in the course of worldly activity. They guide the movement of attention, which in turn is the site of manifestation of the entities with which we engage. The meaning of the mental and physical therefore shows itself in how it guides the very manifestation of entities, in conjunction with the broader understanding of which it is a part. When physicists inquire into the nature of the physical, for instance, their understanding of its nature determines how they themselves are made manifest in relation to the entities with which they engage, how they comport themselves in relation to it, and how the physical itself is understood in relation to them.

But this shows that attention transcends the distinction between the two. For it is how all such entities are made manifest to us, the understanding of which shows itself in how it guides the placement of attention and the associated speech and action. Consider, for instance, the proposition that attention is a mental phenomenon. The meaning of such a statement depends on how the mental is understood, which in turn determines how it guides attention itself when the term is embedded in sentences in the course of life activity. This is how the truth of any statement is determined—we seek to verify it in worldly engagement based on how it is understood, where that worldly engagement is undertaken as centered in attention. The fit between the understanding we bring and what is made manifest in response (how the statement resonates with the new understanding) is how we negotiate such meanings. And in general, to verify the truth of any statement we must see how those deliverances resonate and how they match up with other matters. This is the fit with the understanding, hermeneutical reasoning according to Charles Taylor (see chapter 2). But what is key here is that the possibility of verifying the truth of this particular statement depends on how attention itself is deployed. So we would have to look to attention itself as we go about our lives and ask if it is a mental phenomenon, and ask what is the mental at the same time, all the while sensing how it resonates with our embodied sensibilities.

Attention is neither mental nor physical because it is the essence of the first-person perspective, for which there is no such dichotomy. And given that the third-person perspective is grounded in the first person, from the perspective presented herein the assumed primacy of the physical relative to the mental is a reversal of the primacy of the first over the third person. A relational ontology that recognizes the essential role of attention keeps that priority straight, unlike the predominant view. I now show that support for relationality comes from physics itself, the mathematical study of the physical.[1]

RELATIONALITY IN PHYSICS

On the predominant view, the physical enjoys an ontological primacy that is unquestioned. It is, however, best defined in terms of the mental, its opposite (Montero 2005). This sort of circularity would suggest that a more holistic perspective is appropriate. In particular, I am arguing that attention is a holistic phenomenon that is neither mental nor physical. It is how these notions show up for us, with their meanings unfolding within the dynamic of the hermeneutical circle.

Moreover, the question of the nature of the physical in itself is also wide open, offering no comfort to those who would point to the success of physics as indicating a well-understood physical reality that responds to human interventions. The assumption of the primacy of the physical is meaningless if we do not understand what it is. Although there is certainly something that so responds, and although physical properties can be reasonably identified, the leap to assuming the physical is ontologically ultimate is not justified.

While it is obvious that a wide range of entities can be characterized as having physical properties, this by no means implies that the physical enjoys a primacy. Consider, for instance, the following statement by Searle, which would hardly be considered to be controversial:

> On the account that I have been giving you in this book, it is clear that *rock bottom* is the world as described by atomic physics. . . . We can pretty well conclude that the known world is made up of entities that we find it convenient, if not entirely accurate, to call "physical particles." These particles exist in fields of force and are organized into systems, where the boundaries of the systems are set by causal relations. Examples of systems would be water molecules, babies, nation states, and galaxies. . . . The account bottoms out in what I think of as the real world that exists in a way that is observer independent and ontologically objective. One of the tasks of philosophy is to explain the constitution of these higher-level systems and how they bottom out into the entities of atomic physics. (2015, 222–23, em)

Searle uses the term "rock bottom" to refer to what is most real, pointing to the solidity of the physical reality we experience. Although he hedges somewhat by saying it is "not entirely accurate" to refer to the fundamental entities as physical particles, there is little doubt that this is a version of the building block theory of physical reality where freestanding entities are related to one another extrinsically by the laws of physics. It should be noted that babies and nation-states are included as systems of particles, which has crucial implications for how we understand ourselves and our relations with others.

Searle's description leaves much to be desired even without bringing in the matter of attention. He does not consider, for instance, issues in quantum mechanics that arise because the states of quantum systems are defined in terms of probability distributions over properties such as momentum, position, and spin. When such systems interact, there will typically be correlated measurements between entities within each system, which means that after the interaction each system state must be defined in terms of the other and are thus "entangled."[2] This includes any measuring devices whose interaction with the systems of interest produces observed properties, and in principle means that when we look at the cosmos as a whole it can be the case that all subsystems are entangled with one another (e.g., Horgan and Potrc 2008). This is why there has been interest in relational ontologies in the philosophy of physics, for the notion that entities are only related extrinsically does not apply in the quantum world (e.g., Teller 1986, Esfeld 1999).

Other problems for Searle's account arise because the entanglement of measuring devices with the systems being observed means that rock bottom is not observer independent when it is thought in quantum terms. As Schumm puts it, "The true system under consideration must always be the combination of the system of the observed with that of the observer. In the (thoroughly verified) theory of quantum mechanics, the distinction between the observer and the observed has to be discarded" (2004, 43). In addition, the difficulty in reconciling macro-level measuring devices with microsystems is that classical and quantum views of the world must mix (Faye 2019), in particular regarding the transition from a probabilistic world to the singular and substantive entities we ordinarily think of as being perceived in the course of observation. This is known as the "measurement problem," which is considered below.

Searle says that particles "exist" in fields of force, which would appear to assume an extrinsic relationship between them, but microphysics has brought the notion of extrinsic relations between fields and particles into question. Entities in the standard model of particle physics do not simply exist in force fields with their own intrinsic properties, such as mass, for it is rather the case that the effective mass of the twelve elementary particles is generated by interaction with force fields.[3] Consider Schumm again, who says that "[o]ne of the most basic and common-sense attributes of a physical object—that of mass—has been removed from the conceptual lexicon by the juggernaut of modern physics, having been exposed as the combination of two illusory effects. . . . The notion of mass, it would seem, is a sham" (2004, 306). Along these lines, Wilczek argues that "[i]n modern physics, there's only one thing, and that thing is more like the traditional idea of light than the traditional idea of matter" (2008, ix). Rather than thinking in terms of building blocks, the entire system of particles and forces must be viewed as an irreducible whole.[4]

Properties such as location, velocity, and mass are all relational, as are mental and physical.

Considerations such as these have led to the development of relational ontologies in the philosophy of physics. The classic work is that of Teller (1986), who considers the possibility that objects have relations that do not supervene on their intrinsic (nonrelational) properties. For Teller, local physicalism means that (1) all intrinsic properties of an entity supervene on its intrinsic physical properties, and (2) any relations between such entities supervene on their intrinsic properties (73), which implies that all relations (physical and nonphysical) between entities supervene on the intrinsic physical properties of the associated relata. Teller argues, however that there are instances where such relations do not supervene on intrinsic properties even in the case of purely physical phenomena.[5] He considers such cases in classical physics and finds them more likely when space-time is viewed as inherently relational. He finds it easier to make the case in quantum mechanics, where (as noted above) entanglement arises in the state functions that are used to attribute properties to microsystems. He therefore puts forward a relational holism where there are at least instances where distinct individuals with their own inherent properties also have inherent relations that do not supervene on the former. The implication is that the presence of physical properties is by no means warrant to assume that the ultimate ontological status of an entity is physical.

The key question thus becomes the extent to which physical entities are to be viewed as enjoying an absolute reality with intrinsic properties that serve as a supervenience basis for their relations, or whether there are properties that come about only in relation to other entities. The philosopher-physicist Michel Bitbol takes a phenomenological approach to the question, arguing that the paradoxes in quantum physics can be resolved by taking relationality into consideration. Rather than taking the point of view of a detached observer, he finds it necessary to incorporate the context of the situation and the perspective of the embodied observer to understand how it is that entities are made manifest in laboratory settings (Bitbol 2019).

Bitbol (2008) shows that measuring devices must be present for properties such as spin and position to be made manifest in quantum realities, and given that such devices are extensions of human attention (as discussed below) the implication is that the presence of attention is necessary for quantum properties to be made manifest; otherwise they do not have an absolute reality on their own. Thus he finds that although it had been possible to ignore the perspective of the observer in classical settings, that is no longer the case in the quantum world, where it becomes apparent that besides being physical entities, we also form the transcendental background for the manifestation of all such entities (10). And given that the quantum measurement process comes about by way of a measuring device interacting with the entity under study, relationality lies at the heart of the practice of quantum mechanics, for observed properties show themselves only by way of relations with measuring devices.

I am not suggesting that there is not considerable controversy regarding these matters, but this points to the difficulties involved in assuming the absolute reality of the physical as it is described in physics. What I argue for now is the transcendence of attention with respect to the mental-physical divide, which supports the arguments for the hermeneutical circle and its associated relational ontology. The implication is that human realities are much more like the quantum world than the world of classical physics, for attention is how we are made manifest in relation to all entities, micro and macro. Rather than viewing humans as entities with intrinsic properties such as tastes and interests that clash in political confrontations, those very properties are constituted and made manifest in public spaces. And rather than being information processors who select among incoming stimuli by way of attention to form representations of reality, that very attention is the site where we stand bodily within that reality and come to understand its nature. Thus, ground zero is not inner representations of external realities, for we dwell and participate in the latter by way of the presence of attention and the associated hermeneutical circle, from which may follow further articulation and expression by way of language.

THE THEORY-REALITY DIVIDE

Attention can be conceived in both mental and physical terms. We naturally think of it as associated with the mental, given its role in tending to our work, for instance, but we have also seen that it is regarded as part of the functioning of the brain in cognitive science (Chun, Golomb, and Turk-Browne 2011), which is presumably physical. In addition, it is required for both abstract intellection and worldly engagement, both of which occur within broader life contexts, for it is how the self is made manifest in the course of engaged activity (see chapter 4), how our ontological resources are gathered in deployment in various matters. It is our situated presence in the world, within the whole and in relation to entities, appearing within the lived body-environment at the center of worldly engagement.

My claim is that attention mediates between theory and reality, which can be seen in the practice of physics itself. For we come to understand the theory by way of education and ongoing study of the literature, where attention is deployed in what are typically conceived as "inner" or "mental" pursuits, although there are also material dimensions, such as books, classrooms, laboratories, desks, and the like. Attention is how the terms of a theory refer to represented entities (e.g., Campbell 2002), according to how we understand them and their implications for behavior in the laboratory. We also set up the experimental equipment, which together with observation is administered by way of attentive human presence. We ultimately access the referents themselves in this manner, always within the relational context of the theory, its associated technology, and the implicit practical understanding that enables us to navigate the world in general.

We access the physical itself by way of experimental devices, which are extensions of the human and its attention (e.g., Heelan 2016, Bitbol 2008). Just as the tip of the cane becomes an appendage of the blind person, attention engaged in this manner provides access to the experimental phenomena themselves, or their predicted traces. For what else would explain the efficacy of the theories and their associated applications? Something responds to the experimental interventions, be it "physical" or not. As the argument for scientific realism goes, if the theoretical entities are not themselves real (in a relational sense here, relative to our presence as understanding physicists), the efficacy could only be deemed to be miraculous (Putnam 1975).

Consider the work of physicists in the laboratory. They engage in a wide range of activities in putting equipment in place and conducting experiments. Care must be taken to be precise, for example, in preparing for the entities to be observed in a double-slit experiment. One handles the devices and maneuvers them in just the right way to position them correctly. That is how the physicists are present in the course of the engagement, as attention is literally in their hands as care is taken in handling the equipment. I am bodily centered in the midst of the equipment, my hands are intertwined with it as I act in a purposive manner in the midst of it all. This is being in relation to the entities that show themselves in this way, including myself in relation to them. There is no transformation of the physical into mental representations that underlies it all, for that is redundant, as being in relation happens first. For what else could be the basis for the representations in the first place? We never get outside of that.

Thus, our presence by way of attention is all-pervasive in practice, from the study of the theory to observation of results. It is required in all phases of the process, for it is how the self is made manifest as engaged and how any features that are interpreted to be mental or physical are made manifest in relation to us. That is, features that are made manifest and interpreted as mental or physical are subject to the placement of attention and the associated action of language and understanding. This means that attention traverses the entire domain from theory to reality, which is the basis for the very meaning of the mental and physical, for that is how they are made manifest in the course of engagement and in our understanding. Thus attention mediates between the two, bringing thought and theory to bear on what we understand to be the physical and the deliverances of attention from the physical to the understanding. Attention is itself neither mental nor physical; it is rather extended in its being, ranging from entities that can be characterized as mental to those that are thought to be physical.

This can be seen in the measurement problem in quantum physics, where it is unclear how to determine where the physical ends and the mental begins. Ney, for instance, asks when measurement occurs:

> [Is it]when the electron physically makes its way through the device? Only later when some human experimenter observes the device? If the latter, then when exactly in the process of observation does the collapse occur? When light from the device first hits the experimenter's retina, when it gets processed by the visual centers in the brain? When the experimenter first has the conscious thought, "The pointer is reading x-spin up (or x-spin down)"? (2010, 27)

This is known as the problem of the "cut," which is to determine where the dividing line is between the physical process and concomitant mental events. The "collapse" refers to how the quantum probability distribution over potential outcomes is transformed into an outcome with probability one once it has been observed, and a presumably physical process is transformed into a mental representation. Ney cites Bell, who asks "If the theory is to apply to anything but highly idealized laboratory operations, are we not obliged to admit that more or less 'measurement-like' processes are going on more or less all the time, more or less everywhere?" (1987, 216). My proposal is that these measurement-like processes are the traces of attention itself, for historically the problem of attention has been concerned with where selection occurs, early or late in the perceptual process (e.g., Broadbent 1958). I am arguing that attention does not fit into either category, mental or physical, and that it is indeed present more or less all the time because it is the mark of the human, the essence of our bodily engaged presence in the world, the basis for any act of interpretation that characterizes phenomena as either mental or physical.

Another example is provided by Heelan, a philosopher who worked with Werner Heisenberg. He shows how the cut can take place in various points in the experimental process, and that the very vocabulary that thereby arises varies depending on where the cut occurs. To make the case, Heelan says the observer has two tasks, attending to the medium and attending to the message communicated by the medium, and concludes that "[o]ne and the same scientist is able to act on separate occasions as two different and mutually incompatible observer-subjects by choosing two different embodiments, each responding to two different objective horizons described by two different descriptive languages" (2016, 97). Thus we see the hermeneutical circle here, with the interaction between attention and language in full display in the experimental world of quantum physics.

THE PUBLIC-PRIVATE DIVIDE

In addressing the relation between attention and the mental-physical dichotomy, we have considered the subject-object and theory-reality distinctions. Another approach is to identify the physical with the publicly accessible while rendering the mental only private. Since my claim is that attention as our engaged presence is how we access anything at all, it follows that an entity is publicly accessible if and only if it can be an object of joint attention. That is, we distinguish between the private and the public by way of attention. The private is accessible only by way of the attention of the particular individual, whereas the public is in principle accessible to anyone. This is what makes the proposed relation between public accessibility and the physical attractive, in that it enables intersubjective validation of results. But now the mental and physical are defined in terms of accessibility, which in turn depends on attention. The implication is that attention is neither mental nor physical because it determines which entities fit into the categories under this definition.

The move to distinguish between the mental and physical in this manner fails on its face because attention and language are constitutive of the human worlds in which life occurs, and in which all entities that are presumably mental or physical are encountered (see chapter 7). That is, the public-private distinction cannot withstand the movement of attention that is its basis. It cannot designate entities that are independent of that movement, for we have no means of access to such, which require attention to be so designated. For example, consider the physicist who works with publicly accessible entities and/or their traces,[6] such as quarks, although they are not necessarily the same individuals with which others work. They are considered to be "absolutely identical" physical entities, however, which enables physicists to jointly attend to the same thing, so when they refer to a quark it is assumed that they are focusing on the same public entity which is presumably physical. This is what is essential about language: that it enables the same thing to be made manifest to different individuals by way of joint attention. But the problem is that the attention of the physicist is directed by the confluence of language and understanding, as is always the case. This means that the perception/ understanding of the quark is subject to any differences that may exist across the various communities of physicists. The term "quark" only gets its meaning from the web of theoretical terms in which it exists, together with the action of attention and language in modifying any such meanings. There is no quark in itself that can be determined to exist—indeed, that makes sense independently of that theoretical structure—for some of its properties could very well differ with a change in the structure that could conceivably occur in the future.[7] Thus the "absolute identity" of the quark depends on the existence of a commonly understood theoretical framework that determines its meaning.[8]

To further address the question, consider the following types of joint attention:

1. Mutual attention: In this case, individuals engage in face to face interaction, paying attention to each other. This process begins at birth, in the interaction between child and caregiver (e.g., Trevarthen 1979). A protolanguage enables the interaction here, as the child mimics the caregiver's gestures. This is the basis for bonding between individuals, with obvious political implications, as discussed in chapter 2 on Taylor and further in chapters 7 and 8.

2. Joint attention to the same object, present to both: This is important in the process of language acquisition, as discussed in chapter 2.

3. Joint attention to the same object, not present to both: This is the most prevalent form of joint attention and inevitably involves the full capacities of language, which bridges the divide between the objects of attention. Language is essential here, and any perception will be subject to the limitations of the hermeneutical circle, in that the understanding of the language is essential in guiding attention to the object. In what follows I focus on the first and third definitions.

In general, public accessibility means that a shared understanding enables each to focus on the same thing, not necessarily at the same time, as in the third definition of joint attention. This all occurs in the lived body-environment in which attention moves by way of bodily understanding and language, where the latter is itself the vehicle of shared understanding. An entity that is publicly accessible is thus understood in a particular manner whereby it can be apprehended from the different vantage points of the individuals who occupy the same public world in which the events occur. So any object that is deemed to be physical must satisfy these requirements, that they are recognized by particular features that are perceptible from the various positions in the shared lived body-environment. Each position has its own vantage point that is unique to it, given the historical process by which it has arrived at its state. Thus, an idiosyncratic dimension is always involved in the perception of public entities that show themselves by way of the shared understanding in language, for the bodily intelligence is always present in the movement of attention as discussed in chapter 2.

The same considerations also hold for the private. Indeed, it is always the case for any movement of attention whatsoever that it moves within the lived body-environment, which includes the presence of the lived body itself, which is presumably private and hence mental on this approach. But the lived body is fair game for the perception of such entities, which always takes place by way of the movement of attention, as do all such perceptions. And we have words for the sorts of things we encounter there, such as pain, and we can talk to people about the sort of pain it is, where it is located, if it is hot or sharp, and so on. There is no difference between this and the perception of a tree or any other object in that environment. It is always accompanied by attention and language in making the tree manifest within the body-environment, so the objects that are jointly attended as selected out of that environment are publicly recognized. So any objects apprehended in this manner, be they deemed to be public or private, are always accompanied by an idiosyncratic dimension that goes beyond the extant understanding housed in the language. The implication is that any aspect of the lived body-environment can be public depending on the deployment of attention, language, and understanding that prevails. Thus attention and its circle transcends any such distinction between the mental and physical.

Again, is there anything that can only be perceived privately? No, because language always accompanies the movement of attention, which means there is always a public or shared dimension to its movement, and that is how access to anything supposedly public or private occurs. For instance, just like quarks, our bodies are identical in the sense that they have the same general form and functions. And we can focus interoceptively on our feet or other parts of the body and talk about the experience, coming up with terms that describe what we experience together. So this argues against the idea that bodily sensations are private, not public, and argues again that attention determines whether something is private or public, subjective or objective.[9]

Moreover, we see examples of relations between the lived body and external objects, as in emotional and bodily intentionality. As discussed in chapter 2, Taylor (2016) describes how the language captures the sorts of dynamics involved when we say, "My heart goes out to you," for instance. This suggests that such an experience has been preserved in the language and can be retrieved by way of phenomenological excavation, so that, when in such a situation, one can expand attention to include both the body and the suffering interlocutor and see the relation between the two, which will be discussed in detail in chapter 7 on empathy.[10] It also can be seen in Merleau-Ponty's (2002) example of his hands touching a table, where the body is in relation to the table when attention is centered there. Given that phenomenologists (and others) can conduct these sorts of investigations, the notion that lived bodily goings-on are private and not publicly accessible is put into question.

Consider now the first definition of joint (or mutual) attention, where each pays attention to the other. We can each focus on aspects of the other, either about their bodily or expressive behavior or features of their character that we can glean from their behavior or what we know about them. These are all public in that they are in principle accessible to anyone who is able to attend in the appropriate manner and has an understanding that is suitable for the apprehension, which includes the terminology that makes the apprehension shared. These entail rendering the other as an entity with features that manifest according to the movement of attention in the circle, but this is not the same as being purely physical. More importantly, as I argue in chapter 6, when attention is active, a space can open that enables us to be made manifest together, which is the ground for ontological bonding and the associated terms that come out of that. These terms are not objectifying, for they arise from a being made manifest together in which we are not objects for one another. Thus we are no longer talking about public or private entities because the bond transcends any such dichotomy.

This is crucial for the formation of effective political realities. This possibility, developed in detail in what follows, shows that attention transcends any such dichotomies. In this case we are not separate individuals or bonded in union, but identical and different at once (as in the circle), for now there is a shared space in which we transcend the individual-communal dichotomy. This is important as we go forward, for it is not just attention that transcends the dichotomies but our relations themselves when we bond ontologically in this manner.

Thus the hermeneutical circle serves as the underlying dynamic for manifestation of all entities in relation to us, for unlike what Taylor (2016) refers to as the HLC position, under HHH they are not given to us in advance, at least in the form in which we encounter them. That is the key distinction, and we see it in at play in quantum mechanics. In any engagement there is an existing stock of terms that is always expanding by way of articulation in support of the webs of relations that make up human worlds, which means that the background understanding that supports the manifestation is always changing. This is discussed further in chapter 7.

Under a relational holism, we engage things as they manifest in worldly activity, for their essential nature is to be in relation with other entities. This is because we can access nothing beyond what can be made manifest at the center of attention, where things come into focus and thus become intelligible in the course of theoretical and experimental activity. Only then can they be understood and discussed; otherwise, they can be thought only in the abstract. That is, only what can show itself in relation to us is accessible in itself. The quark is thus subject to the circle and is made manifest according to how it is understood within the community. The deliverances of attention can change the understanding, which itself depends on how such entities have been made manifest in the past at the center of engaged activity, which again includes theoretical and experimental activity.

A VIEW FROM NEUROSCIENCE

I now turn to the work of Jennings (2020), who presents a philosophical treatment of the neurophysiology of attention. Although she draws primarily on literature from philosophy of mind and neuroscience, I show that even in this context attention is a switching point between the mental and physical, thereby transcending the distinction. For Jennings, there is an essential link between self and attention, in that the self (which consists of more or less enduring interests, motivations, etc.) directs attention. In doing so, attention shapes perception according to the current interests of the self, rendering the objects of perception meaningful and informative. However, her reliance on traditional metaphysical assumptions renders her ultimate view of attention problematic. I contrast her position with that of enactivist thought, including Fuchs (2018) (discussed in chapter 1, who also has expertise in neurophysiology and phenomenology) in arguing for a holistic ontology.

Jennings distinguishes between top-down and bottom-up attention, where top-down inputs come from the subject and bottom-up inputs come from the sensory system, which, when combined, produce the objects of conscious perception. She focuses on brain waves as essential constituents of mental activity, and given that the subject is a macro-scale phenomenon, top-down attention is determined by macro-scale wave dynamics, while bottom-up attention operates on the micro scale. Jennings argues that this setup allows for a form of mental causation, because "it allows macro-scale wave dynamics to determine the influence of bottom-up stimulation" (2020, 67). What is essential to note here is that for Jennings, attention is the site of the relation between the mental (top-down) and the physical (bottom-up) in that it enables the subject to shape the manifestation of physical entities that are processed through the sensory and perceptual systems.

But this causes a problem for the conclusion that attention is a mental phenomenon, where it is defined as "the prioritization of some mental and/ or neural processing over other processing" (Jennings 2020, 50). Jennings argues that attention is mental because it enables the subject to shift between tasks and thus is task sensitive. Since tasks are mental phenomena, the implication is that attention is mental because it engages with the mental. But it is also the case that attention is partly composed of bottom-up attention, where "purely bottom-up attention would be a case in which the relevant mental and/or neural prioritization is not at all sensitive to the subject's current task" (50), and where the neural is considered to be physical and responsive to inputs from other physical entities. We can also see this in Jennings's statement that "an attention system is a set of specific brain areas that work together to bring about one's attention to a stimulus or internal process" (45), where that stimulus will generally be considered to be physical in nature. She also writes, "The question is what exactly makes sensory input available to the perceiving subject. . . . In my view early visual states are the data that become information for a subject only once they are integrated by attention" (77). Thus, attention engages with both mental and physical processes, representing part of the process whereby the physical is transformed into the mental. It is difficult to posit attention as a purely "mental" phenomenon under these conditions. Thus, Jennings provides support for the claim I am advancing, in that attention enables access to both the mental and the physical in both perception and mental causation, rather than being merely associated with mental representation.

A Narrow View of Attention

As Jennings argues for a conception of the self arising out of brain dynamics, which is responsible for the movement of attention, most of the attributes that are typically associated with attention, such as first-person experience, focusing, concentration, and mindfulness, are excised to fit the scientific findings. The focus is only on task shifting, which has much in common with the notion of executive control, which is posited in the attention literature, but in so doing she ignores most of the features that are commonly associated with self and attention.

Jennings argues that the self is a phenomenon of the brain that directs attention: "In the picture I have provided, the attending mind controls its world by managing information about the body. I have argued that the fact of attention points to a self, or subject of attention, whose powers are directed inward, even while its motivations are directed outward" (2020, 189). Attention is considered to be a process of mental selection by a subject, which is to be contrasted with habitual activity, conscious entrainment, and strategic automaticity. She argues that attention is paid only to new and novel stimuli, while others are handled by automatic processes.

But the notion that attention is required only for novel stimuli misses the nature of engaged human action, which always has something new that can be encountered in a given situation. Consider, for instance, the study of the attentional deployment of experts in various areas, where it is sometimes assumed that they need not pay attention as they engage in their profession. Suppose one visits a doctor for what may be a serious illness. One certainly does not want a doctor who only goes through the motions, whose mind is elsewhere, thinking, say, about an upcoming vacation. Or even if the doctor is not so distracted, one would want the doctor to be fully attentive to the complaint, for any nuance could be crucial in getting to a favorable outcome. The notion that experts do not have to be attentive is far from true.

Or consider the case of expert chess players. It has often been noted that such players can perform great feats, such as playing blindfolded against multiple players. In this case, however, the notion that attention is not required is laughable, for extraordinary attention is required to remember the positions and come up with appropriate moves. Given the well-documented relation between attention and memory (e.g., Pashler 1998), it is clear that this cannot be achieved without attention. Indeed, even in the more ordinary case of playing without a blindfold against a single player, the expert must still be acutely attentive to take in the patterns on the board and quickly make a move. The opposite of attentive is distracted, regardless of the presence of very advanced automatic skills, and doctors and chess players who are distracted will not perform up to the standards that are expected of them.

Holism in Jennings

For Jennings (2020), the self is a phenomenon of the brain that arises by way of "contextual emergence" and "machretic determinism." She needs these notions to posit mental causation, so that this is not an inert notion of self. Interestingly, these approaches incorporate holistic and relational notions. Contextual emergence means that other environmental factors account for the emergence of the entity beyond the entities that are directly responsible for its arising, which is a relational notion, while machretic determinism means that a new property arises at the level of the whole that arranges the constitutive parts in a particular way, which is a holistic notion. Jennings, however, assumes that global (not local) supervenience on the physical holds, which means that she assumes what I refer to as the primacy of the physical. I argue, on the other hand, for the primacy of attention, in that the very notions of the mental and physical presuppose the lived reality where attention is fundamental.

Jennings argues for a self that controls attention, which in turn enables mental causation. She argues (2020, 64) for a stronger form of weak emergence by pointing to the phenomenon of "self-organizing complexity," where an organizational structure emerges from the interaction of its components, pointing to examples such as earthquakes, social networks, and the flocking behavior of birds, which is similar to scale-free correlations in brain activity. Importantly, this applies to how the self itself should be understood: "As I have been describing it, the self or subject should not be understood as a single controlling agent or leader within the system, but as *the organizational structure that emerges*—the tendency for the system to be a certain way" (64, em). Jennings argues that this is a stronger form of emergence, which points to a self with its own causal powers (65). She does not, however, cite the enactivism literature, which is founded on the notion of *autopoiesis*, a complex form of self-organization that applies to living systems. This literature, which has developed in opposition to the predominant computational theory of mind that Jennings relies on, puts in question many of the assumptions that form the basis for her notion of attention.

Thus Jennings must confront this body of thought, for like her text it is science based and it draws on phenomenology, and yet it puts many of her presuppositions into question. This is most apparent when Jennings says, "I see macro-scale brain dynamics as becoming functional in the context of a macro-scale body in its macro-scale world. In other words, the extra ingredient required for emergence would be constraint at the level of the emergent entity: constraints faced by a body in a particular environment" (2020, 67).

The seminal work in the enactivism literature is Varela, Thompson, and Rosch's *The Embodied Mind: Cognitive Science and Human Experience* (2017), which argues for the active role living organisms play in shaping the meaningful worlds they inhabit. As Thompson (2011) puts it, living beings enact meaning in the course of worldly engagement—they are not passive recipients of information that is transformed into inner representations of reality. The theory is biologically based, where autopoietic organisms are organized circularly, in that constituent processes are both enabled by and enable one or more other processes, so that together "they form a recursive and interlocking network" (119). Thompson also notes the reciprocal relation between organisms and their environment, where each acts as a "control parameter" for the other (120). Relational holism is prominent here, for while interactive processes and relations are necessary for maintenance, they presuppose the system as a whole that controls them (116).

Enactivist thought also incorporates phenomenology, in that it attends to life as a purposive and normative process. What is essential for a life form is *adaptivity*—being able to monitor and regulate the autopoietic process in relation to conditions registered as improving or deteriorating, viable or unviable (Thompson 2011, 115). Autopoiesis can thus be conceived as the "self-production of an inside that also specifies an outside to which it is normatively related" (116). The interaction between self and its environment shapes them both, while at the same time the world as a whole shapes the self-environment interaction. This is the sort of relational holism that is put forward in enactivist thought.

For Jennings, the combination of the input of self and world produces the objects of conscious perception. It is important to note that these objects consist of mental representations, which she notes, citing Yantis (2013): "Perception refers to the later steps in the process, whereby the initial sensory signals are used to form mental representations of the objects and events in a scene so that they can be recognized, stored in memory, and used in thought and action" (2020, 75–76). Thus we gain access to objects in the physical world only by way of a chain of physical events that culminate in the transformation of these stimuli into mental representations by way of the subject's attention.

This sort of input-output model is put into question in the enactivist paradigm. Fuchs (2018), for instance, considers the ecology of the brain in terms of reciprocal causation, loops, cycles, the lived body, and the body subject. Moreover, instead of mechanical models and global supervenience on the physical, he puts forward an organic model that is holistic and insists on the primacy of the life world. While Jennings thinks in terms of mental representations, Fuchs thinks in terms of resonance with the body of understanding.

Thus, in Jennings, what is in fact part of the supporting network for action at the personal level is raised to the level of the self, and along the way most of the attributes which are associated with attention, such as first-person experience, focusing, and concentration are eliminated. This attempt to argue for a neurophysiological phenomenon that directs the movement of attention also fails because it must engage with the larger context in which it operates to be effective. And in fact Fuchs argues along these lines, that although the brain is certainly a most important bodily organ, its action can be understood only within the larger ecological context in which it operates.

I am arguing that attention is a holistic phenomenon that is how the embodied self is made manifest in the course of worldly engagement. It is how we are centered as we engage the world, how the body is poised to interact with the entities with which we engage. For instance, suppose I am dealing a deck of cards and I am attending to the deck as my hands are engaged in the act. There is activity in the brain and nervous system that supports the effort, but my whole bodily orientation is centered on my hands as I deal the cards. I feel them as I deal them. I am left-handed, so the deck is in my right hand. My right thumb pushes the top card to the left, which enables my left thumb and forefinger to grasp the card and deal it to the various players, including myself. That is where I am centered as I deal the cards, in the midst of that bodily activity. This all depends on where my attention is, because I have assumed initially that I am fully attending to the process as I engage in it. But suppose I am also talking to one of the players as I am dealing. Then I am engaged in two activities: talking and dealing. Generally there will be more attention on one task than the other. If dealing is more or less automatic, then less attention will be paid to that and more to the talking. But in any event, the manner in which I attend to the act is how I am engaged in the task as a whole human being. My body, brain, and nervous system are centered on the task depending on how I am attending. That is, attention enjoys a primacy here in that it ultimately determines how these supporting systems are deployed. If I am feeling the cards as I deal, if I am focused on that, then I am in direct contact with the cards as I deal them. That is my presence, how the self is made manifest in the course of the engagement, and if I am feeling the cards there is no representation mediating the relation between me and the cards. It may very well be the case that there is corresponding coding in long-term memory (in cognitive science terms) that occurs during the task, but that is only possible because I am in contact with the cards in the first place. I can later re-member that embodied engagement, but the original "membering" is necessary for the memory to be possible in the first place.

Now I may in other circumstances be in a situation where I am deploying representations that were produced in such a manner, where, for instance, I am imagining something, or where I am perceiving an object without being extended to it, but rather by way of activating corresponding representations from long-term memory. It all depends on how attention is deployed. But the primacy of attention means that the way I engage in any situation at all depends on how attention is deployed, and any representations that develop ultimately depend on some sort of direct worldly engagement that is their source. That is the site of my presence and my freedom, which cannot be reduced to neurophysiological phenomena.

The Indubitability of Attention

Jennings (2020) ignores the possibility of human presence and the action that can be undertaken by way of that presence in the world. She wishes to reduce it to the workings of the brain and nervous system in engaged activity, but that misses the key dimension that attention can provide, which is the indubitability of my presence by way of active attention, which enables an explicit self-awareness and the possibility of transcendence and transformation (see chapter 8).

Attention is how we are placed in the lived body-environment, which is the support for capacities that engage the world from that posture. Ordinarily its movement takes place unawares, at the sub-personal level, but it is possible to stay with it, either by intentional placement or by being extraordinarily attentive to one's present engagement with the things of this world. All human activity takes place in this manner, including the highly theoretical and complex experimental activity of physicists. Of course, thought is included in such activity, as attention must be placed so as to enable this "inner speech" (linguistic as it is) to occur.

The key distinction, of course, is that between active and passive attention. When attention is passive, our placement takes place without awareness, which means that the basis for action is concealed from us. But when it is active, we stay with its very movement, and we cannot help but know how we are presently engaged, indubitably. Our indubitable presence in the world under active attention is the ontological ground on which we stand, which is always accessible as the ongoing support for worldly engagement.

This is the same process Descartes went through. While undergoing a thought process seeking the source of absolute indubitability, he came to himself and saw the thought taking place within his embodied presence. Thus he came to the embodied center of attention itself. Indeed, attention plays a significant role in his thought. So when he saw the thought in this manner he concluded that its occurrence was indubitable. His own presence to himself enabled that insight.[11]

When we are lost or immersed in thought, that is literally the case, in that attention is fully absorbed in the thought process and there is no awareness of being embodied and in the world, as one literally disappears. But as we have seen, it is possible to be aware of thinking and being embodied at the same time. We are explicitly aware of being so engaged because attention brings us ourselves to bear on the task. This is the Cartesian truth, which is contingent upon the deployment of attention in the world, not in an inner realm, as in Jennings. This aspect of our experience cannot be denied based on theoretical musings that arise out of that same experiential field, out of our very presence in the world.

Representations cannot replace the living experience we have at the embodied center of attention, of being present to the things of this world. For we can deepen that experience by sustaining that presence, and know more fully that we are there, directly engaged with, in the midst of the living reality in which we dwell. I can stay with myself and feel myself ever more grounded in that presence. The freedom I enjoy to ground myself in this manner, ever more deeply engaged with the things of this world, is antithetical to a system that magically transforms physical stimuli into mental experience. Rather, the deliverances of attention are already interpreted by language and understanding, and can be expressed linguistically either in thought, speech, or writing. That is, they are made manifest at the site as such and such—as Heidegger puts it, we hear the creaky wagon first, not its component parts (SZ: 164/207). Entities come already articulated by the guiding confluence of language and understanding, which shows itself in this manner.

Attention is *my* presence in the world, how the self is made manifest, as I show in the next chapter. When I stay with it, I know that I am there indubitably, and if I stay with that presence while extending it to an act of speech in which I say, "I know I am here, speaking to you," that very act will also indubitably be the case. It is not a third-person fact, but rather my living presence in the moment, that has a primacy Jennings must admit to stay true to the notions of the self that we all hold to, as is her stated aim.

THE NATURE OF THE PHYSICAL

The question of the physical is crucial in this work because the central claim is that attention is human presence, which flies in the face of the notion that we are in a physical world, which is impervious to any "mental" incursions. Perhaps, though, we are in need of a definition of the physical in order to more forward more convincingly. My approach has been to determine the difference between the mental and physical, for if one cannot do that, how is one to define the physical in itself? If one is able to do the latter, then presumably the mental is everything else, so it is essential to be able to distinguish the two. But I have argued that any such distinction depends on how attention is deployed, which suggests that there is no mental or physical in itself.

When we assume the physical is what is publicly accessible by way of distanced observation, the implication is that we live in private realms that are cut off from others and the world. On this view, we do not dwell in what is deemed to be the physical, we only observe it from mental perches as the stimuli stream in. This is crucial for how we conceive ourselves and our relation to others and world. The key question I have addressed is whether we inhabit our own bodies. It is difficult to suggest otherwise, and Kant agrees. If not, we just live in the brain, or head, but the point is that even they are part of the body, so we do dwell in the body even under such highly constrictive notions. Indeed, how do we reach the point where our theories lead us to claim that we do not inhabit our own bodies, that the brain merely processes physical input in producing the illusion of freedom and a presence in the world?

The question is key for interpersonal relations, affecting as it does our self-conceptions and how we comport ourselves—how we understand self, others, and the value of human life. As I turn now to the central question of self-manifestation, we shall see that self-understanding plays a large role in directing attention, which is how the self is made manifest in the course of worldly activity. It is free to be placed where it may, which points to a realm of freedom that is not bound by the "physical," for attention and human presence transcend any such dichotomies.

PART II

Attention and the Self

I now turn to the central claim of the book, which is that attention is how the self is made manifest in the course of worldly engagement, in particular how we are made manifest in relation to one another as we go about communal life. In order to motivate the approach, I consider the broader context in which the question arises, which is the phenomenological study of experience where metaphysical assumptions regarding the true nature of encountered entities are held in abeyance (bracketed). Specifically, I consider the work of Dan Zahavi in considerable detail because the central question he considers is this very matter, which is how the self is made manifest in the course of experience. Largely inspired by Husserl, while drawing on the work of other phenomenologists, Zahavi has made significant contributions to bridging the continental-analytic divide by writing on topics in philosophy of mind such as empathy, shame, and intersubjectivity, while also pointing to our openness to the world and the limits of representationalism. He thus brings a sophisticated philosophy that is much in concert with the work that is put forward here, which is hardly surprising given the relation between Husserl and Heidegger, but he generally limits himself to knowledge of the early Heidegger.

My aim is to show how Heidegger can contribute to this work. There is much at stake, as I will argue that Zahavi puts limits on the sorts of bonds that can develop between individuals because of his insistence that pre-reflective self-awareness is not intersubjective. The claim that I put forward is that we participate in the manifestation of all things by way of attention, which is the ground of our presence in the world. We can sense each other more profoundly as whole human beings when we are actively present together, thereby sharing open spaces that can bond us ontologically.

Zahavi is known for his focus on the givenness of first-person experience as essential for any conception of selfhood, and he argues that there is an associated pre-reflective self-awareness that is the basis for the reflective self-awareness that arises when one turns attention to experience itself. Following Husserl and his analysis of inner time consciousness, Zahavi sees that as the basis for the self-awareness that accompanies all experience, which he refers to as the "minimal self."

Most importantly for our purposes, Zahavi argues that an individual's first-person experience is not accessible to others. For instance, when I attend to someone who is grieving the loss of a loved one, no matter how acutely I listen and attend to her and how much I feel for her loss, I cannot experience her grief the way that she does. There is an ineliminable difference between self and other, which, according to Zahavi, is what inspired Husserl to investigate the question of intersubjectivity. I cannot know what it's like for her to go through that experience because I do not share that perspective, I am not in her body feeling what she does. Although there is much to be said for Zahavi's emphasis on this phenomenon, I argue that it limits the sort of bonding that can occur between individuals, which is the focus of part III of this book.

My approach is to argue that attention is our presence in the world, which is the most originary basis for self-awareness of any type: pre-reflective, reflective, and what I refer to as explicit self-awareness. My body as it is brought to bear by way of attention is how my presence is made manifest—that is why my experience is mine. It is true that there is always an idiosyncratic aspect of an individual's experience, but I argue that we can merge with the presence of others in open spaces and feel them bodily, which enables the sort of ontological bonding that is essential in developing robust communities where all aspire to articulate and achieve common visions of the good together.

Chapter 4

Attention as the Manifestation of the Self

I now argue that attention is best understood as self-manifestation, or how the self comes into presence in the course of worldly engagement. Thus when James ([1890] 1983, 381–82) says that everyone knows what attention is and that it varies from vivid focalization to dispersal, it follows that the self manifests itself in tandem with these states, for when James says that we are all familiar with the latter state and its associated lethargy and that something eventually "enables us to gather ourselves together," it is implicitly assumed that the gathering of attention is a gathering of oneself. The implication is that as attention goes, so goes the self; when it is gathered, so are we, and when it is dispersed and distracted, so are we. Or so I argue.

There are many ways in which to understand the notion of self. I begin with notions that are prominent in the phenomenology literature, namely those put forward by Husserl and Zahavi. I focus on Husserl's conception of the transcendental or pure ego in this chapter and consider Zahavi's minimal self and the associated approach to self-awareness and manifestation in the following three chapters.

There are considerable commonalities between Husserl's transcendental ego and the conception of attention that I have been putting forward in this work. The notion of transcendental in Husserl refers to conditions for the possibility of manifestation, and the ego is understood there as how one is made manifest in relation to other entities. That is exactly how I understand attention, within the context of the hermeneutical circle of attention, language, and understanding, where the center of attention is indeed how and where the self is made manifest in the course worldly engagement. Moreover, for Husserl, rays of attention are directed into the world, which corresponds to my notion that attention is an extended presence within the lived body-environment. He also sees the ego as a spatiotemporal center,[1] as part of the structure of experience, and I also understand the center of attention in this manner, in that it centers us in the present moment (where past and future are also operative), and it centers us in the various spaces/places in which we dwell. Moreover, both are centers for the coordination of activity, both intra- and interpersonally, as well as for various forms of perception and control. Finally, both are imperceptible in that we only see traces of their effects in the course of engagement. Thus I identify the transcendental ego with the center of attention, where self-understanding within the hermeneutical circle accounts for the other functions of the ego.

There are also, however, important differences between the conceptions:

1. While the notion of a transcendental ego is controversial, I would argue that the hermeneutical circle consists of moments that are essential for human existence. But while the pure ego is an abstract structure (e.g., Zahavi 2021b, 10) that integrates the human being, active attention represents the *possibility* that one can be more integrated, or more present, and points to a depth dimension that can be the basis for more profound ontological bonds between members of communities, as I discuss below.

2. Rather than there being a distinction between an ego pole and the thematic intentional object, I argue that the center of attention is the only center to be found in experience, which is itself the site of agency. Moreover, active attention enables explicit self-affection and self-awareness, thereby fulfilling functions of the pure ego such as centering and unification. Thus, the extent to which the self is centered and unified, which is the essence of selfhood itself, depends on the state of attention.

3. The hermeneutical circle has a historicity that includes its own spatiotemporality. In particular, the possibility of active attention enables one to see that the experience of space and time itself depends upon its deployment (see chapter 6). This is consistent with the intimate relation between attention and Heidegger's notion of the clearing, and his claim that spatiotemporality arises out of that clearing.

The claim in brief is that attention brings the lived body to bear in the course of engagement, which makes the experience mine. My bodily resources are made manifest in a unique configuration that fits the situation as it is understood and as oriented to the entities that appear at the center of attention, which is how I show up as engaged in the world.

ATTENTION AND SELF-MANIFESTATION

Attention is often conceived in philosophical discourse as being restricted to reflective activity. Of course, reflection is an important dimension of the human being, but on the view presented here, attention is much more than reflection; it is rather how the self is made manifest in *all* of its modes of worldly activity. The self as it is made manifest is how the self shows itself, which aspects are made manifest as modes of engagement (e.g., Husserlian noetic modalities, or what I refer to as embodied resources and sensibilities) are deployed in the turning of attention in worldly activity. The self is more or less centered and unified in its manifestation, which is always individuated with respect to the circumstances in which it finds itself.

The implication is that rather than assuming that the human being is unified under a given ego structure, the claim here is that we can be more or less gathered depending on the state of attention.[2] That is, I argue that attention as my engaged presence is the de facto ego/self, the center of experience, how I am occupied, the basis for integration and explicit self-awareness and affection. The state of attention determines the extent of such centering and unification, and therefore enables "control" over action by way of a unified, overarching presence. The explicit self-awareness that is associated with such gathering compares favorably with the fissured looking-back of phenomenological reflection.

This sort of constitutive activity is usually associated with transcendental structures, such as the transcendental ego, and indeed attention is part of Husserl's egoic transcendental structure, but the difference I am pointing to is that the movement of attention is typically passive, proceeding as it does unawares. Husserl does recognize that the ego is subject to external influences that can attract its attention and cause shifts in orientation, but besides such events the ego (when active) is assumed to be in control of cognitive activities such as judgment, evaluation, and other processes of active objectification, whereas I argue that these processes can all occur under passive attention as I define it.[3]

On the approach presented herein, the movement of attention is seen as the action of the whole human being. It only comes "under control" when there is a gathering of one's entire being that enables a unified presence that could be the source of such a movement, although it always requires the same extraordinary effort of attention to hold together what tends to fissure. If attention is not held by way of such an effort, the stability of the worlds that are subject to its movement depends on that of the background understandings that direct it. Such stability can be due to sedimentation, which results in a petrified understanding and little or no response to attentional deliverances,

Chapter 4

or it can be due to the exercise of active attention, which enables a grounded understanding and hence a more stable world order. This is what is at stake in understanding the movement of attention and its determinants (see chapter 8 for more discussion).

The claim is that attention and self-manifestation are intimately bound up with one another. I understand self-manifestation as follows: The self is made manifest as bodily modes of engagement are brought to the foreground to meet worldly demands at the center of attention (see figure 4.1). They are oriented to the center as called for in the present circumstances, directed to the thematic object that is the organizing focus for the activity. Thus, the center is how I am presently occupied; it organizes me in my presence. It is how the self is made manifest as presently engaged.

Bodily resources can be more or less gathered, engaged, and related to one another, depending upon the extent of active attention. Under passive attention, the centering and unification of the self comes about by way of the independent action of those resources, which is habitual or automatic, meaning it occurs without an overarching presence; that is, I am unaware of its action.[4] The extent of self-relation rather depends upon any implicit awareness that may arise due to the unattended action in the background, and I do not enjoy an explicit self-awareness.[5] I am (attention is) rather *immersed* in the acts, occupied with content at the center of, instead of being aware of the action of, the resources themselves. The latter may be subject to the influence of entities that exert the most allure or interest, and I can be more or less present depending upon the passive effects of such activity.[6]

Under active attention, on the other hand, the self as manifest *gathers itself* and is thus more awakened and unified in relation to the center. Active attention stills the habitual action of bodily resources and opens them more

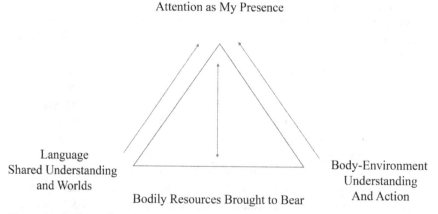

Attention as My Presence

Language
Shared Understanding
and Worlds

Bodily Resources Brought to Bear

Body-Environment
Understanding
And Action

Figure 4.1. Self-Manifestation

profoundly to new and fresh intuition. In this manner, attention holds open a space for self and things to show themselves, and is thus essential for the turn to the things themselves that is called for in phenomenology. It withstands the allure of particular activities in light of the needs of the whole, and in so doing enables the action of bodily resources themselves to come to the fore, thereby enabling an explicit self-awareness.

The fundamental claim is that the self follows attention, for the center of attention is the center of engaged presence in the world. All action issues forth from there; all movement, thought, and feeling emanate from the center. As such, attention is intimately related to the ego, which Husserl describes as the "center of life and lived experiencing" and as "the center as the wakeful radiating center of active striving" (2001, 17, 128). It is also the basis for access, for (in Husserlian terms) the Now is the source of the primordial impression, where fresh contact is possible with all things, and attention is where we are in the here and now.

The movement of attention is guided by self-understanding, which means that we pay attention to what matters most to us, implicitly or explicitly. The self is made manifest as the particular configuration makes manifest who we are in a given situation, which is intelligible to others as they relate to us. Thus the manifestation of the self is the manifestation of a self-understanding that speaks to others. That self-understanding, in turn, is intimately bound up with the bodily expression of emotion, which plays a large role in how attention moves.

All aspects of the self follow the movement of attention. Suppose, for instance, that one is walking along a street while deep in thought. One's attention is literally immersed in thought. There may be some peripheral awareness devoted to walking, but that proceeds largely by way of habitual, sedimented capacities. If for some reason the center of attention shifts to the act of walking itself, the deployment of bodily resources is completely refigured. The thoughts recede to the background, and capacities of movement that were heretofore latent come to the fore. One's very gait changes as more of the self is present to the body and the act of walking. Suppose next that one's attention is taken by a violent altercation across the street. The center of attention literally flies out of the act of walking and into the sights and sounds that have suddenly become prominent. A different set of capacities is now aroused, as fear and confusion take hold. All of these reactions depend on the deployment of attention, for the self follows attention.

The key move is to assume that there is no higher-order unifying structure such as the pure ego beyond that afforded by attention and the associated language and understanding. This means that under passive attention, individual modes can direct attention with little or no coordination with the whole, and thus without the benefit of a more global understanding. Emotion is quite powerful in this regard, for instance, when fear of a predator keeps one alert for signs of danger,[7] and the body has its own highly skilled intentionality that can be disrupted by intellectual activity, as Dreyfus (2005) has argued. Of course, thought too can direct the movement of attention with little or no regard for the emotions or the body, in which case it is cut off from the whole. Under passive attention, there is no unifying structure beyond the implicit awareness that coordinates the action of the resources. Under active attention, on the other hand, the awakening of resources that are ordinarily dormant enables a more global understanding to prevail, the effects of which can persist in the resulting constitution in spite of the inevitable reversion to passivity.

I now turn to the role of attention in Husserl's conception of the ego to understand how important it is there, and to show how my conception improves upon it. The central claim is that there is a metaphysics of constant presence operative in Husserl and Zahavi, in contrast to the abyssal ground of attention.[8] The latter opens up the possibility of depth dimensions that can be made more or less manifest by way of acute and sustained attentiveness, or mindfulness. This dimension can also show itself in more profound bonds between individuals and an associated stability in worldly affairs by making the possibility of joint action in pursuit of commonly understood goods more feasible.

ATTENTION AND THE EGO IN HUSSERL

There is considerable support in Husserl for the relation I am positing between attention and self-manifestation, in that attention for Husserl is how the ego reaches out to objects of intuition in the course of worldly activity, as discussed in chapter 1. For Husserl, the "ray of attention" is considered to be part of the transcendental structure of the pure ego. It is "inherent in the cogito itself," the basis for its acts which is not an act itself: "*In every act a mode of attentiveness holds sway*" (2014, 65). That is, attention as the engaged presence of the ego is the basis for any acts that may be associated with it, such as willing, valuing, judging, etc. In §84, entitled "Intentionality as the Main Theme of Phenomenology," he lays out the intimate relation between attention and the ego:

> In every currently actual cogito, a "focus" radiating from the pure ego is directed at the "object" of the respective correlate of consciousness (at the thing, the state of affairs, and so forth), achieving the quite diverse sorts of consciousness *of* it. . . . This advertence of the ego in presenting, thinking, valuing, and so forth—i.e., this *current* preoccupation-with-the-correlative-object, this being-directed-at-it

(or even away from it—and yet with the focus on it)—is not to be found in every experience, though it can still contain intentionality in itself. (161)

For Husserl, attention is the ray that emanates from the ego to the object, thereby relating the former to the latter. This is the basis for the *occupation* of the ego, how the self is deployed, made manifest. Other background experiences can still be intentional, but not thematic, in this sense. Importantly, attention is essentially related to the ego in its structure: "The radiating is not separated from the ego but instead itself is and remains the ego radiating" (2014, 184). He also says that attention is the basis for egoic activity:

> In general, we can say: The investigation into the active accomplishments of the ego, through which the formations of the genuine *logos* come about, operate in the medium of an attentive turning toward and its derivatives. Turning our attention toward is, as it were, the bridge to activity, or the bridge is the beginning or *mis* [*sic*] *en scène* of activity, and it is the constant way in which consciousness is carried out for activity to progress: All genuine activity is carried out in the scope of attentiveness. . . . (2001, 276)

Thus, for Husserl, attention is the bridge to the activity of the ego, for its awakening, which must be sustained for activity to progress. We shall see below that active attention is the basis for the integrated action that is implicitly assumed in Husserl's ego conception.

As the ego-ray, attention is the presence of the ego, how it engages in the world, reaching out to the entities in the course of interaction. In addition, it is the basis for the action of all other noetic modalities, in that higher-order intentional acts are founded upon attentional apprehension, as noted above. Zahavi similarly sees the ego as a principle of focus for Husserl, and attention as "the specific actionality mode of our intentional acts" (1999, 147).

The Center of Attention

Husserl assumes two poles that are present in all egoic activity: an act-transcendent ego-pole and an object-pole (1950, §30), while attention is assumed to be a ray issuing from the ego that is the basis for intuitional contact at the object pole. He argues that he in fact has phenomenological evidence for the existence of such a configuration:

> The ego that is at issue here can be manifest in each lived-experience . . . as their outward radiating or inward radiating point. . . . This can be seen by the fact that in order to grasp this outward radiating point thematically, we must exercise a peculiar [*eigen*] reflection, one going in an opposite direction. . . . The structure of the lived-experience, its directional structure that goes toward what is

presented, toward what is wished for, etc., points back to an outward radiating point and to the directedness of this ego toward its intentional theme. (2001, 17)

Husserl claims that the ego can manifest in each lived experience as its center; it shows itself as such, which can be observed in phenomenological reflection. He says that the directional structure of lived experience goes toward what is presented, thereby pointing back to an outward radiating point that is the identical ego itself. How is such a "peculiar" reflection to be executed, where one reflects in "an opposite direction"? I assume Husserl means eidetic intuition of the ray of attention emanating out of the ego-pole. What is interesting is that to come to such a perception of the ego and its ego-ray, it is necessary for the attention of the phenomenologist to be appropriately directed to experiential contents in retention, and it is crucial that these contents be held by way of attention during the entire exercise. That is exactly what phenomenological reflection is, attention oriented to retentional experience itself, which enables cogitation on those contents. The fact that it is ongoing experience in the living present (1950, 102) guarantees the apodicticity of the contents, which enables the reflection to be well grounded assuming veracity of execution. We must ask how Husserl directs reflective attention so as to make the prior attentional ray thematic in such a peculiar manner, where it would seem that the ego-pole must attend (or imagine itself attending) from the vantage point of the prior intentional object itself, which is the recipient of the prior attentional ray, so we can see the rays directed at the object from that vantage point (so it is "opposite" in this sense). But that is indeed a strange maneuver, in that initially attention is directed outward to the intentional object, and immediately thereafter, while holding on attentively to the original experience as its new intentional object, attention is directed by the ego from the prior intentional object (in imagination or in actuality) back toward the ego, which directs the prior attentional-ray outward to intuit the latter. How do the ego and its attention move in such a manner? Is it possible to sustain the attentiveness in which such a maneuver is executed while holding on to the contents of retentional experience at the same time?[9]

In any event, a more fundamental question concerns the nature of the directional structure of lived experience that Husserl is reflecting upon. My claim is that this is a mischaracterization of the nature of attention. The error in Husserl's depiction of the ego-attention relation is that attention should not be characterized as a ray; it is rather the center of self-manifestation, where the shape it takes can be any of a variety of unitary formations.[10] Any perception that is taken to be a ray is rather the action of the body in response to the movement of attention, for as we have seen, bodily resources are brought to bear to the site of action at the center of attention. The ray is thus the body being oriented to the center.

To see this, consider the following: As noted above, Husserl discusses how he can focus on the things in his immediate field of perception and how he can focus on more or less familiar objects that are not in that immediate field. For instance, he can move from the desk he has just seen to "unseen parts of the room behind my back to the veranda in the garden, to the children in the bushes, and so forth, . . . —a knowing that has nothing of conceptual thinking in it and only changes into a clear intuiting when attention is turned toward [it], and even then only partially and mostly in a very imperfect manner" (2014, §27). Similarly, in §92 he discusses how attention can radiate through various noetic layers such as remembering, enveloping, and reflecting, sometimes focusing on something as a whole or in parts, and then turn to the perception of objects. My suggestion is that when Husserl describes attention as an ego-ray, he is relying on observations similar to these to conclude that all experience has such a directional structure. But it misunderstands the nature of the movement of attention to conceive it as being directed from an identical ego-center. I argue that it is rather the case that attention is directed according the present manifestation of the ego/self, which is itself a particular configuration of embodied resources that are oriented to the center of attention.[11] Rather than attention being a ray that is directed by an awakened ego, there is instead a reciprocal relation between the bodily resources and the center of attention (see figure 2.2 in chapter 2), where they are awakened by and oriented to the center at the same time that the body directs it in its movement. For this purpose, let us consider Husserl's observations regarding the body as bearer of localized sensations, where we shall see that the question of what directs attention calls for an examination of its entire movement.

The Movement of Attention

Husserl begins §36 of *Ideas II* (1989) with a discussion of how the lived body is perceived by the body itself as the subject's perceptual organ. He considers the case of the right hand touching the left and finds touch appearances that arise out of a "soft, smooth hand, with such a form." Here the left hand is objectified by way of the touch of the right, where the indicative sensations that are the basis for the recognition of movement and representation of the left hand are located in the right. He also finds, however, that the left hand has a series of touch-sensations that are located in it ("localized") but are not properties associated with the objectified hand. He then goes on to discuss the sorts of sensations that can be experienced in the lived body in general:

> I find on it, and I *sense* "on" it and "in" it: warmth on the back of the hand, coldness in the feet, sensations of touch in the fingertips. I sense, extended over larger Bodily areas, the pressure and pull of my clothes. . . . My hand is lying on

the table. I experience the table as something solid, cold, and smooth. Moving
my hand over the table, I get an experience of it and its thingly determinations.
At the same time, I can at any moment pay attention [*achten*] to my hand and
find on it touch-sensations, sensations of smoothness and coldness, etc. (153)

After exploring the sensations of the body, Husserl looks at the specific relation between his hand and the table. He experiences the objective properties
of the table and then shifts attention to the sensations of the hand itself in
relation to the table. What is key here is that all of Husserl's descriptions are
produced by the movement of attention, which is free to roam from the body
to the environment and vice versa.[12] This is not surprising given the relation
between attention and the ego; for Husserl, it is how we go out from the ego
pole to the world. What is telling is his use of the term "I" in the descriptions.
For example, he begins with "I find on it, and I sense 'on it,'" indicating the
presence of attention, which in turn enables the manifestation of the described
events. This holds, of course, because he is describing the movement of attention in the lived body-environment, which he purports to direct while at the
same time he himself is being made manifest as engaged in such a manner *by
way of attention*, as the modes are oriented toward the focus of inquiry. That
is, Husserl posits the existence of the ego-pole as the basis for the emergence
of the modalities, but as it is put forward herein, the presence of "I" in these
statements requires the associated movement of attention, which is how the
"I" emerges in the first place. My difference with Husserl is thus that the
emergence of a particular configuration of embodied modalities oriented to
the center of attention *is* the manifestation of the self (as a moment of the
hermeneutical circle), rather than an identical ego-pole that manifests as the
center of lived experience that directs such activity.

The observations derive from the movement of Husserl's attention, and
they are in fact brought about by *active attention* because he is aware of its
movement, which is the hallmark of the state. For instance, he senses warmth,
coldness, and touch in the fingertips, after which he moves attention to the
table's objective properties and then to the correlated touch sensations. This
means that Husserl is consciously engaged in moving attention to explore the
phenomenology of the body. He reports this explicitly:

In order to bring to perception here the tactual thing, paperweight, I touch it,
with my fingers, for example. I then experience tactually the smooth surface of
the glass and the delicate crystal edges. But if I attend [*achten*] to the hand and
finger, then they have touch sensations which still linger when the hand is with-
drawn. . . . In the case of the hand lying on the table, the same sensation of pressure is apprehended at one time as perception of the table's surface (of a small
part of it, properly speaking) and at another time produces, with a "different

direction of attention [*Aufmerksamkeit*]," in the actualization of another stratum of apprehension, sensations of digital pressure. (1989, 154)

Thus, the movement of attention that ordinarily proceeds unawares is directed by Husserl, and the resultant shifts enable movement from objective properties to the associated touch sensations. This is an instance of active attention, but the key questions concern what leads to the initial interest in exploring bodily phenomenology, what determines the movement of attention, and how the associated reflection and written expression are conducted. My claim is that all of this activity similarly requires attention to proceed, but in this case it is typically passive.[13] We can surmise that Husserl is initially engaged in phenomenological studies and writing, and decides at some point to explore the lived body. All of this is of great interest to him and he is absorbed in the thought and writing that is involved, which means that attention is passive in that its movement proceeds unawares.[14] But when he actually wishes to see what there is to see in the body, Husserl must be acutely attentive to what is there to be seen, which enables an awakening from immersion and therefore awareness of his own presence in the lived body-environment. That is, the claim is that Husserl must be engaged in active attention, which is always accompanied by an explicit self-awareness, to produce phenomenological observations.

This is because he himself is made manifest at the site of manifestation of the observed entities, for this is not the distanced observation that is said to hold in the natural sciences. If that is the case, how is Husserl to see the things themselves, to have fresh intuition of what presents itself to him? When attention is passive, the configuration of modes that is presently manifest directs it, but since they are constituted on the basis of past experience, that action in itself does not enable the manifestation of fresh intuition. Sustained presence is required for that, for when attention is active, the constituted action of the modes is held in abeyance as they become open and receptive to what is presented.[15] This is what is required for phenomenological observation and description when we ourselves are made manifest at the site of manifestation of the entities that are to be observed.

Now Husserl attends to the hand and reflects on the results. In the case of description, he does not need to hold the experience attentively and conduct an eidetic analysis, for he is merely reporting what he sees, but the actual seeing is achieved by way of active attention, which enables him to come to the intuitive directness that lies at the heart of the phenomenological method. After this insight he falls into activity where attention is passive, for, as James [1890] 1983 says, short bursts of active attention are typically followed by more extended periods of passive attention to affairs with more intrinsic interest.[16] This does not mean that Husserl is uninterested in the act of phenomenological observation itself, but rather that such interest must momentarily be held in abeyance as the modes (including emotion) are stilled, ready, and receptive to what is about to present itself.[17]

We cannot discern the order in which such events may have transpired, but we can speculate in this regard. For instance, he could have started by touching his left hand with his right, and then reflected and written down some notes. We must ask, though, how the ego-pole and ray would have been deployed under these circumstances. Consider first the act of sensing the left hand with the right. I am arguing that the only center of experience that could have been observed would be the intentional object, such as the warmth in the left hand. After that, say that attention moved to reflection in the region of the head. Then the new center of attention would have been the basis for that act, for reflection also requires attention to be made manifest. That is, it is just another mode of worldly engagement in the lived body-environment, another way that the self can manifest, and as such requires attention. In all this, there is no discernable ego-pole that is directing the attentional ego-ray in its tasks, there are merely the purported effects of its action, which can also be explained by the hermeneutical circle.[18]

Consider, for instance, the act of writing. I must pay some attention to the paper as I write, or it may not be legible. I see that I write a bit, and then touch my mouth as I move to thinking about what I have written and will write. Attention has moved to the head area to support that activity. I then scan what I have written to see where I am. It seems that attention can stay on the page while I do that, as I process what is there, so there is no need to move to thought for this purpose unless something strikes me. I resume writing and see that I digest what I am writing at the same time, all while attention is on the paper. Attention then moves quickly to thought, then back into further writing. As I reflect on these movements, there is no experience that corresponds to the notion of ego-pole and ray. There is only the center of attention that moves in support of the various activities.

All the while, attention has not moved to the hand that is doing the writing. That action is habitual and as such remains in the background, by and large. But I can actively move attention to the hand and see the muscular contractions taking place as I write. The experience of writing changes when I do so as the center moves to the hand, and with extraordinary effort I can keep attention on the hand and write thoughtfully at the same time, expanding the center to accommodate the activity. Similarly, I can actively attend to my head while thinking and see its character change to inner speech, given that I am now centered and manifest as engaged in the activity. Otherwise I am immersed in the activity of writing and thinking and do not see what is to be seen. What is key is that my presence varies with the movement of attention in this manner, thereby affecting what is made manifest.

Similar sorts of observations pertain to experiences where emotion is prominent. Colombetti (2011, 296), for example, describes the experience of guilt as spanning the middle of the body from the throat to the lower abdomen. Emotion experiences can manifest as localized (one's heart is beating), diffuse (in action readiness, or urges), or localized and diffuse, as in the case of grief, where there can be a knot in the stomach and a diffuse feeling of being weighed down (296). Colombetti also considers how bodily feelings are affected when they appear in the foreground: "In many emotion experiences, one's body somehow 'stands out' from the field of awareness and engrosses one's mind—as when I perceive my heart beating very fast. In all these cases, the body comes to the *foreground* of awareness, as I shall put it: it comes into relief, it makes itself apparent, it asserts its presence" (294–95). The "I perceive" indicates one's presence by way of attention at the foreground. Colombetti recognizes this when she says that the foreground and background "differ in the degree of self-presentation." In the terms presented herein, this means that the self is made centrally manifest at the center of attention—in this case, with emotion as a significant element of the modal manifestation—whereas the self is by definition only peripherally present in activity in the periphery.[19]

Or consider the example considered in chapter 1 of leaning on a desk with both hands, then moving attention to the shoulder and back. In all of this there is no ego-center and ray to be found, in spite of Husserl's claim that it manifests as the structure of all egoic experience; rather, the thought arises to move attention to the shoulders and back, which thought itself requires attention. All the activities described above involve me as centered in them in the course of their manifestation at the center of attention.[20]

Naturally the question arises as to how attention moves if there is no entity directing its movement. Since attention in itself seems to be nothing but a tool for exploration, we would appear to need thought or some other intelligence as the basis for its movement. And indeed, there is no doubt that if I wish to move it to my hand, it will respond to the wish. But do I also direct it back to thought to reflect on the experience in the hand, and then direct it to the notebook and pen to write down the results? No; the movement of attention ordinarily proceeds unawares. In general we are absorbed in worldly engagement with little or no explicit awareness of ourselves as embodied and in the world. Its movement is passive in that we typically do not choose to attend to thought or reflection, willing, and so on. We are thus unaware of the primordial action of the self, of our very self-manifestation, which is the movement of attention. It is rare that someone like Husserl explicitly explores the lived body-environment by way of conscious control of attention. So how, then, does attention move? The claim here, of course, is that it moves according to the hermeneutical circle of attention, language, and understanding. It may be argued that discursive activity is what moves it, and that is indeed a prominent example of the circle at work, where language is one of the vertices of the triangle. In this case, the discursive act event is understood in a certain way that is made manifest performatively in the resulting movement of attention. My view is that in general the movement of attention proceeds according to the deliverances of attention (which include discursive events) in conjunction with the historically constituted background resources that move it.

ACTIVE ATTENTION AND UNIFICATION

As our presence, attention is the possibility of integration and depth of openness to other entities. Active attention can gather ourselves in and out of ourselves in what is an ontological effort. It is true that any movement occurs within the circle, and thus in conjunction with language and understanding, but we do not act directly on these ourselves, only by way of our presence in attention. Both foreground and background operate within the circle, but the possibility of insight, for instance, at the center of attention means that attention enjoys a primacy. We know that we come to the insight and that it shapes us going forward.

The background is brought to bear on the present situation by way of attention. What is brought to bear is the body of understanding. When attention is actively engaged in the lived body-environment by way of attending to its inner sensation, we see the action of these resources of understanding as they are deployed in our life situations. This is an immanent reflexivity, because we do not take a detached perspective and reflect upon ourselves as objects, but rather stay with the very action of ourselves as it occurs in worldly engagement and deepens as we proceed in this manner. There is the possibility of transformation via insight in this manner, as discussed in chapter 2.

The sustained staying with the sensation or object that occurs in active attention is a grounding in which one is rooted, for the self follows attention. One is there and one knows it, impervious to any influences that may take one away. The objects that support the grounding may change in the course of activity, but what is essential is to be aware of shifts in attention rather than being absorbed in activities, unaware of the very movement of the self. Such a holding/grounding enables one to see what ordinarily takes one away and become aware of the event of manifestation itself.[21]

We can become grounded at the center of attention and either resist the indications or follow them in a more conscious manner. Steinbock (2004, 38) chooses the latter approach in his discussion of the highest level of attentiveness, which is called phenomenological reflective attentiveness. He describes it as an active remaining open while stepping back. Rather than being disinterested, this mode of attentiveness is the most receptive to affection of all the attentive attitudes, which is consistent with his claim that higher gradations of affection accompany higher modes of attentiveness. We are disposed to be struck in whatever way the phenomena give themselves. Steinbock suggests that such an effort may require self-transformation and may enable religious insight. It is motivated by the self-givenness of the matters themselves, a "forgetfulness of self as openness to the allure" (41), a motivation in terms of the call. We will return to the question of transformation of affect in chapter 9.

Steinbock says that as a phenomenologist, one must dispose oneself toward the phenomena in an open disposition and dispose of the self. We must let the phenomena flash forth as they give themselves, as we become dispassionate about ourselves. But how is one to dispose of the self or become dispassionate about oneself? Rather, the primacy of attention must be recognized, and it can be seen that events such as transformation, being disposed to openness, and self-forgetfulness are possibilities that are contingent upon the exercise of acute attentiveness. One cannot will to forget oneself, but one may undergo transformation, one may achieve a higher order of awakening as a result of the disciplined exercise of sustained attentiveness. It is possible for such a discipline to be sustained by way of a communal understanding that deepens with the awakening and transformation. I consider the question of the institutionalized practice of mindfulness in chapter 8.

The call for such discipline is not new; rather, it is the basis for spiritual practice over the ages. The importance of mindfulness in Eastern religions such as Buddhism is well known, and has also been noted with respect to Western practices. Hadot, for instance, discusses spiritual exercises that were practiced by the Greeks, Romans, and early Christians: "Attention (*prosoche*) is the fundamental Stoic spiritual attitude. It is a continuous vigilance and presence of mind, self consciousness which never sleeps, and a constant tension of the spirit" (1995, 84). Similarly, in their discussion of the relation between phenomenology and the wisdom traditions, Depraz, Varela, and Vermersch distinguish between "*genuine* attentiveness and simple attention" (2003, 217). Arvidson puts it this way: "If I am capable of having a "quality of mindfulness' with regard to a text that I am reading, of being present to myself at the same time as I am attentive to my reading, and if a person drops a glass behind me, this does not make me start, for my attention is not only focalized on the reading but embraces, with a certain panoramic vision, all of the space that surrounds me" (2006, 147). Such a statement could just as well apply to Steinbock's example of reading a newspaper and being irritated. Instead of being taken by the irritation, mindfulness enables one to stay with and embrace one's very presence in the world, enabling inner communion and a more profound awakening.

An Experiment in Active Attention

As discussed above, Husserl shows how attention can move between perception of objective features of objects and the sensations that reside in the lived
body itself. This indicates that from the perspective of attention, the lived
body-environment is a continuum, for it can move effortlessly from the body
as lived to the features of objects in the environment itself. To pursue this
thought and further address the question of the structure of lived experience,
we can engage in phenomenological experimentation along these lines.

In producing phenomenological descriptions, Husserl actively attends to
the lived body-environment, after which he tends to go into a more passive
state of attention. Under some circumstances, of course, he calls for extended
efforts of active attention, as in reflection upon retentional experiential contents. But I now offer an alternative to reflection and its attendant difficulties
and propose that the reader simply attend to the sensation of the body for
the sake of seeing what happens and stay with the sensation as long as possible in an effort of one's whole being. For instance, one can attend to the
sensation of one's head and trunk, which will result in a self-manifestation
in which one is deployed in this fashion. That is, the fullness of effort here
means that one is fully engaged in the effort, and there is thus a corresponding self-manifestation. The difference between this and phenomenological
reflection is that retentional experience is not the object of attention, which is
rather the simple ongoing sensation of one's body and trunk. In fact, one can
go about ordinary activities when engaged in this manner, which will increase
attentional demands but also open the possibility for greater insight. It should
be noted that this is not mere "staring," for attention is on the sensation of the
body itself, which Husserl has shown to be possible in his reflections.

As noted above, to sustain that action it is desirable to ground oneself in
the lived-body environment, such as staying with bodily sensations in this
manner, keeping attention so grounded. One simply sits and attends in this
way or goes about activities that are ordinarily pursued as immersed and thus
passive. Such activities can be pursued with active attention when the site of
immersed activity (the center of attention) is expanded or deepened to include
an awareness of being grounded in the lived body-environment.

My claim is that when active attention is exercised in this manner, it will
be evident that there is only one center of experience, and that is the center of
attention.[22] We are in fact made manifest at the center, in this case, at the site
of the head and trunk, and the task is to sustain that presence. Now, as attention flags it may fall into thought, which will be seen as taking place in that
vicinity if attention then goes back to the task, for when one gathers oneself
one can get a glimpse into how one was preoccupied, as in phenomenological reflection. Or, as noted above, if considerable effort is exerted, one may

be able to think while at the same time attending to the body by way of an expansion of the center of attention. There may also be thoughts that remind us to return to the task, which shows it is not the ego that directs attention but rather instances of thought (or other modalities), which themselves require attention, which must be diverted from the task into thought for it to occur. In such a case, one will see the action of this mode of engagement while it takes place, because attention enacts the thought to return to the grounding, which will be an instance of explicit self-awareness. And to the extent that we exert enough effort, we will be unable to doubt that we are there ourselves, present at the center of attention, which is another form of explicit self-awareness (as discussed in the next section). Thus, the claims that the ego-center directs attention, and that only phenomenological reflection can produce explicit self-awareness (e.g., Zahavi 1999, chap. 8), are put into question.

The Indubitability of Active Attention

I now show that Husserl's argument for the apodicticity of the pure ego relies on an assumption of active attention. When this is recognized, it follows that the self (understood as its bodily resources and their manifestation) can be more or less present, more or less gathered, unified, open, and centered, depending upon the extent of active attention, which implies that selfhood is an achievement, not a given state of affairs. What is therefore key for phenomenological verification of the claim of attention as self-manifestation is that I can stay with myself, I can affect my self, gather myself by way of active attention. I must be self-aware when putting myself together, for I am intimately involved in both initiating and being made manifest in the process. In this gathering, the resources of engagement come to the fore and I am aware of their action, as they constitute me and my very coming into presence. Thus, the application of the thesis is itself essential for its own verification.[23]

Consider Husserl's treatment in *Ideas II* (1989, 109–10) where in arguing for the absolute existence of the ego he says that the ego can grasp itself indubitably, in the manner of Descartes. For it can be established by way of pure intuition that the pure ego does not arise nor vanish, which intuition is itself achieved by way of the ego's own attention; indeed, Husserl is explicit that this is a self-grasping of the ego itself. He says that if we try to doubt the existence of the pure ego, and see by way of pure intuition that it does indeed arise or vanish, then "[t]he pure Ego itself of such intuition, namely the regarding, focusing Ego, on the one hand would be living in *the continuity of this regarding* as *what is identical* in the corresponding duration, and yet it would have to find at once, precisely in this duration, a time-span in which it itself was not and a beginning point in which it first of all entered into being"

(109–10, em). Husserl is arguing that if the presumed absolute existing ego were to seek to verify the possibility of its impermanence, it would be impossible because in the course of the inquiry it would never be able to intuit any such evidence. This is because, by definition, as it were, the pure ego is *continuously present* as the court of adjudication; indeed, that is *what is identical* in the corresponding duration, which is an essential feature of the pure ego. But this continuity of the regarding, attentive ego, the sustained attention to the inquiry that is the basis for the apodicticity, is exactly the active attention that is being considered herein. For the ego is watching to see if it indeed arises or vanishes while it is watching, and therefore cannot help but be aware of its own presence, which is the very movement of attention. Thus when Husserl characterizes the ego as being endowed with such a capacity, he assumes a fixed ground for its sustained presence, which is in question in the present work and in Heidegger's thought in general. The entire argument rests upon this assumption.

We may ask, what indeed is the nature of such an active presence? For this purpose, consider again the experiment in chapter 1 on the reversibility thesis, where one hand is the subject and the other is the object depending on the placement of attention. I invite the reader to put all attention on the sensation of the left hand, from the perspective of the lived body, while at the same time grasping the right. One must devote full, active attention to the task, with the force of one's whole being. With such an effort, one knows that attention is there and that I am there, as readers can verify for themselves. The question is, can one doubt that one is presently engaged in such a task in the course of executing it? No, for one's very presence is fully engaged in the act, and one must know that this is so, for it is how one is manifest as so engaged. Now doubting it would mean that one is no longer engaged in the task, and that attention has moved to a doubting thought rather than sustaining the presence to the hand. One would no longer be engaged in the task, as attention would have been diverted to another activity. So if one is engaged in the task, it is not possible to doubt that one is so engaged, because one's full attention is there.[24]

In fact, in the terms put forward herein, in this case the self has been made manifest as centered in the sensation of the hand. One has devoted one's full attention to the task with the force of one's whole being, and thus the self is made manifest in this manner; I literally gather myself together there. I am centered and unified to the best of my ability by way of attending as fully as possible to the left hand, which is now how the subject is centered. It is the hand that touches, or is touched, whereas the right hand is in the background and thus peripheral to the central activity that occurs in the left. This is a gathering of the self, a self-affection, as all bodily resources are deployed in the effort, to the extent possible. It is the effort of active attention that serves to unify the self, which is not a given ground for presence, or a metaphysics of presence, in Heidegger's terms. I invite readers to test this for themselves, for this claim is central to the thesis put forward herein.

My contention is that this is virtually identical to the experiment that Husserl puts forward, for his inquiry into the status of the pure ego also requires sustained and full attention; he is explicit about this in identifying attending and intuiting, and in positing attending as an essential capacity of the pure ego. Now it is difficult to actually achieve full attention to the hand, in part because we are not accustomed to such efforts, rather being habituated to occupation with thought or other modalities. So the typical experience will be one of attending to the hand and then struggling to keep attention fixed while being constantly diverted into thought or other occupations. This is a struggle at the heart of selfhood. It is a struggle to take a stand with regard to one's very being presently engaged in the world. But regardless of the difficulty involved in the effort, it exemplifies how the self comes into presence. In the course of the experiment we know we are there, explicitly aware of being engaged in the activity. Attention brings the self to bear on the situation, and we cannot help but know that we are presently engaged in that manner.

The explicit self-awareness that is associated with active attention is thus the key to indubitability, which is contingent upon the exercise of such presence. Furthermore, we cannot imagine ourselves without the ability to pull ourselves together in this manner. Husserl does note in *Ideas II* (1989, 110) that the ego steps forth and steps back in engagement, but he says that both of these are moments of lived experience itself, and the same applies to the act of gathering ourselves at the center of attention. It is important to note, however, that active attention is to be distinguished from Husserl's active egoic modalities (e.g., 2001, part 3), for activities such as judging and explicating can take place without explicit awareness of the movement of attention. In addition, references to the absorption or occupation of the ego (e.g., 2001, 16) suggest that Husserl does not conceive here of the ego as actively attending to the movement of its own attention and as thus enjoying awareness of its own coming into presence, unless, of course, that ego is involved in an activity such as phenomenological reflection, which requires it.

In the next three chapters I turn to Zahavi's treatment of the question of self-manifestation and awareness. My proposal is that attention is the empirical, functioning I, which is spelled out over the next two chapters, and where the transcendental ego can be replaced by self-understanding and the associated self-referring emotions (Taylor 1985) that accompany it.

Chapter 5

The Primacy of Attention

I now apply the findings of chapter 4 to Zahavi's position on self-awareness and manifestation. I argued there that attention is how the self is made manifest, which means it is the very condition for my experience, for I have to be *present* for it to be mine. Indeed, that presence determines the very spatiotemporality of experience itself (see chapter 6). I also argued that the center of attention is the only center to be found in experience and that active attention enables explicit self-affection and self-awareness, thereby fulfilling functions of the pure ego such as centering and unification. Indeed, the possibility of active attention attests to its primacy, for bodily resources can be readied, unified, and potentially transformed by way of such sustained and acute attentiveness, which can eventually show itself in the shared language. Thus, the extent to which the self is centered and unified, which is the essence of selfhood itself, depends on the state of attention.

In turning to Zahavi, I look at some recent work where he contrasts phenomenology with introspection and mindfulness. I show that attention plays an essential role in all three practices. In particular, I have already shown that it is where self meets world, which Zahavi argues is the central concern of phenomenology, and I show that the distinction between pre-reflective and reflective self-awareness is subtended by the passive-active attention dichotomy.

To provide some background, I discuss the difference between attention considered as a type of reflection and as the necessary basis for all experience and reflection. For this purpose, I turn to Zahavi's treatment of "Reflection and Attention" in *Subjectivity and Selfhood* (2005, chap. 4).

ZAHAVI ON ATTENTION AND REFLECTION

In this chapter, Zahavi says that Heidegger's approach to phenomenology responds to Natorp's (1912) critique, which argues that subjectivity cannot be grasped with categories from the objective world. Natorp assumes that we do not have direct access to our own functioning subjectivity, and that reflection can only grasp a "paralyzed and objectified subject" (Zahavi 2005, 75). Zahavi says that Heidegger's approach responds to such criticism by developing a phenomenology that speaks from the phenomena themselves, and as such is not subject to Natorp's critique. For Heidegger starts from "factic life experience" and its associated articulations, which enables the development of a reflexivity (my immanent reflexivity) that is already present in life (79). Life is acquainted with itself, as there is the immediate experience that enables it to come to itself with its own categories and modes of access. For Heidegger, what is essential is to get a foothold in lived experience that enables one to stay within it, to go along with it as it is lived. Since self and world are co-given, this enables a codisclosure of self, which means there is no need to turn attention back to the primary act. Reflection, on the other hand, is too late to grasp functioning subjectivity in its originality.[1]

Much of this is in concert with Zahavi's views on phenomenological method, although he finds an apparent inconsistency in one aspect of Heidegger's thought, given that the notion of "going along with life" would seem to be at odds with the struggle that is required to resist the tendency to fallenness and bring factic life to genuine self-givenness. I show below, however, that this is related to the paradox associated with attention, that since it is how the self is made manifest, how is the self to gather itself, to affect itself, when the impulse only remains operative for so long? One can just go along with life, with the movement of one's own attention, but that takes effort. However, who is there to make the effort, when we are considering the very manifestation of the self itself? Staying with the movement of attention is where the effort is required, paradoxical as it may seem.

Zahavi contests the idea that there is more than an artificial difference between phenomenological reflection and Heideggerian attention. He argues that there are varieties of reflection, and that attention is simply a form of reflection that enables an accentuation or awakening of life experience. He cites Fink (1992), who says that phenomenological reflection is itself a more articulate and intense form of self-awareness, or simply a type of attention (which still requires the epoché). We turn attentively in reflection, which then articulates pre-reflective experience, in a consummation of experience that articulates its own sense (Zahavi 2005, 88).

We can see this when Zahavi discusses Jean-Paul Sartre's distinction between pure and impure reflection. While impure reflection operates with an epistemic duality, pure reflection provides a true thematization of what is reflected on, but as a result "never learns or discovers anything new" (Zahavi 2005, 87). Although Zahavi favors the former type of reflection, he recognizes the potential value of a mode of reflection that is simply a type of attention. But since for Zahavi the notion of attention comes from the realm of object consciousness, pertaining to the structuring of the field between thematic and marginal objects, there are limits to what it can achieve, because pre-reflective experience cannot be viewed as a marginal object that lingers in the background. In addition, while attention is a feature of our primary acts, reflection is a new, or founded act: "Thus, reflective self-awareness must be appreciated as involving a *relation* between two different experiences. . . . As Husserl also frequently put it, it entails a kind of doubling or fracture or *self-fission*. Following Husserl, Fink even speaks of reflection as a *self-multiplication*, wherein I exist together or in communion with myself" (90).[2]

The implication is that such reflection is required for self-critical deliberation, and that it enables experiences to be situated within egological and intersubjective contexts. As such, they are subject to intersubjective validation, the absence of which Zahavi considers to be a limitation of introspective techniques (see below). He does admit, however, that the self-fission that is involved means "there will always remain an unthematic and anonymous spot in the life of the subject. . . . Reflection will always miss something important, namely itself qua anonymously functioning subject pole" (2005, 92). So the question for Zahavi is, what is the value of such a self-awareness when the core, essential part of oneself is not included?

Earlier in the text he notes similarly that while we are typically absorbed, immersed, and preoccupied, this pre-reflective mode of engagement is implicitly self-aware but not thematically, and when I do thematize myself, that very act is itself not thematic. We must therefore distinguish functioning subjectivity from thematically experienced subjectivity, which forms a key dichotomy at the heart of reflection. When I take myself as object, I am always unthematically co-given as the functioning I, which is in turn accessible by way of reflection and so on. While functioning subjectivity is anonymous, it is implicitly self-aware.

In fact, our presumptive absorption is essential for how Zahavi defines reflection. While we are typically absorbed and immersed in the mode of pre-reflective awareness, any move to withdraw or otherwise distance ourselves from such immediacy is what Zahavi calls reflection. That is why he admits the possibility of both attention as a form of (hermeneutical) reflection and the phenomenological reflection that he champions.

Zahavi now turns back to the question of Heidegger and his hermeneutic phenomenology and finds that as a species of attention it is a form of reflection that merely accentuates aspects of lived experience. "Heidegger's real contribution might be taken to consist in an analysis of a phenomenological type of reflection that can precisely *provide us with an access to lived subjectivity* that is not vulnerable to the objections posed by Natorp" (2005, 96, em). That is, while Husserl's phenomenological reflection always has a blind spot when it comes to access to functioning subjectivity, *that is not the case for Heidegger*. He goes on to downplay this by saying it is simply paying attention to things we normally live through (are absorbed in, preoccupied with) but fail to notice. He concludes that the distinction between the two modes of reflection is "utterly artificial." My claim is that, in fact, the functioning subjectivity that goes unnoticed *is attention itself*, which means that when one attends to one's own mode of being, one attends to the movement of attention itself, which is the very mineness Zahavi champions as the minimal self. But this is not reflection in the retrospective sense that Zahavi favors.[3]

The key question is the nature of the functioning subjectivity that is impervious to reflective awareness. I have argued that any experiential structure is contingent upon the deployment of attention. What Zahavi misses is that any reflective move requires the movement of attention. So when we say that one is absorbed in experience, that means one's attention is so absorbed. When the motivation arises to reflect, it is attention that withdraws and moves to reflection, be it in thought or other mode of engagement. When he says that attention belongs to the primary act, while reflection is founded on that act, which supposedly distinguishes attention from reflection, he misses the fact that the anonymous subjectivity that enables the reflective act is attention itself. Attention, as my presence, belongs to all acts to the extent that they can be called mine. Thus, what reflection cannot grasp is the attention that enables it.

Zahavi's thinking would imply that the move to attend to attention itself is reflective because any such withdrawal from immersion is included in his definition, but it certainly is not retrospective, for this can only take place in ongoing life. For attention is always about the ongoing Now, about our presence in the lived body-environment, where the absent can be made manifest as present in absence. Such a move is rather a gathering of oneself, a self-integration rather than the fissuring of reflection. For when one attends to the very process of one's own bodily being drawn into presence, there is a union between the part that initiates the attention and the factical being that is made manifest, which enables an explicit self-awareness in the course of worldly activity.

Attention is the site of functioning subjectivity, as it is required to support bodily engagement. When we are grounded by way of active attention, we can see the action of such subjectivity, as aspects of factical being come to the fore as they are deployed in worldly engagement. Since these embodied modes of engagement have their own temporality, their own unfolding, their action can thereby be seen while it is ongoing, in contrast to the phenomenological reflection that must always look back at the "experience" that has already occurred.

When attention is active, our presence is transformed by way of the associated gathering, and hence our experience is also transformed. Zahavi (2005, 90) thinks that attentional modification is limited to the change from marginal to thematic focal object, but that is far from the case. Gathering enables things to show themselves in a more profound light, to emerge from the depths in which they are concealed because the self itself, which enables the things to show themselves in relation to us, is also made manifest more profoundly. That is, this also pertains to ourselves, as we also emerge, are made manifest from hidden depths depending on the extent of active attention. This is the depth dimension that Zahavi misses.

Passive/Active versus Pre-Reflective/Reflective

It is well known that reflection occurs when attention is turned to one's own experience, but it is less often remarked that prior to that, attention is essential for the original, or pre-reflective, experience itself, which points to the importance of what I refer to as active attention, or mindfulness. The implication is that attention is essential not just for reflection but for the quality of worldly engagement in general. Thus, the distinction that trumps that of pre-reflective/reflective is that between passive and active attention. Now Zahavi says that we are often absorbed and immersed in daily activities, which is typical of pre-reflective engagement. And when attention is passive there will be such absorption, because there is no awareness of being engaged in the lived body-environment. On the other hand, activities that are considered to be active, such as judging and willing, will also often involve passive attention. One can be fully immersed in such activities, along with a driving emotional state, which means that one is unaware of one's movement, one's spatiotemporality. As such, attention is passive. Likewise, reflection cannot grasp its own movement, the movement of the attention that enables it, for only attention can stay with itself as the condition for the possibility of all other modes of comportment. Its movement cannot be objectified; it can only be lived by staying with it. In fact, when Zahavi says there is a blind spot in reflection, the implication is that attention is passive, for lack of awareness of the movement of attention is its hallmark. So there is immersion inherent in a retrospective reflection that seeks to objectify its very movement. I would argue, however, that when Husserl is engaged in activities that call for extraordinary attention, such as in phenomenological description and reflection, the effort involved makes it more likely to be aware of one's very movement, the movement of functioning subjectivity that is the movement of attention, and he often recognizes the latter explicitly, as we have seen.

Thus, attention is not a form of reflection, but is rather how we engage in worldly activity in general, the very basis for experience and reflection, and active attention is a more collected and intensive way of being in the world. Under passive attention we are dispersed according to the varying deployments of bodily resources, whereas under active attention there is an effort to maintain one's presence, to hold it constant regardless of any impulses that may arise to take one away. It is not a distancing that removes one from engagement but rather a more profound awakening and engagement in life activity. One remains actively engaged while at the same time being aware of one's living, embodied presence, thereby enabling explicit self-awareness and integration. It is a distancing in the sense that it withdraws from the typical immersion in experience that is associated with passive attention; one can continue in the same activities, but with more self-awareness and depth as engaged and in the world.

ZAHAVI ON INTROSPECTION

I consider now the debate between Zahavi (2011, 2017a) and Bitbol and Petitmengin (2011, 2013a, 2013b) on the relation between phenomenological reflection and introspective techniques such as micro-phenomenological interviews.[4] What is interesting is that they both rely on the notion of attention in the course of argumentation, and in fact there are similarities in the ways they deploy it in the study of lived experience. I wish to show that understanding attention as the manifestation of the self has considerable implications for the debate.

Zahavi begins *Husserl's Legacy* (2017a) by arguing that phenomenology is more than a form of introspection because it seeks to lay out the transcendental structures of all experience. While some argue otherwise that phenomenology's dependence upon introspection renders it ill-founded, practitioners of introspection such as Claire Petitmengin and Pierre Vermersch argue that phenomenology is worthwhile precisely *because* of its reliance upon introspective techniques.[5] In arguing for phenomenological reflection, Zahavi (2017a, 12–13) cites a passage from Bitbol and Petitmengin as an example of introspection:

> I am in a *café*, absorbed in a lively philosophical discussion with my friend Paul. At the beginning of the conversation, my attention is completely focused on the content of the ideas. But as the discussion goes on, my mode of attention progressively changes and I start to become aware of other dimensions of my experience. I first realize that we also speak with our hands, and that I was initially unaware of our gestures. I then realize that I am feeling many emotions triggered by the ideas we are exchanging, that these emotions are experienced in several parts of my body (especially my chest and my throat), and that I was

not clearly aware of this. Suddenly, I also become aware of a vague and diffuse, yet intense and specific feeling which is likely to have been within me from the very instant I was in Paul's presence: the energy, the rhythm, the special "atmosphere" that emanates from him, his highly personal way of being present. At the moment I become aware of this feeling, I keep on participating in the conversation, but the field of my attention is now broader and defocused. I do not try to capture this feeling but it imposes itself on me. It is as if instead of trying to fetch it, I am allowing it to come to me, to pervade me. While I adopt this open and receptive form of attention, I am present and awake but lightly so, effortlessly and without tension. (2011, 33)

This is a rich example of phenomenological description where the movement of attention is explicitly followed. It is initially absorbed in the conversation, but it eventually expands to include more of what is present. Note that the narrator continues to participate in the conversation, but her field of attention is now broader and defocused. She sees that she experiences emotions in different parts of the body, and that there is "vague and diffuse, yet intense and specific feeling" in relation to Paul's presence, which may have been present the whole time.[6] I argue that sustained attention enables this feeling (see Taylor's felt intuition in chapter 2) to come into awareness, and that Paul's presence is itself made manifest by way of his attention and associated bodily resources in the course of the conversation. In fact, open and receptive attention enables the interlocutors to be made manifest together, in communion with one another, which will be an important theme in chapters 7 and 8.

After providing the above citation, Zahavi (2017a, 13) asks if this is the stuff of phenomenological description. For Zahavi, phenomenology is neither about "fine grained descriptions of thin time-slices of experience," citing Bitbol and Petitmengin (2013a), nor broadening "our field of attention in such a way as to allow us to discover hitherto unreflected and unnoticed aspects and details of lived experience," citing Bitbol and Petitmengin (2013b). While recognizing that both disciplines study consciousness and seek to discover invariant structures of experience, he cites Husserl for insight into what distinguishes phenomenology from all other scientific disciplines: "All their questions refer to a world which is given to us—with an obviousness belonging to life—prior to all science, but they fail to notice that this pre-givenness conceals a true infinity of enigmatic problems, which are not even noticed from within the natural perspective" (Zahavi 2017a, 16). Thus Zahavi says that while psychology accepts a number of "commonsensical metaphysical presuppositions, [phenomenology] is engaged in a transcendental investigation of those very presuppositions" (16).[7] While the introspective psychologist sees consciousness as a "mere sector of being, . . . the phenomenologist realizes that an investigation of consciousness cannot take place as long as the absolute existence of the world is left unquestioned" (17). Both rely on the deliverances of attention and its associated hermeneutical circle (in my view), but Zahavi's understanding is informed by Husserl's theories and those of other phenomenologists. The question I raise is whether or not those theories aid in or prevent us from gaining access to the things themselves, which is the aim of phenomenology.

Moreover, the other question to Zahavi is, how can an investigation of consciousness take place as long as the nature of attention is not explored? For he does not address the essential role it plays in the work of Petitmengin and her colleagues. He does not comment on the notions of stabilization of attention, broadening of focus, and taking on a posture of openness and receptivity, which enable awareness of, for instance, emotion experiences in different parts of the body, and the particular presence of the other person, saying that it merely opens us to otherwise unnoticed aspects of lived experience. He also says that the introspectionists turn attention inwardly, while the gaze of the phenomenologist is always on worldly engagement (Zahavi 2017a, 25–26), but that is hardly the case when considering the question of Paul's presence in the above citation, which is a novel contribution indeed.

Zahavi's understanding of attention is that it serves to structure experience into foreground and background, but otherwise it merely accentuates what is already there. He may be relying for this position on Husserl (2014, §92), who argues that attention is part of the structure of the pure ego. For Husserl, the ray of attention extends to thematic intentional objects, thereby enabling access to them, but its action does not affect any intentional structures that may be operative. In this regard he refers to attention as a spotlight that merely illuminates, but I am arguing that attention is much more than that. Indeed, Zahavi misses the possibility of opening up to a depth dimension that he himself points to when he says, "[I]t must be recognized that there are depth dimensions in the constitutive processes which do not lie open to the view of reflection" (2002, 8), which for Husserl can only be disclosed by way of an "archeological effort."

ATTENTION AND EXPERIENCE

The question now is how we are to investigate any posited structures of experience when the findings are produced by the deployment of attention. For the problem is that experience (including any such investigation) is contingent upon the manifestation of the self, making the experience mine, which in turn requires attention. We have seen that Husserl depends on active attention in his phenomenological explorations, and Bitbol and Petitmengin (2013b) call for stabilization and an open and receptive attentional stance toward what may be made manifest. The attentional posture must be such that the self (or its bodily resources) "is stilled," as it were, to enable the entities to make themselves manifest more profoundly. What is to be seen is then an open question, something to which we ourselves are to stay open.

Even in the brief citation from Bitbol and Petitmengin (2011) provided above, we can see that the deployment of attention is a key determinant of the experience that is described. Being actively attentive rather than absorbed sets the stage for insights such as how emotion is experienced and how the presence of others is made manifest. Not only does Zahavi fail to consider how it is understood in Bitbol and Petitmengin's work, but he goes on the use the term in support of *his* understanding of phenomenology. It is as if its use is obvious and requires no explanation, even though it is what is closest to us as the manifestation of the self itself.

The first time Zahavi uses attention this way is in discussing phenomenological reflection: "Our attentive examination of a bottle does not change the bottle beyond recognition, so why should the attentive examination of *an experience of* a bottle necessarily change the experience beyond recognition?" (2017a, 22, em). But what does it mean to examine an experience attentively? That is much different than an object that presents itself to someone, given that the experience must presumably be conjured up retrospectively. What is the ontological status of such an entity, that it would admit to attentive examination? How does one enter into a posture that would enable it? In fact, we need to understand what the self and attention are to address the question, which, beyond recognizing the ego and its attention as a structuring principle for experience into center and periphery (e.g., Zahavi 1999, 146–48), are not forthcoming in Zahavi's work.

Another instance of Zahavi's use of attention is when he argues that phenomenology is not about turning attention inward as in introspection, but about "paying attention to how worldly objects and states of affairs appear to us" (2017a, 25). The phenomenologist does not perform "mental gymnastics" where an inner attention replaces the object of experience with a mental object; rather, "it is by intending the object of experience that I can attend to the experience of the object" (26). The problem, however, is that Zahavi wants to pay attention to how things appear to us, but they come into presence for us *only by way of attention*, so it is only by way of altering one's attentional stance in some manner that it is possible to gain such insight. He goes on:

> By adopting the phenomenological attitude, we pay attention to the givenness of public objects. . . . We do not simply focus on the object; rather, we investigate the object qua experienced as well as the structure of the respective object experience. That is, by attending to the objects precisely as they are given, we

also uncover the subjective side of consciousness, thereby becoming aware of
our subjective accomplishments and of the intentionality that is at play in order
for the objects to appear as they do. (26)

Thus we see that, for Zahavi, attention is crucial for the practice of phenomenology, as it is for Bitbol and Petitmengin's version of introspection. It is
not, however, a term with a transparent meaning, where the phrases "we pay
attention" and "we do not simply focus" are clear to all speakers of the language, and it is not a transparent "window" by way of which we view things
"as they are." For I have been arguing that it moves according to a historically
constituted background of bodily understanding and language, a transcendental "structure," if you will, which is the basis for any such phenomenological
investigation. But it is not transcendental in the Husserlian sense because, as
Heidegger argues, Husserl does not situate those structures in the ultimate
context, which is Heideggerian *being*. My ultimate aim in this work is to situate the hermeneutical circle in this manner.

Let us consider, for instance, what it would mean to attend a bottle and
likewise the experience of a bottle. Three things can be attended here—(1)
the bottle, (2) the bottle as experienced (the way the bottle manifests), and
(3) the subjective side of the experience, as stated by Zahavi above. But the
notion that there is a difference between attending to the bottle and attending
to the way it manifests is problematic, for we have nothing by definition to
attend to except the manifestation of the bottle. That is what manifestation is:
the way that it presents itself at the center of attention and its periphery, where
both are determined by the deployment of attention in relation to what shows
itself. This means it would be better to specify the options as attending to (1)
the bottle as it is made manifest to me as I come into presence, (2) the way the
bottle is made manifest to me as I come into presence, and (3) the way I am
made manifest in relation to the manifestation of the bottle. But in all these
cases attention is already operative as what enables me to be made manifest
in relation to anything at all. So the question becomes, if Zahavi seeks to pay
attention to the manifestation of self and object as it occurs pre-reflectively,
in the course of life as it is lived through, how is he to do it when attention is
always already engaged in these very events themselves?

Let us look more closely at the difference between attending to the bottle
as it is made manifest to me and attending to *the way* it is made manifest to
me. Zahavi is not clear here, but I believe the best way to understand the
difference is that the first case occurs pre-reflectively, where for Zahavi one
attends to the bottle but is absorbed and unaware of the process of manifestation itself. This means it is possible to attend to the bottle but not be reflective in the phenomenological sense. In the latter, reflective case, I am able to

examine how the bottle manifests itself while I am attentively engaged with it. Let us look at these cases in more detail:

(1) Suppose, for instance, that I plan to buy a bottle of mustard in the supermarket. I have a long list to go through, but the bottle still has a place in the recesses of my mind, so it is manifest in a peripheral sense. I finally get near the aisle where it is and start looking for it. I scan the shelves, see the right section, and focus in on the required bottle. In all this the bottle is made manifest in a variety of ways, when I am thinking about what I need, how it appears on my shopping list, when I see the aisle I expect it to be on, when I see the right section, when I get it in my hands and into the shopping cart, and when I get it home and into the pantry. These are some of the contexts in which the bottle is made manifest, either focally or peripherally. The key is how attention is deployed and whether it is stabilized, so that its movement within the lived body-environment is explicit rather than flitting about as I am absorbed and unaware of the process of manifestation itself.

During this excursion, the question is how context affects how I attend to the manifestation of the bottle. It is assumed that I am not engaged in phenomenological reflection but rather absorbed in the process itself. But my understanding of the situation still determines how I attend to the manifestation of the bottle. For instance, I might be concerned that the bottle is defective in some manner, because there have been some recent cases where that has occurred. Or I could be worried about the ingredients and how they may affect my health, so I look at them very carefully. But the point is that the way the bottle shows up during this process depends on the fact that I am absorbed in it. If it were undertaken with an active attention, which is necessary for phenomenological reflection, it would still be possible to go through the very same process, shopping for the bottle and looking for the right aisle, examining the same features, and so on, but the experience would be very different.

The understanding of the situation plays a large role in how attention is deployed, determining how context affects its movement, which is a historical, holistic process that is not reducible to the interaction of noetic modalities and noematic essences. The associated changes in understanding are much more intricate than this, as are the bodily changes which accompany them. The effect of mood, for instance, can be all-pervasive, and shifts can be sudden, due, for instance, to changes in social atmospheres. These are features that Bitbol and Petitmengin point to, but which Zahavi dismisses as irrelevant, and when the situation is understood as calling for active attention that has a large effect, as I have indicated.

(2) and (3) Zahavi says that we can also pay attention to the manner in which the bottle manifests, the lawful manner in which such an entity comes into presence. And he would be the first to agree that it is always coordinated with the manifestation of the self in relation to the bottle, which I argue occurs by way of attention and the associated language and bodily understanding in the hermeneutical circle. Indeed, Zahavi often states that manifestation always

has a dative, and the claim here is that the dative is made manifest by way of attention, which is how the lived body of understanding is brought to bear in the course of engagement. So what can it mean to attend to the way in which the bottle manifests? Perhaps it means to stay with the bottle thematically, and to continue to do so as it unfolds into presence. But that would render all of the nonthematic manifestations of the bottle problematic. For instance, when entering the supermarket, the bottle is peripheral to the enterprise, given that I have several items on the list and many other things can be occupying me at that time. So what would it mean to attend to how it is made manifest in that case? At a minimum it would require that the entire track of the enterprise be disturbed, so it would appear that the experience of the bottle that I can attend to in this manner must be thematic.

This requirement entails that we ourselves must be thematically present to the bottle the whole time, meaning that bodily resources of understanding must be so deployed, with the specific historicity that inheres to the researcher performing the investigation. So now, the question becomes, how do we separate that presence, which manifests as the structure of the experience (Zahavi 2017a, 26) of the bottle, and the experience of the bottle itself? This is Zahavi's key claim here, cited above, that "by attending to the objects precisely as they are given, we also uncover the subjective side of consciousness."

The key in distinguishing between attending to the bottle and attending to the experience of the bottle lies in the fact that when engaged pre-reflectively we are absorbed in the process, unaware of the movement of attention, which is literally absorbed, immersed in the activities, with no distance from the processes in which it is absorbed. In fact, Zahavi (2017a, 23) says that reflection fulfills a need to step back from the activities in which we engage, and I have shown that attention enables such a distancing immanently by expanding or deepening the center of attention. I have referred to this as the immanent reflexivity that comes about by active attention, which is the antidote to the immersion that typically holds. But such an expansion can mean a dramatic change in the experience itself, contrary to Zahavi's claim that attending to an experience, in this case while it is ongoing, does not change it beyond recognition (22), at least when that attending is active in the sense put forward in the present text. It is true that the bottle is still included in the experience, but the required active attention, which provides the material for any reflection that may then occur, necessitates a significant change in the associated historical understanding that is brought to bear and the deliverances of attention itself, which then indeed includes more that can be reflected upon. This is similar to Husserl's explorations discussed in the last chapter, where active attention was paid to various bodily sensations that would otherwise stay in the background but are nevertheless present but not attended to because the focus is ordinarily immersed and hence narrowly construed. So the idea that the experience does not change beyond recognition when attention is expanded to enable an awareness of the process of manifestation itself is questionable. Zahavi does note that reflection indeed changes the experience (23), citing Husserl, but he misses the fact that the required shift in attention also affects it, changing it from an absorbed experience in which little can be recalled beyond the activities in which one was engaged to a temporally altered (see chapter 6) opening that changes everything, from immersion to an awakening to one's own presence in the lived body-environment and the ability to see the action of embodied resources as they are brought to bear in the course of engagement.

Zahavi says that awareness of the manifestation itself is achieved by adopting the phenomenological attitude, which consists of notions such as the epoché and reduction. But these are merely theoretical shifts in understanding, which themselves vary depending on how they are interpreted and are subject to considerable controversy (e.g., Zahavi 2021a, 260). My understanding, for instance, is that the epoché calls for setting aside the typical assumption that the entities we encounter are independent of any constitutive achievements, which allows us to see those achievements themselves, and reduction simply calls for a focus on certain regions of the consciousness-world relation that is under study (e.g., Zahavi 2021a, 263). How these attitudes play out is that they enable attentional postures that can uncover the desired structures. But I would propose that setting aside the way in which we typically perceive worldly entities is most problematic, given that it involves an all-pervasive understanding that is deeply rooted. Another approach is to simply stay with the entities as they unfold, which enables us to see how they manifest in relation to us, and to ignore a device such as the epoché, although focusing on certain regions as in the reduction certainly seems innocuous enough.

So, can we see both the self (manifesting as the experience of the bottle) and the bottle at the same time? I argue that this can be achieved only by way of an opening of the center of attention to include both the body and the object simultaneously, and to shift from body to object within that expanded presence. That is, the actual work of separating out self and object comes about by way of effort of attention, which means that Zahavi's statement that we attend to the objects precisely as given is to be taken literally. For when we attend to the bottle, the self comes into presence as so engaged at the same time, manifesting in correlation with the bottle and informed as it is by the understanding of self in context, which is why the experience of the bottle is mine. So what can it mean, in this case, to pay attention to the manifestation of the bottle when we are made manifest at the same time, the we that is attending to the way the bottle is made manifest? Does that mean how it unfolds over time? For that to occur, I must stay with myself as I move and see how the aspects arise. In this manner, I speak from within the situation and not about it, so there is no fissure within and I can see the action of the self itself in the course of engagement.

For instance, suppose I am talking to a friend and I notice a peculiar expression on his face. The question is, how does our relation affect how his face appears to me? Why have I focused in that manner? What if any contribution can be referred back to me rather than to him? We know that any contribution comes about as my bodily resources are brought to bear in the encounter. What I can do is move attention from his face to my lived body while the encounter is ongoing, in what could be considered to be an introspective move. (This is the vaunted freedom of attention that Husserl points to and will be important in our consideration of the political in chapter 8.) I turn back not retrospectively to my own experience, but in the present moment to the lived body itself as so engaged, from which any resources in the encounter are deployed and make the experience what it is. Much like Bitbol and Petitmengin's (2011, 33) description of the meeting in the café, instead of attention being absorbed in associated feelings that arise in the background, I stay with its movement to see what is taking place in the body-other relation and get the required distance while it is fully immanent.

As attention moves to the lived body, I can see various aspects that are constitutive of my presence, such as feeling tired, aches and pains, moods or emotional stirrings in various parts of the body, together with feelings that are related to our shared history. This is the path to sorting out my contribution to the manifestation of my friend's face. Moreover, this kind of inquiry can be pursued by way of something like Gendlin's Focusing technique (see chapter 2), where one places attention on the lived body with the aim of attending to various sites of emotion and staying with them, speaking from them with various phrases that resonate with the feeling, which itself must be sustained. This would, of course, be facilitated by being somewhat removed from life situations, but one can even attempt this in the "wild," so to speak, and seek to do so in the course of engagements similar to that with the friend. When pursued in a therapeutic setting, the aim is to invoke various situations in which we find ourselves that are implicit in the emotion, noting that Gendlin argues that these situations are ever-present as the most important objects in our lives.[8] Thus even in a remote setting the subjective side of our feelings about life situations can be similarly explored.

We can also apply this sort of approach to the work of the phenomenologist, whose bodily understanding is also brought to bear in the course of investigation of the life world. That is, phenomenologists are themselves made manifest in the course of worldly engagement, informed as they are by the required attitude, and in this case in relation to the experience of the bottle. Zahavi's understanding, for instance, is informed by Husserl's theories and those of other phenomenologists, and that is what he brings to bear in the course of investigating the bottle's manifestation, and thus any such investigation has this sort of historicity embedded in it. The question is how one is to come to eidetic intuitions when the understanding that is brought to bear varies from person to person, when (according to Zahavi; see chapter 7) streams of consciousness cannot fuse with one another, and when such intuitions require shared attention for intersubjective validation.

Zahavi says there is no change in experience due to attention, that it is a mere accentuation, but all experience is produced by way of attention, and that is how the intuitive material for reflection comes about. But we can focus more on the subjective side, or on both sides at once, and see the interaction between the body and an external object, or on intrabody interaction as in the reversibility experiment in chapter 1, by expanding or deepening the center of attention and sustaining the holding open. The center of attention can be held anywhere in the space between subject and object, accompanied as always by the required deployment of bodily resources, and that placement determines the shape of the experience. This is hardly mere accentuation, but is rather the basis for exploring a world that we inhabit with our embodied presence.

There is thus an alternative that does enable a practice of phenomenology along these lines. On the view put forward here, we attend to the manifestation of the bottle when we stay with the movement of attention itself by way of active attention, for in this case we stay with the joint manifestation of self and bottle, their joint unfolding. These always occur together, and such a reflexive move enables attention to the manifestation of both. This is the essence of hermeneutic (Heideggerian) phenomenology, as discussed above. But we would still be attending to the bottle along with our own bodily manifestation, which includes more than just movements of the physical body, but also resources such as thought and emotion. Turning attention inward in this context is just another placement of attention. The key is if it intentional or not, where we stay with our own movement.[9] Reflection on such findings can indeed occur, but it is essential to recognize the role of attention in producing the intuitive matters for reflection and in the actual process of reflection itself.

Perhaps Zahavi means that we do not "simply focus" on the object, meaning just a blank sort of staring, but that rather more is involved in phenomenology. He says it is about "paying attention to how worldly objects and states of affairs appear to us," and investigating "the object qua experienced." My approach is to focus on both the lived body and the bottle and see how bodily sensibilities and resources are engaged in the course of the action. Now, when he talks about attending to the experience, Zahavi means to attend to (reflect on) what remains in retentive memory. The way Husserl describes it, the phenomenologist must continue attending to the bottle in retention (which is part of the "thick moment" and thus apodictic) while going through variations either in actuality or imagination to get to the essence of the bottle. But this

These sources of value (or strong goods) provide power and motivation when their point is understood, which can be contested with the same hermeneutical reasoning process. Strong goods have the appeal of higher ways of being that are intrinsically motivating (Taylor 2016, 210). We often feel that there are truly important ways of being that we are not living up to, and we strive to go in those directions when we feel lost or dissatisfied with our current trajectory. We talk about true vocations, and answering the call, higher ways of living together, and progress (203). Indeed, often the only way to understand the goods involved in these situations is to strive to rise above the morass of our lives, and in so doing discover what is really important. Taylor says that working in this manner gets us closer to the source and strengthens its hold on us, be it contact with nature, or another human being, or a general sense of the common good (215).

It can happen, for instance, when a parent really sees their child, and what she needs and wants. "You have to focus beyond yourself; set aside your deep investment in the child to let her appear" (Taylor 2016, 209). There is a sense in which we are then "on the path," as it were, which enables a sense of both the sources and the impediments to getting closer to them. In all of this, once we do get closer there is a power associated with them due to the intrinsic motivation they provide to act in ways that live up to what they are about. When that power is gathered in a community it can be a force for achieving the common good, but it must always be tested by staying with the associated felt sense to further articulate and assess the validity of the understanding that is so generated. This will be an important theme when we consider the question of political engagement in chapter 8.

is simply another species of manifestation by way of attention. Manifestation is always in the course of worldly engagement, the types of which can vary widely but all of which require my presence by way of attention. Certainly, new understanding can come about by way of such an exercise, as it does by way of any other mode of engagement, depending upon the quality of the attention and the understanding that enables the manifestation to take place. But that makes the point, that focusing on the bottle does not mean staring at it vacantly; no one is advocating that, but rather that any mode of investigation of the nature of the bottle requires my presence by way of attention. For why was attention being paid to the bottle in the first place? There must have been an understanding that guided attention in such a manner, which could have included vacant staring to see what comes of that. That understanding guides attention and leads to a manifestation and revision of understanding depending upon the quality of the attention that brings things to the fore in a particular manner. Intuition is essential.

Thus the distinctions that Zahavi makes do not hold up when considered from the perspective of attention. In fact, we are now closer to Bitbol and Petitmengin's position. They argue that attention is typically absorbed in the content of experience, which Zahavi readily agrees with, and as such is not available for awareness of the process of manifestation itself. Zahavi, following Husserl, believes it is necessary to reflect retrospectively to become aware of that process and any associated structures of experience, which on his view is not possible while the experience is ongoing. But Petitmengin's approach, when augmented by considerations from Heidegger, enables one to be aware of the process of manifestation while it is ongoing by staying with the movement of attention itself.[10]

ZAHAVI ON MINDFULNESS

More recently, Zahavi has turned his attention to the relation between phenomenology and mindfulness. In an article entitled "Phenomenology and Mindfulness" (Zahavi and Stone 2021), he argues that phenomenology is not a kind of mindfulness, nor is it limited to mere description, but rather seeks to solve philosophical problems in areas such as ontology, epistemology, and ethics by way of a focus on the correlation between subject and world. Moreover, he claims that "being a skilled practitioner of mindfulness is neither necessary nor sufficient for being a good phenomenological philosopher" (Zahavi and Stone 2021, 178), but he misses the essential role that mindfulness (thought in terms of active attention) plays in phenomenology. Indeed, when discussing both mindfulness and phenomenology in this article, terms such as "attend," "attention," "focus," and "attentive" appear more than sixty times, by my count. So while he emphasizes his differences with both introspection and mindfulness, he misses the common dimension that underlies all of these disciplines, which Husserl (cited above) recognizes when he says that "turning our attention toward is, as it were, the bridge to activity. . . . All genuine activity is carried out in the scope of attentiveness." (2001, 276).

Moreover, when attention is thought in terms of its presence in the hermeneutical circle, it is immune to the sorts of criticisms he levels against these approaches. For instance, Zahavi argues that rather than thinking in terms of a "bare attention" that connects with direct experience rather than being immersed in the distorting effects of thought, reflection, and beliefs, phenomenology "aims to make us realize the extent to which what we encounter in experience is inescapably intertwined with our cognitive and affective contributions" (2021a, 19). But since language and the body are essential for the movement of attention, as we see in the circle, these contributions as well as the "social, communal, and transgenerational dimensions of the human lifeworld" (Zahavi and Stone 2022, 13) are indeed included in the general framework for human presence that I am putting forward here. Moreover, given the primacy of attention within the circle, in light of (1) the foreground-background relation where human action and its effects occur in the foreground with implications for the formation of background resources and (2) the importance of direct experience that is emphasized in the phenomenology literature itself in its consideration of intuition and its relation to attention, we see that the emphasis in mindfulness practice on staying with the present moment is also consistent with this wider framework. Of course, we have also seen how phenomenological reflection depends on active attention, and most importantly, the emphasis in mindfulness practice on active attention and the self-integration and openness that can result is completely missing in Zahavi's account.

Moreover, Zahavi claims that absorption is the key feature of pre-reflective experience, but he fails to see that at least some forms of reflection are also absorbed, such as judgment and imagination, and that the key for emerging out of absorption is the explicit self-awareness that comes about by widening or deepening the center of attention in whatever activity one finds oneself in, and recognizing that one is present, here in the lived body-environment by way of the active attention that phenomenology shares with mindfulness. And as I show in what follows, by focusing on two-dimensional streams of consciousness instead of the lived three-dimensional embodied reality in which attention is placed, he puts up a metaphysical barrier between self and other that would stand in the way of the more robust bonds between members of communities that can come about by way of the institutionalized practice of mindfulness. For active attention opens a depth dimension (including within the human being itself) that can serve to unify us all. This is the promise that Zahavi misses due to his metaphysical commitments, as I discuss in chapter 7.

Chapter 6

Attention as the Minimal Self

Dan Zahavi is perhaps best known for his notion of the minimal self, which is described as the first-person perspective that makes any experience "mine." He associates it with Husserlian inner time consciousness, which he says is the minimal condition for self-awareness and hence conscious experience. He does note, of course, that there is more to the concrete reality of personhood, all of which is developed in Husserl's work. In fact, Zahavi (2021b, 10) says that the idea of inner time consciousness is merely formal, and he (1999, chap. 8) notes two other basic levels, attention and an act-transcendent ego. But the question is, why not incorporate attention right away to come to a more satisfying notion of a minimal self? It would certainly seem to be necessary, for it is difficult to conceive a self without attention. Indeed, there can be no experience or first-person perspective without it, for there would otherwise be only a "buzzing, blooming confusion," according to James ([1890] 1983, 462). If we think of attention as a "selection mechanism," as conceived in cognitive psychology, then it is necessary to filter out extraneous stimuli to make manifest something intelligible to self and others, and therefore be able to say that one has had any experience at all.

THE MINIMAL SELF

Zahavi's key claim is that the minimal self is intimately related to pre-reflective self-awareness, which in turn is related to inner time consciousness. He does note that for Husserl, attention is essential for the structuring of experience, but Zahavi does not see it as essential for the minimal self. I argue, on the other hand, that attention, as always within the context of the hermeneutical circle, is how the self manifests itself, and (in Husserlian terms) it is intimately related to inner time consciousness and the duration block (the "thick moment") that arises therein.

129

Not only do I agree with Zahavi that my first-person experience is indeed mine, but the very attention that brings my resources to bear in the course of engagement *makes* it mine, thereby producing the experience that is constitutive of those very same background bodily resources. For as we saw in chapter 4, as human presence, attention enjoys a primacy within the hermeneutical circle, in that we gain fresh access via its ecstatic openness at the foreground, the deliverances of which shape the background resources of body and language.

My approach is to demonstrate the role that attention plays while providing a different setup, inspired by Heidegger, which includes spatiotemporality. This will build on claims I have made already, such as attention being our extended presence in the world, and how we are placed as mediating the subject-object divide. Attention accompanies all experience and enables it to be experienced as *mine*, as owned by me in that it brings my factical being, my embodied resources and sensibilities, to bear in the course of engagement. It is *my presence*, how the self is made manifest, and as such determines the structure of experience and its ownership. This is the "minimal" self, how I am occupied, the "I" that is made manifest in the course of everyday worldly engagement. It is a full-bodied placement in the world,[1] in contrast to the two-dimensional notion of "streams of consciousness" that Zahavi employs, as in the movie theater of the mind. And the fact that the center of attention is in movement attests to the relation between attention and spatiotemporality, all of which I argue in what follows.

Zahavi counts all objects, foreground or background, as objects of experience *for me*, where the me is the minimal self. In this manner he finds pre-reflective self-awareness to be associated with all objects of experience, foreground and background, which is consistent with the position he takes in *Subjectivity and Selfhood* (2005, chap. 4), where he argues that the dichotomy attention produces does not establish the distinction between reflective and pre-reflective experience (discussed in chapter 5). Thus for Zahavi, the minimal self is the pre-reflective self-awareness that is associated with all experiences in this manner, but this assumes a very weak conception of experience and a passive notion of selfhood with no agency, no center, and little or no memory and unification except for the notion of a thick moment. Moreover, in the absence of attention and the associated demarcation between foreground and background, there would be no self-manifestation at all, for in that case we would be in the position that James points to, with nothing that stands out in a blooming, buzzing, confusion, or a state of "undifferentiated fusion with the environment," as Zahavi and Rochat (2015, 546) put it. But in this case it is not possible to discern a self and self-awareness at all, because it is only when we "gather ourselves together," as James puts it ([1890] 1983, 382), that there is anything we could refer to as experience, or any distinction between self and other which is so important for Zahavi.[2] Thus attention must be assumed for pre-reflective self-awareness to be possible. This is in concert with the fact that the minimal self is a formal analysis that abstracts from the larger context of the full human being, which, importantly, includes the phenomenon of attention. No minimal self could exist outside of that context, just as animals cannot survive in the wild without the attention that enables them to focus on food sources and predators.

It is the presence of attention that enables the distinction between foreground and background and the associated distinction between thematic and peripheral objects, together with an awareness of self as bodily resources are brought to bear in the course of engagement. Indeed, there is no pre-reflective self-awareness without the existence of reflection, which, as noted in chapter 5, comes about by way of attention as the basis for both experience and reflection on that experience. Moreover, the very experience of spatiotemporality would not take place without attention, for, as argued above, it is our spatiotemporal center, how we are placed in the here and now. Since there must be a reference point for time to be experienced as passing, and our very attentional placement is the basis for the experience of movement in space, there can be no minimal self that arises out of spatiotemporality without the presence of attention.[3]

To make the case, I turn first to the subjective feel, or "something it is like" to have a first-person experience, which is the essence of Zahavi's minimal self, after which I turn to the relation between attention and spatiotemporality.

ATTENTION AND WHAT IT IS LIKE

Zahavi says that the first-person givenness of an experience such as tasting a lemon is itself ineliminable, in that that there would be no experience without at least implicitly knowing that I am having it. He argues that it is inaccessible to others, at least directly.[4] He also distinguishes between the intentional and subjective aspects of our mental lives and claims that we can pay attention to either. The question I address is, how do we gain access to the subjective side of tasting a lemon, and how do we tell someone what it's like to taste it? The latter is necessary because the notion of "what it's like" implies that it is like something that others are familiar with; that is, it is a shared understanding housed in language where it is put into words.[5]

As we have seen, a difficulty is that the attention of the inquirer must be deployed to be able to ascertain the nature of the experience, while at the same time any such experience is produced by that very same attention. For again, there is an essential link between attention and experience, as when James says famously that "my experience is what I agree to attend to" ([1890]

1983, 380). I engage in a particular manner depending on how I am placed, which depends on attention, which in turn can bring my resources to bear in a more or less gathered, open, and coordinated manner. So we now must ask, how is one's attention placed while tasting a lemon? How does that determine what it's like to undergo the experience? The claim here is that any alteration in that placement will affect the experience. For instance, if a perception is marginal to the center of attention, it will be more difficult to recall the details of the experience and reflect upon it. So if we intend to proceed reflectively, the question is how phenomenological inquirers can recover the original movement of attention that produces the experience, given that all they have is their own reflective and selective attention. The role of context here is crucial as manifest in the self-understanding that directs attention, so there is no experience of tasting a lemon without accounting for the historical context in which the experience occurs. This suggests that there are no experiences "in themselves" out of context, which would imply that any conception of a stream of consciousness and its associated noetic and noematic structures must take account of the historical context in which they occur beyond any genetic accounts.

For instance, I may not be paying much attention to tasting the lemon. I may be in a conversation, or thinking about what I'm doing tomorrow, or driving a car—these are all possibilities for how I can be engaged while tasting it. Or perhaps my entrée is flavored with lemon juice, in which case the tasting most likely occurs in the periphery, not at the center of attention. Under the latter conditions, is it appropriate to say something like "I experienced tasting lemon juice" and ignore the context? It would appear that the most we could say would be that I experienced the taste of lemon, say, while eating dinner, where my attention and thus the associated bodily sensibilities and capacities were primarily focused on the eating. So the experience of tasting a lemon was peripheral at the time, and it is difficult to recall many of the details to be able to reflect on it and tell others what it was like.

The problem is that, as is well known, attention is selective, and I am arguing that the selection process takes place by way of the hermeneutical circle. One can reflect only after the fact, and that reflection by way of attention is itself necessarily selective depending on the context, as was the original experience, both of which are produced by an attention that operates within a historical context of language and bodily understanding.

As another possibility, suppose one approaches the question phenomenologically, and wishes to explore what the experience is like. My proposal is that the only way to do this is to, say, pick up a lemon and stay as actively attentive as one can during the entire process, and then describe what it is like while staying with the tasting, for reflecting after the fact is subject to a new set of conditions for selection. So let us start at the "beginning," and the question is, what is my experience at that moment? Suppose I am thinking about the phenomenological project, in which case there are two possibilities: (1) I am passively absorbed in thought because I have not yet decided to actively attend, or (2) I have already taken up the intention and am actively attending while thinking about the project. In the latter case, I am aware of where my attention is: not absorbed in the content of thought, but in supporting and being aware of the actual thought process as it occurs in the lived body-environment. The question in this case is how to sustain the attention while engaging in the act, especially because I also have to describe it, which means I must know where my attention is at all times because that is how experience arises and how I am present to whatever entities or bodily processes present themselves.

In this regard, Zahavi (2013, 329) cites G. E. Moore: "When you try to focus your attention on the intrinsic features of experience, you always seem to end up attending to that of which it is an experience." Notice that attention is deployed here for inquirers to ascertain the nature of their own experience. As Zahavi himself says in discussing this, the only way to go about it is to pay attention to what we are experiencing when it happens. So we don't find experience *as such* when we focus on the process of attending itself, but rather find ourselves in the midst of worldly entities as postured in various manners as our attention shifts in and out of engagements. We find it only after the fact, when we reflect upon what has transpired and express it to others.

But putting all this aside, I begin and reach out to take the lemon in hand. Where is attention now? Well, there are many ways in which it can be placed in this situation. I can have attention on my hand itself, or it can be on the lemon and the hand would follow automatically in the periphery, or in any of an uncountable number of other ways in which attention can be placed, on the floor, thinking about the task, worried, and so on. So going from there, I now have the lemon in hand; I cut it open, take a slice, and put it in my mouth. I feel the slice as it touches my lips, I feel my teeth as I take that bite, it feels cold on my teeth and tastes very sour, which gives me a shudder. All of this is describable to someone else, and we share that understanding, so what distinguishes my experience from that of another person, therefore making it mine? The key is that the movement of attention of the other person will invariably differ from my own, even if we undertake the same task. The question is how my attention is deployed just before tasting it. The specific context matters here because it determines the sort of focus that is brought and which resources are guiding and being reconfigured over the course of the engagement, as they are in movement themselves.

The difference in movement lies partly in the fact that we have different bodies with different histories, because language and the body determine how attention moves in a holistic manner. Our attention during the same process as just described will thus differ depending on how our particular bodies react to the events, and how we understand the task. Most importantly, attention will vary even if it is appropriate to describe the experience in the same terms and phrases. For language provides us with common frames with which to think about experience, but that all takes place within a hermeneutical circle of attention, language, and the body of understanding that is the basis for our presence in the course of worldly engagement.[6] Language is constituted by way of the action of attention in the lived body-environment, and it directs attention according to how it is understood, which will vary from person to person according to their bodily endowments, historical context, and the state of their own attention.

It is interesting that Zahavi agrees when he says that what distinguishes one experience from another is not the content but rather "the first-personal how of experiencing" (2017b, 412), for two people could have the same kind of experience without becoming identical to each other. For I have been arguing that the how of experiencing is the movement of attention itself, not a stream of consciousness without that dynamic, especially without the possibility of more or less presence on the part of experiencers. Indeed, this statement would appear to put in question Zahavi's emphasis on the "what it's like" of experience, which, as discussed above, must be able to be put into words, which is the definition of the content of an experience.

To see this from another perspective, consider further the thought process that takes place before beginning the phenomenological task of seeing what it's like to taste a lemon. What do I do to prepare myself for the engagement, where I hope to be fully attentive every moment while engaged in tasting it? Perhaps I start by noticing that I am looking at the table where the lemon is placed. But that means attention has moved from its initial position to seeing how I am bodily placed, and then perhaps to thinking that I am looking at the table. The problem here is that I cannot be separated from the movement of my own attention and thus the movement of my experience. So the very idea that I "have" an experience (or have it on reflection), or that there is something it's like for me to have an experience, is problematic because it assumes that "I" am detached from the experience, and I can describe it and tell someone what it is like. Of course, in retrospect I can tell someone that the lemon tasted very bitter, that I wouldn't do it again, and so on, but when I aspire to be truly attentive to the event so I can describe it more carefully I see that I cannot be separated from the experience at all. This is the essence of Moore's insight. It is only upon reflection that I can selectively articulate what it was about, unless I am able to stay with the experience and speak at the same time, although in that case the experience includes the act of speaking itself. Thus, experience is always retrospective unless one is able to speak from the ongoing event itself.

In the case of approaching the tasting, there are an uncountable number of ways in which attention can be directed. I start by looking at the table, and the question is how I eventually come to move my hand and reach for the lemon with the aim of picking it up. In staying with what it's like to experience, I am present to such particulars at each potential inflection point, and thus the desired event may never come to fruition because there can always be more inflection points before I get to actually taste the lemon. That is, as we shall see below, under active attention, time slows down because when I stay with my presence in the moment I am aware of myself as embodied and engaged in the body-environment, which counts as what I refer to as an ontological event, that which engages the whole human being. Thus we have another take on Zeno's paradox, for the state of attention determines how time unfolds in taking an action intentionally in this manner. The point is that the movement of attention is itself more primordial than the notions of "what it's like" and reflection in Zahavi, where it is implicitly presumed that attention moves in a habitual manner, but this becomes problematic when attention is seen as essential to the practice of phenomenology.[7]

Moreover, as we shall also see below, the question is how the intention to taste the lemon is to be sustained as the process of reaching for it unfolds. For there is no fixed entity that guides the movement of attention, rather being a holistic process that makes manifest the self-understanding that is operative at any particular moment, which is subject to shifts due to the reaction of background resources to the deliverances of attention on the way to tasting the lemon.

What is most fundamental is that attention is placed and in movement and is thus intimately related to how we experience space and time. Whereas Zahavi's notion of the minimal self draws heavily on Husserl's study of inner time consciousness, I consider now the spatiotemporality of attention from a Heideggerian perspective.

ATTENTION AND SPATIOTEMPORALITY

I discussed in chapter 4 how attention centers us in the present moment (where past and future are also operative) and in the various spaces/places in which we dwell. Thus we see that the movement of attention is fundamentally spatiotemporal, as it is placed in the present moment. It is how I am occupied, how I occupy (or inhabit) space, and it has an associated temporality. And of course attention as presence is intrinsically related to the present moment, and its state will have a large influence on that moment's constitution.

For it is where we are in the present, thick moment, as we are placed in situations. My claim is that the state of attention determines the thickness of the moment, which follows immediately from the fact that, all else being equal, more bodily resources are brought to bear in the course of engagement, which in particular enhances memory. This relation between attention and memory and the action of the past in the present thickens the moment.[8] Thickness also determines how slowly time is experienced, for more events occur in that case, at least events that I attend to bodily, as grounded in the lived body-environment.

We can ask, of course, what presence is, which will vary with the metaphysical assumptions that are employed. If we believe that the physical is what is ultimately real, then presence is physical, but under a relational ontology, presence is how we enter into relation with all that is. In that case my presence and thus attention is ecstatically and intrinsically open. Since, under such assumptions, there is no determinate ground for its movement (it is abyssal), this means that presence can be more or less open or gathered, not static, for it is itself the ground for all that is made manifest (it is an abyssal ground) in relation to us.[9]

There are significant implications for temporality, which varies according to the state of attention. We can be more or less present and endure within thicker or thinner moments, which means that more or less is made manifest (events occur) in relation to us. Assuming that the number of such events determines the experience of time, the implication is that the more that is made manifest the slower that time goes for us. The key is whether we are absorbed in bodily processes or whether we know we are present, here, grounded and placed in the world, where the general rule is that time passes more slowly in the latter case.[10]

Stated alternatively, we can be more or less gathered as a whole, so the movement of attention also includes the possibility of gathering ourselves by way of active attention. One becomes explicitly self-aware when one gathers oneself in this manner, which is an ontological event engaging the whole person. Moreover, it is an event because attention is how we relate in a relational ontology, and the quality of attention determines the quality of relations and the very constitution of related entities. This means that such a gathering may be transformational, in which case it would be an event that effects the very being of the related entities, and in the case of political realities it would mean the strengthening of the ontological bonds that hold between individuals, whereby we are more deeply related as members of communities.

The key claim is thus as follows: Attention is how we are made manifest, which occurs by way of movement and placement. Under passive attention, in the absence of ontological gathering, time goes relatively quickly (fewer events) and our placement is absorbed and closed to others, while under active attention and the associated gathering and deepening, time goes slowly (more events) and our placement is more expansive and open to others. Thus, the movement of attention is our unfolding and more or less deepening presence and openness in being placed. The unfolding and deepening is *how we are made manifest*, where what unfolds is our background resources, to which we now turn.[11]

The Temporality of Background Resources

Bodily resources have their own temporalities, which unfolding shapes how we engage and thus how we experience time. I focus here largely on the role of emotion, given its importance in disclosing what matters to us and hence moves attention, which (more or less) coordinates that unfolding (see chapter 4). We can consider longer-term emotional states such as depression and loneliness, or episodic emotions such as anger and excitement. There are a wide variety of states that can be more or less operative in a given situation, and which influence how we engage the world by way of their action on attention. As such, our temporality will be influenced according to the associated temporalities of the engaged emotions and the extent to which they lead to either immersion or an awareness of our placement in the lived body-environment. Pain will also, of course, tend to take us out of any immersion and put us back in the body, at least temporarily, with a resulting slowing of the experience of time.

Another interesting example is how thought tends to unfold over the course of time. We can be very much absorbed in thought without a corresponding bodily awareness of its occurrence. In particular, when one goes to sleep while still processing various matters, one will often wake up having made progress on the issue, which highlights the passivity that can be involved in the thought process. As I argue below, in the case of thought as well as other such events, the unifying potential of active attention will typically enhance such outcomes, because being grounded in the lived body-environment brings more of the self to bear harmoniously on the activity, which enables a more efficient deployment of resources in the process.

Inhabiting Space

We inhabit space by way of the placement of attention. Experience takes place from that vantage point, which corresponds to Zahavi's insistence on the perspectival nature of first-person experience. In order to explore how this occurs, we can see how it is possible to intentionally inhabit our own bodies.[12] Suppose we are initially absorbed in thought, or reading, and we then intentionally shift attention to the sensation of the left arm, say, which is part of the lived body, the body we experience from inside as placed in the lived body-environment. This opens us up to a more profound, deeper relation with the lived body-environment in which we are placed. We are no longer lost in thought or reading, merely living in our heads, but are manifest as more in touch with the environment when we more fully occupy the body, due to the intimate relation between body and environment.

In fact, it is very common in the practice of mindfulness to perform "body scans" in which attention is intentionally placed in various parts of the body. This takes one out of absorption in habitual engagements and into postures where one goes more deeply into the lived body, which enables a more profound relation with others and the environment at large.[13] For instance, suppose I am making breakfast and am able to be more deeply placed in the body while being so engaged. As I go about spreading my avocado on toast, I feel more directly connected with that very act because I am placed as such in the body as I go about the activity. This is an *opening* to environmental events that issues from my profound placement in the body, which typically goes uninhabited by my presence due to the passivity of attention. I am now more present to environmental events, which occur more slowly and profoundly as I am ontologically closer, nearer to them.

When active attention is sustained, I stay with how I unfold and am placed in the lived body-environment, while I am made manifest myself as what unfolds and is placed. That attention becomes an overarching, centered presence (see chapter 4) that integrates the bodily resources that are brought to bear in making myself manifest, and that harmonizes and grounds them. I stay with their unfolding and I am thus closer to them, and the unfolding seems slower because *I am with it*, not cut off from it. I myself unfold with it, it is *my* unfolding, so it is near to me. In the plural, *we* unfold together, and thus we go deeper together. Thus the movement of attention is intimately bound up with space and time, and determines my experience because my very movement occurs therein. When I gather myself in such a manner, I am brought into a more profound relation with myself (my body and its sensibilities) and am thus more self-aware, explicitly so instead of the implicit self-awareness that Zahavi emphasizes in pre-reflective states. Thus, rather than merely determining my experience of space and time, in fact the very movement of my extended presence is spatiotemporal, thereby producing that experience. And as noted in chapter 5, this Heideggerian approach avoids the self-fissioned reflection, the blind spot that Zahavi sees as inevitable in reflection.

MINDFULNESS AND SPATIOTEMPORALITY

I turn now to the effect of mindfulness on spatiotemporality, but before doing so it will be useful to discuss the definition I employ in contrast to others that are in currency. I define it as active attention, which can be thought of as an acute and sustained attentiveness or as the intentional placement of attention. The two are closely related because the former necessarily involves explicit self-awareness, and attention is always placed. Some other definitions refer to attending to or being aware of the present moment, nonjudgmental attention, and the notion of "bare attention." My claim is that virtually all of the definitions in currency involve attention in some form, and that acute and sustained attentiveness is necessary for it to be an effort of the whole human being. Given that the practice originated as a quest for "union with the divine" (Yoga, see Morley 2008), nothing less than an effort of the whole human being could be sufficient. Such an effort is associated with attention because that is how we are brought to bear in the course of worldly engagement. I now turn to a consideration of the alternative definitions.

1. Regarding the first, attention is always employed in the present moment, as discussed above. It is an act that occurs in the lived body-environment in the present moment, not the past or the future, although of course the past and future are present in the thick moment as constitutive of the background resources that are operative there. What is meant by this definition is that we should not be absorbed in thinking about the past or the future, but rather be aware of our presence in the lived body-environment, in which case we can think about or otherwise relate to anything we wish. So what is key is the lack of absorption, which is in agreement with the notion that I am putting forward.

2. Jon Kabat-Zinn is well known for recommending a nonjudgmental attention (e.g., Kabat-Zinn 2005). Zahavi and Stone (2021) contest this notion, arguing that judgment is part of the human being that cannot simply be put aside in this manner, and I agree to a certain extent. From the perspective of the hermeneutical circle, acts of judgment emanate from the body of understanding and thus cannot be excised from their influence on the state of attention. But this ignores the fact that under active attention, background resources can be stilled and at the ready, which is what the notion of bare attention is alluding to. While the notion of refraining from judging others is most useful, on the view presented here nothing shows respect like paying full attention to the other. Thus I argue that the essence of mindfulness is active attention, as I have employed it in this work.

Relaxation is also an important part of mindfulness, as is gentle, nonviolent movement. Relaxation is lack of tension (a-tension), which can obstruct the sort of holistic harmonization that can occur under active attention, and non-violent movement is called for since we must stay with our own movement as we find ourselves in the course of worldly engagement, for otherwise one part of the self may do violence to the other if it acts without cognizance of the whole. The staying with oneself, on the other hand, is a self-integration, a self-possession.

I am arguing that the movement of attention is *my* movement, which is essentially spatiotemporal, thereby going beyond Zahavi's claim that first-person *experience* is my experience. He also argues that the first-person perspective arises out of Husserl's inner time consciousness, which enables a pre-reflective, implicit self-awareness that makes the experience mine. My claim, however, is that under the hermeneutic approach it is essential to distinguish between passive and active attention. In the present case, this means that when attention is passive my movement is implicitly spatio-temporal, while when it is active that spatiotemporal movement is *explicit*, meaning that we stay with our very presence in the lived body-environment in its movement and placement, with the varying depth and openness that is correlated with varying presence. Moreover, that very movement is itself subject to shifts in ontological composition from dispersal to collectedness, or self-integration, to which we now turn.

Self-Awareness and Integration

Zahavi distinguishes between pre-reflective and reflective self-awareness, but as discussed in chapter 5, there are many forms of reflection that do not produce the sort of explicit self-awareness that is associated with active attention (mindfulness). Moreover, although we use the same language of absorption and immersion in describing pre-reflective awareness and passive attention, respectively, we have diametrically opposed interpretations of the meaning of these terms. For while Zahavi discusses how reflection produces a self-fission or dislocation within the self, I argue that the true and perpetual dislocation lies in passive attention, where absorption means that we are cut off from the lived body-environment in which we dwell. Active attention, on the other hand, enables a self-integration, where the effort of acute and sustained attention enables a more profound relation between foreground and background, or between attention and its associated bodily resources, which under passive attention do not enjoy the overarching presence that enables enhanced coordination and harmonization.[14]

Thus, when attention is passive the implication is that we are scattered, dispersed, cut off, or distanced from our bodily resources of understanding and the associated lived body-environment. We are less present and the resources we bring are deployed according to their own logic in response to environmental demands, which may be less conducive to the needs of the whole, thereby producing instability and discordance. But when attention is active, bodily resources can become more integrated by way of the presence that is produced by steadfast attention. For, as noted above, attention brings resources to bear that have their own temporalities, which can in turn be more harmonized by way of the presence that a gathered attention can bring. This is diametrically opposed to Zahavi's position on the question of pre-reflective and reflective self-awareness, where the latter brings dislocation, not self-integration.

Stated alternatively, it is possible, in light of the intrinsic openness of attention, to "hold open" its center, the space in which we dwell, to stay with its very movement and watch the action of bodily resources as they come to the fore and pass to the background. The sustained staying with the lived body and the field of activity and experience is a grounding in which one is rooted, for we are made manifest at the center of attention. One is there and one knows it, explicitly self-aware and impervious to any influences that may take one away. Rather than being dispersed or distracted, one's state can be characterized as being more collected or gathered. The resources that support the grounding may change in the course of activity, but what is essential is to be aware of shifts in attention rather than being absorbed in activities, unaware of one's very movement. Such a holding/grounding enables one to see what ordinarily takes one away, and become aware of the process of coming into presence itself.[15] This is the essence of the practice of mindfulness.

The action of background resources comes to the fore when the movement of the center is grounded and one becomes explicitly aware of oneself as embodied and engaged in the world, thereby enabling insight and potential transformation. Stabilization is achieved as one is less susceptible to movement that issues from unseen sources. The state (or quality) of attention refers to the extent to which the movement of attention is stilled in this manner, which is the basis for movement toward insight and transcendence. That stillness is how lived time slows down and the places we inhabit open and deepen.

Spatiotemporal Effects

The claim is that attention plays a large role in the experience of space and time because its very movement is spatiotemporal, varying as it does according to the state of attention, or the extent to which attention is active, intentionally placed and moved. When it is passive and hence absorbed or immersed in activity, time is typically experienced as going faster, although as discussed above that can vary depending on the action of background resources that drive attention in the absence of a more active presence. And when there is such a presence, those resources are held in abeyance as attention opens the space of activity and readies them for responsiveness to the demands of the situation.

Put another way, the more present we are, the higher the quality and intensity of what shows itself, two terms that appear extensively in Husserl's (1991) work on inner time consciousness. We experience more detail and are more in contact with events in the same objective duration block, and time goes more slowly.[16] At the same time, our spatial presence is more profound when we are no longer immersed and absorbed in the lived body-environment.

What this does is slow down the passage of time, as there is more contact with the lived body-environment, and the experience is richer, filled with more events that produce the experience of time slowing down. So instead of flitting about on the surface, we are open to what presents itself and able to go more deeply into the reality in which we dwell. This assumes a metaphysics where entities are made manifest out of concealed depths that can be plumbed by way of acute and sustained attention (see chapter 9), rather than the sorts of naturalisms that abound.

Active attention enables a quieting of our movement, a stilling that enables us to inhabit places more deeply and slow the experience of time, rather than staying on the surface and being absorbed in engagements. As discussed above, another way in which we come in contact with the lived body-environment in the absence of active attention is when an event occurs that takes us out of the habitual modes of engagement in which we are typically immersed. When we are no longer occupied with the various pursuits that typically absorb us, we may become bored, for instance, in which case time drags on slowly as we are forced to "stare at the walls," as it were. We are thus pulled out of immersion and faced with the lived body-environment in which we dwell.[17]

When we are habitually occupied, these background processes consume our attention, and we are at a remove from the lived body-environment in which we ultimately dwell. This is what Heidegger refers to as living on the surface, where the associated language becomes the well-worn coin of the realm. But when attention is active, we go from the surface to explore the depths of the reality in which we always already dwell, from which a richness can be made manifest by way of our ecstatic presence (see chapter 9). In the practice of mindfulness, the deepening relation to the lived body-environment is often achieved by way of a focus on objects or the breath, to which we now turn.

Empirical Evidence

The question of time perception is important for both James and Husserl, as is attention, and there has recently been considerable interest in the relation between the two notions. Tse (2010), for instance, surveys literature going back to the 1970s on attention and the subjective duration of time intervals. The general finding in this literature is that the perception of duration depends on the perceptual processing of events, where attention plays a large role. For instance, Tse discusses experimental results where perceived duration increases when attention is fully dedicated to estimating duration, and decreases when there are other demands that distract from the task, therefore supporting what he refers to as a "standard attentional model" of time perception (2010, 138). He suggests that this is the case because attention directs information processing to events that are more important or interesting, and therefore run "in slow motion" as they are processed in greater depth than would otherwise be the case (148). Notice that the notion of depth appears here, even though it is implicitly assumed that the manifestation of any such entities is not affected by the presence of attention. Those sorts of metaphysical assumptions are, of course, in question here, for under a relational ontology the very manifestation of entities depends on the state of attention, as argued above, as we unfold in space and time in relation to all things accordingly.

The question of the relation between mindfulness and the perception of time has also been investigated, with similar results. For instance, Wittmann and Schmidt (2014, 201) study expert mindfulness meditators and find that the associated ability to be more aware of sensory experiences, feelings, and body states leads to a slowing down of the prospective perception of time, which is consistent with the assertion above that active attention enables explicit self-awareness.[18] Moreover, they say that regular meditators report fewer negative mood states and ruminative thoughts because they are more aware of them, which enables more emotional control (204–205). They also note that the enhanced memory associated with mindfulness leads to a subjective lengthening of past duration.

Wittmann and Schmidt consider affective states such as boredom and find that in the absence of distraction, attention is directed to the passage of time itself, which leads in turn leads subjective time slowing down (2014, 205). This literature often refers to attending to the passage of time, which in my parlance is rendered as being brought back bodily to one's environmental placement and unfolding. In fact, Wittmann and Schmidt state that in mindfulness "a practitioner focuses on the experience of the embodied self at the present moment," from which it follows that "because the feeling of time is created through attending to the embodied self at the present moment, being exceptionally mindful slows down the passage of time" (206).

Tse (2010, 146) also finds that an attended stimulus may appear to last longer than a less attended stimulus that lasts the same objective duration. There are similar results with regard to *spatial* perception that have been discussed by Block's "Attention and Mental Paint" (2010). Block defines "mental paint" as qualities of perception that are not captured by what one is directly aware of or by representational content, claiming that experimental results in attention point to its existence. He says that focal attention changes experiential qualities such as perceived contrast, color saturation, object size, and speed (33) in a manner that is entirely mental. For instance, Block discusses how perceived size changes with attention when there is no change in the objective situation, which is characterized by features of objects in the environment and the subject's relation to those objects. Although there is little discussion in the paper of the metaphysical implications of these findings, Block comes down on the side of a "philosophical" dualism, meaning there are features of perceptual/mental activity that are neither the result of direct awareness of the things themselves nor their representations. There is thus for Block a "mental" dimension in which attended objects are larger than those that are unattended, while the physical world does not appear to change at all. I am suggesting that it is rather the case that instead of assuming a fixed world that is represented by mental representations, the very center of worldly interaction moves with respect to the entities we engage with, which are themselves made manifest in relation to us in this manner.

Let us compare, for instance, the statement of Broad that Block cites as an example of introspection when discussing direct realism:

> In its purely phenomenological aspect seeing is ostensibly saltatory. It seems to leap the spatial gap between the percipient's body and a remote region of space. Then, again, it is ostensibly prehensive of the surfaces of distant bodies as coloured and extended. . . . It is a natural, if paradoxical, way of speaking to say that seeing seems to "bring one into direct contact with remote objects" and to reveal their shapes and colours. (1952, 5)

Block also mentions Heidegger in this context, but he does not consider the notion of de-severance, which Rowlands (2010, 200–202) discusses, where attention brings one closer to the objects of experience. Thus the question arises as to whether it is the objects that appear to be larger when they are attended, or if we are somehow brought closer by way of attention.

AUTONOMY

I argued in chapter 2 that attention plays the role of a command center, in that the body follows the commands that emerge (implicitly or explicitly) from the center of attention, which includes, of course, thought itself. That is, rather than there being an entity (such as a transcendental or rational ego) that determines its movement, it is instead the case that attention itself, as placed in the body-environment, "controls" how the body and its resources are engaged in worldly activity in a holistic manner. We have also seen that when attention is passive it is directed by background resources, which then react to its deliverances, which leads to shifts in their constitution and further direction, very much in the spirit of a circular relation, but ultimately attention commands because the resources are always reactive—they have no presence of their own. On the other hand, when attention is active it gathers and harmonizes the action of those resources, thereby enabling more insight into how they affect our worldly presence and engagement. It produces an overarching presence and self-integration instead of assuming some entity which guides activity on a more or less "rational" basis.

This means that in the case of active attention, the overarching presence is in command because it is how I carry forward those resources in an action that paradoxically enables me myself to be made manifest in a more holistic and appropriately engaged manner. Instead of being driven by the relatively independent and isolated action of bodily resources, which are deployed habitually, that is, without my presence, I (or my watchful presence) am in command as long as that stance is maintained. The problem is, however, that this can be difficult to sustain because the background resources must still support the movement, since we never leave the hermeneutical circle, and their posture will be affected over the passage of time by the very same deliverances of attention that command them. Due to this paradox, there is the need to institutionalize the practice of mindfulness to facilitate its sustained execution.[19]

Background processes that are presently more active have more influence on how resources are engaged.[20] For instance, if an individual is perpetually sexually fixated, situations will typically be encountered by focusing on those aspects that relate to sexuality. If one is lonely, one engages according to that emotional state. These processes often operate unseen in the background, depending in part on the extent to which one is aware of the movement of attention itself. Moreover, foreground processes that lead to shifts in attention typically set off background processes that then take further control of its movement unawares. One is then absorbed in the action of the resources and unaware of the movement of attention itself. Thoughts may arise to engage in a certain way and the shift follows, but the very movement of attention goes unseen.

The language of absorption, immersion, distraction, attraction, and dispersion is appropriate in the case of passive attention, for there is neither awareness of nor resistance to impulses that may take control of attention. Absorption and immersion suggest an emotional dimension that keeps one engaged in an activity with little or no awareness of the lived body, while distraction and dispersion suggest a lack of sustained engagement and susceptibility to be taken by whatever background process should happen to arise. In both cases, one is not present to the movement of attention, and the forces that are determinative can be described in impersonal terms because one is unaware of their action.

Under typical circumstances the movement of attention proceeds by way of background processes. But when one gathers oneself, one comes in contact with the field of experience in a direct manner, and that contact is achieved by way of our presence in the world itself. What we can control is how and where we come into presence, and my claim is that this is the basis for self-control. That is, only by way of command of the movement of attention itself is it possible to have a sense of control of any of the resources, such as thought and movement, in which we typically engage. We must be present in a bodily manner to an activity to be able to "control" it.

Consider the following example: Suppose I am at a cocktail party, engaged in conversation with an official who is important for my professional life.[21] I am absorbed in the conversation, making sure I am very attentive so as to make a good impression. At the same time, another conversation begins that concerns my ex-wife, leading to emotional arousal and a keen interest on my part in hearing what is being said. However, it is crucial that I pay full attention to the first conversation, because the official will certainly notice if I am distracted and could very well think poorly of me as a result. In a case such as this, there are competing demands on attention, and effort is necessary to resist being distracted by the second conversation. Although I experience the emotional arousal bodily, I must make a considerable effort to stay with the official, to keep him at the center of my attention. This is a situation that calls for significant effort, where I must resist the arousal and potential distraction from the conversation that competes for attention. In this case a background process is oriented to the second conversation, but it is only by way of the effort of attention that I remain centered on the first conversation.

Before the second conversation arose, less effort was required because background processes were not vying for attention. I was absorbed in the conversation due to the emotional force of concern for my professional well-being, but at the same time, background processes were monitoring other potentially interesting events and picked up the second conversation.

Is this a case, then, of self-control, where I know that my professional well-being is of paramount concern and must therefore act accordingly? There are in this case two emotional currents, as it were, that compete for attention. The one that dominates is determined by my self-understanding, which typically arises from communal materials in the course of intersubjective interaction. I understand that my professional life comes first. Is this a choice? In all likelihood it is not an instance of self-control but rather a case of competition between background processes where the forces in operation are not transparent to me. Even though I become more explicitly self-aware (and time slows down) due to the discomfort of being in a situation that demands such an effort, there is not the transparency, the insight into the forces that beckon that would enable one to say there was a true sense of control. What that calls for is a truly extraordinary effort of active attention, where the center is held purely for the sake of presence, to be able to resist the impulses that could overtake me. This would be a superhuman effort, but it points to the possibility of breaking the cause-and-effect circuitry that stands in the way of human autonomy.

Thus, when I am acutely attentive and grounded, I endure in deepened engagement. Rather than being taken by the flow of affective impulses, I stand my ground, watching as the affections come and go. If we are taken by affective impulses we move to their rhythm, but if we resist, our movement is stilled as we open to all that is.

PART III

Attention and the Political

As we turn to the political, I am now able to state more fully the thesis of the book:

Attention is how we are made manifest as individuals and communities in the course of worldly engagement. It is how we come into presence, unfolding together spatiotemporally as bodily resources formed in the past are brought to bear on present situations understood in terms of future possibilities. The state of attention determines the depth of that unfolding and the extent of ontological bonding within and between members of communities. It is how open we are to others in public spaces, and how integrated, stable, and responsive we are to the social and environmental challenges that are encountered therein.

In particular, I argue in the next chapter as follows: I address the perennial question of the relation between self and community. We see from the hermeneutical circle that both the individual body (self) and the shared language (community) are constitutive of our worldly presence, so both play an essential role in the activity that is enabled at the center of attention. I also show that attention and language are world constitutive, and in this regard they are dimensions that exceed us as individuals. Active attention in particular enables us to engage in ontological activity, that which affects the whole, and as worldly creatures we have a duty to make it a better world by engaging in that practice. It enables more harmonious ways of being together that can be institutionalized through their effect on the language and associated social structures. All such structures, however, require the sustained effort of mindfulness to remain robust and responsive to changing conditions, as they are subject to the dynamics of the hermeneutical circle.

Chapter 7

Attention, Language, and World Constitution

I draw again on the work of Zahavi, who has long been interested in the question of intersubjectivity, beginning with *Husserl und Die Transzendentale Intersubjektivität* (1996). He has more recently addressed the question of collective intentionality (Zahavi 2018, 2019b, 2021c, 2022, forthcoming; and Meindl and Zahavi 2023) and has made important contributions by demonstrating the relevance of phenomenological thought to the field. Prior to this the focus of inquiry was on collective action, which has obvious political implications, but Zahavi has demonstrated that the consideration of beliefs, common experience, and self-understanding is also quite relevant. In particular, he emphasizes the role of face-to-face interaction in developing reciprocal self-understanding and bonds with other members of the community, but although attention plays a large role here, he does not address its nature systematically. The hermeneutical circle provides a framework for integrating the elements he employs, which enables a discussion of the importance of mindfulness for the development of self and community.

SELF AND COMMUNITY

In considering the relation between selfhood and the collective, Zahavi begins with the notion of the minimal self, which is based on the formal analysis that Husserl (1991) conducts on inner time consciousness. As noted in chapter 6, he sees the need to extend the analysis to come to a more concrete and comprehensive vision of the self and the relation between "we and me," as he puts it (Zahavi 2021c). He does so by inquiring into how normative relations and narrative structures emerge in support of membership in communities, focusing on the importance of face-to-face, or dyadic, interaction and expression. And in order to delve into these questions, he finds it necessary to introduce an empirical "supplement" of joint attention, which together with language forms the basis for such interaction (Zahavi 2015, 154). Thus, although he does not include attention in the minimal self, he finds it necessary to incorporate it here to bridge the gap between the two dimensions of selfhood.

In considering this question Zahavi draws on his work on empathy, which he conceives as "how we at the most basic level come to understand concrete others," or as "a form of intentionality directed at foreign experiences" (2010a, 290). He argues that this is achieved by way of direct perception of the other's experience, although not from their point of view but rather as the experience of another person who has their own unique perspective and experience (2015, 151). This is perceived bodily in a direct manner as the experience of the other person, such as grief at the loss of a loved one, not one's own experience. Zahavi contrasts this with simulation-theory and theory-theory, where the former is a form of analogy and the latter depends on theoretical inferences regarding the intentions of others. He considers these theories to be about projections based on beliefs regarding the other person's experience, not on the direct perception of others experiencing such events themselves.

Zahavi explains that on the phenomenological view, a proper account of communal being-together and shared intentionality requires an exploration of how individuals are experientially interrelated (Zahavi 2019b, 251). We develop as selves in relation to one another in a public space of norms (2015, 145), where each serves as a mirror for the other and each sees the other in their own unique individuality. Under the gaze of the other we come to understand ourselves in relation to one another. He sees the "we" as a way of being and relating to others, experienced from within due to participation in community (156), where group identification is based on the self-understanding that comes about in interpersonal interaction. In this regard, he discusses the role of second-person engagement in the constitution of we identities (2019b, 252), where such engagement occurs as face-to-face interaction where each focuses attention on the other.

Zahavi goes into considerable depth discussing social interaction in this manner. He sees social acts as requiring a special kind of reciprocity (2019b, 254), where each sees the other *as* other, as having their own point of view. He discusses the role of immediate communication, where both individuals "look each other in the eyes" (254) and are mutually aware of one another. Zahavi emphasizes the direct and intuitive nature of such face-to-face, dyadic interaction, where the other's experience is "given directly to me as present here and now" (2015, 151). He distinguishes between, say, imagining what it is like for another person to be sad, compared to being directly aware of it in the face-to-face encounter, which "has a directness and immediacy to it that is not shared by whatever beliefs I might have about him in his absence" (151). Importantly, he argues that *being aware of each other's attention* is necessary but not sufficient for such an intuitive engagement. What is also required is the will to "intimate" or commune with the other (Zahavi 2019b, 254), which under the hermeneutical circle means that self-understanding plays a large role in the deployment of attention.

But although he posits this direct relation between the experiences of self and other, he argues that experiential selfhood (the "for-me-ness" of experience) and intersubjectivity are constitutively independent (Zahavi 2015, 148). As indicated above, he introduces a supplement to bridge the divide: "A possible answer, that simultaneously suggests that *the two notions* are in need of a supplement, is to point to pre-linguistic forms of sociality with a direct impact on the formation and development of the self" (154, em), after which he discusses prelinguistic forms of joint attention, which (as discussed in chapter 2) is the basis for the acquisition and development of language. It is important to note, however, that from Husserl's point of view attention is already part of the pure ego. Zahavi himself (148) notes that for Husserl, the pure ego is poor in content due to its formality, but attention is also poor in content, all of which comes from our extended presence in the world, together with language and bodily understanding. Thus I continue to argue that attention must be part of the minimal or experiential self, and it is not a "supplement" because there would be no experience and hence no experiential self without its presence, as discussed in chapter 6. It produces the bodily form of experience, which enables it to be re-membered by oneself, articulated in language, and thereby expressed to others.

LISTENING TO THE OTHER

Zahavi emphasizes the fact that community formation requires individuals to identify with the group, meaning they must understand themselves as being its members. He says we need to consider both the self-understanding and the first-person perspective of the individuals (2015, 157), which is consistent with the hermeneutical circle where self-understanding is so important in directing attention. In this way, for Zahavi, we can understand what a "we-experience" involves, one that can be attributed to everything that goes beyond the individual perspectives which he insists cannot fuse with one another. It requires a preservation of plurality, a balance between difference and similarity (157). We need the reciprocity that comes about in the second-person perspective, as discussed by Schutz (1967, 156–57), who Zahavi cites as follows:

> I take up an Other-orientation toward my partner, who is in turn oriented toward me. Immediately, and at the same time, I grasp the fact that he, on his part,

is *aware of my attention to him*. In such cases I, you, we, live in the social relationship itself, and that is true in virtue of the intentionality of the living Acts directed toward the partner. I, you, *we*, are by this means carried from one moment to the next *in a particular attentional modification* of the state of being mutually oriented to each other. The social relationship in which we live is constituted, therefore, by means of the attentional modification undergone by my Other-orientation, as I immediately and directly grasp within the latter the very living reality of the partner as one who is in turn oriented toward me. (2015, 157, em)

Schutz begins with the notion of an Other-orientation, which refers to how attention is directed to each other based on their respective understandings, and says we are mutually oriented to one another by way of mutual awareness of that deployment of attention. He indicates how the relation unfolds by way of attentional modifications, as it is in movement over the course of the interaction. Thus he points to the deep link between attention and temporality, in that the very unfolding occurs by way of its movement. Indeed, although attention is not visible in itself, its state is not without its effects. We can see this in the practice of mindfulness, understood as attending to the here and now, to where we always already are, and what happens as a result (see chapter 6). For Schutz, in this manner we can each "immediately and directly grasp . . . the very living reality" of one another in the exchange. This is the basis for what I refer to as an ontological bond.

Earlier Schutz discusses how such a relation comes about, how we know about the orientation of the other and make contact with them:

For instance, he may affect me, and I may then become aware of that fact. Or I may turn my attention to him and find that his attention is already on me. In both these cases, the social relationship is constituted through my own Act of attention. . . . But all this is not so much a description of how a person knows he is in a social relationship as it is a description of how such a relationship is generated. (1967, 156)

Thus our acts of attention are the basis for the we-experience, which in my conception requires a space to open where we are made manifest together bodily and fuse in a way that indeed maintains our individuality. The key is that it is not about *knowing* one is in such a relation by way of attention, but rather an *ontological* statement about how such a relation is generated. Thus, for Schutz, the statement is ontological rather than epistemological.

Compare this, however, with Zahavi's (2019b, 254) statement that truly social acts require a "special sort of reciprocity," in which they are apprehended by each party to the interaction. He first notes that each could be attending to the other without being aware of the other's attention, and then discusses the possibility of mutual awareness, where each experiences (and is thus aware of) being attended to by the other. He goes on say that this is not enough, as indicated above, in that (in my terms) a sustained state such as this requires an understanding of its importance. But I wish to contest the very possibility, on Zahavi's terms, of such a state of mutual awareness and show that this brings to light certain metaphysical commitments on his part that stand in the way of a better understanding the role of attention in interpersonal interaction, and its possibilities in the development of self and community.

My argument proceeds in two parts: I show that (1) attention can be variously deployed in the face-to-face relation, which determines the sort of bonding that occurs between the participants, the most profound of which is under active attention, and (2) each cannot know how the attention of the other is directed unless they are united in an overarching presence at the center of attention, which is the core of our living presence in the world.

The Deployment of Attention

Expressive phenomena play a large role in Zahavi's work on empathy (e.g., 2015, 152–53), but the emphasis is on bodily gestures and expressions rather than speech. Only at the end of "Empathy, Embodiment and Interpersonal Understanding" (2010a, 303) does he mention that we can always ask our interlocutor what they mean. But obviously the role of voice and nuance of expression in speech is the essence of the face-to-face relation, and bodily expression is merely ancillary to this, in expressing what the whole person is about. Thus the ability to listen to one another is the key to determining the extent of any communal bonding that may occur.

But the problem is that while I am face-to-face with the other I can go from listening to what they have to say to another activity with little or no awareness of having done so, because the events occur passively, that is, under passive attention. For instance, I can wander off and imagine I am somewhere else, or worry about something I have to do tomorrow, all the while remaining in the face-to-face relation. The other person may notice that I am not as attentive as before, depending on how absorbed *they* are in the course of the conversation, and they may try to get my attention back, but the point is that direct experience of the other is not to be taken for granted even when we are facing one another bodily. That is the essence of a metaphysics of presence, where such presence is assumed to be sustained. Indeed, Schutz (1967, 156) discusses how one can shift between direct experience and beliefs about the other person and their motivation in the course of the interaction itself.

This is a very common experience, as has been discussed in previous examples. Face-to-face relations typically involve conversation, and it is well known that many times people do not listen well under such circumstances. I can be standing face-to-face with you and be judging you, or thinking about what I am going to say next, so the point is that merely being in face-to-face relation has nothing to do with my experiencing the other in a direct manner. It all depends on attention. We can *listen and go more deeply* into the living reality of the other, and bond thereby as we meet in the space that opens between us. This is related to the sense of togetherness that Zahavi (2015, 157) mentions, but it involves an ontological merger that is at odds with his insistence that the "mineness" of experience is not constitutively dependent upon social interaction (148). It may be the case that one is aware of the living presence of the other in a manner that is peripheral to the central focus of attention, and the other can have a vague feeling that the first is not present, but that would have significant implications for the quality of the relation, as does the explicit self-awareness that comes about by way of more active attention.

This is clear from the overall context surrounding the Schutz citation. In the beginning of the paragraph from which the citation is extracted, Schutz (1967, 156) says that in the face-to-face relation one can either take the objective point of view of the social scientist or just live through the experience of the other. So he recognizes that even when face-to-face one can go into cogitation about what is going on in the mind of the other, and not on their living presence.[1] This means that the question of direct perception versus simulation-theory and theory-theory, among others, is still quite live when considering the postures that individuals take toward one another in the face-to-face interaction.

Earlier Schutz (1967, 140–41) says that while one is living through the experience there is a background understanding which is taken for granted and thus escapes attention because there is no interest in those particulars at the moment. But that can change with a shift of attention, where, for instance, I ask my interlocutor if I have understood them correctly, or what they mean by a particular action. But when I do so, I abandon "the living intentionality of our confrontation. . . . My attention has shifted to those deeper layers that up to now had been unobserved and taken for granted. I no longer experience my fellow man in the sense of sharing his life with him; instead I 'think about him'" (141). The point is that attention can occupy the space between individuals in different ways. It can support thought or other bodily events, or it can extend to the other lived body and support our meeting in the moment.

In addition, even when my attention is directly on the other person, it can still vary in quality. The epitome of such quality comes about when I intentionally hold attention on the other simply for the sake of being present, not being driven by any emotions that may exert their pull, but rather seeing all of that background activity as it seeks to take me away, as I simply stay present to the person in their lived presentation. When both do this, a space can open where each shares in the living reality of the other, which is where a bodily, ontological bond can form, the possibility of which has significant implications for interpersonal relations and the political. Along these lines, Fuchs and De Jaegher define *mutual incorporation* as "a process in which the lived bodies of both participants extend and form a common intercorporality" (2009, 465). They argue that social solidarity does not require each to inter-pret the bodily expressions of others, but rather comes about by way of such an interaction that enables mutual understanding to emerge.

Schutz gestures toward the importance of the state of attention when he says, "The directly experienced social relationship of real life is the pure We relationship concretized and actualized to a greater or lesser degree and filled with content" (1967, 164). The ontological dimension is clear when Schutz talks about actualization, concretization, and contact with the lived reality of the interlocutors, which I argue depends on the state of attention. Zahavi also picks up on this when he says there are "different degrees of intimacy and intensity" in these relations (2010a, 298), but he does not see the possibility of mindful sustained attention for the sake of mutual presence.

Rather than trying to direct the other's attention to achieve my aims, which we can see in Schutz,[2] I simply seek to commune with others and understand them as worthy of respect solely on the basis of being another miraculous human being such as myself. Thus, the ultimate context matters here, how I understand the nature of humanity in relation to the whole, and, in particular, that of myself and the other with whom I engage. The political dimensions are clear.

Zahavi (2010a) does discuss some of these issues, but he does not consider the role of attention in Schutz. He notes that there are many forms of inter-personal understanding, but argues that the face-to-face relation is primordial, much in concert with the theme of the primacy of attention that I am arguing. He also says that Schutz's "thinking in terms of beliefs" is often projection after the fact (297), but he misses the fact that it can also take place in the face-to-face relation itself, thereby minimizing any contact and bonding that may occur. Now Zahavi (254) does note, citing Husserl, that we do not "just stand next" to each other, but motivate each other and establish a unity of willing as we speak and listen to one another. But this assumes a particular attentional posture that is unspecified, requiring the active attention that I insist is essential for such a bonding and willing to be sustained for any length of time.

Mutual Awareness of One Another's Attention

Zahavi considers the case where each is aware of being attended to by the other, but if one is, say, thinking about the other, how does the other know that? Indeed, how is it possible to perceive the attention of the other? Zahavi (2019b, 254) considers three cases: (1) we experience each other but are not aware of each other's attention; (2) I may be aware that someone else is attending to me, but the person does not know that I am so aware; and (3) we are aware that each is attended to by the other. As I discuss these cases, I ask what is attention, that its deployment is subject to being known by someone else? My claim is that each cannot know how the attention of the other is directed unless they are united in an overarching presence at the center of attention.

The Direct Experience of the Other

As mentioned above, Zahavi focuses on bodily expression in coming to understand the other in the course of face-to-face interaction, discussing how experiences occur in expressive phenomena, as a sort of primary perception. He cites Scheler (2008, 9–10): "It is *in* the blush that we perceive shame, *in* the laughter joy" (Zahavi 2015, 152). But this betrays a limitation of the analysis because he assumes a position similar to that of an outside observer looking to the body for meaningful signs. In so doing he puts little emphasis on our engagement with others by way of speech and the need for deep listening to come to a robust understanding of the other.

As noted above, Zahavi says that empathy is "a form of intentionality directed at foreign experiences" (2010a, 290). In my terms this means that the noesis is what manifests according to what we bring to the experience, and the noematic object shows itself on the basis of what is understood intersubjectively. So the object is the shame in the blush, and the noesis is presumably a capacity we bring to comprehend such foreign experiences. The key question is, however, what can that capacity be other than an understanding and ability to focus on the blush itself? It is true that I am constituted in a similar manner to the other, and I will typically have the ability to blush, but that would be a form of simulation that Zahavi seeks to go beyond. Otherwise what I bring is my particular understanding of who the person is and what their life circumstances are, which includes the existence on this earth that we all share.

I understand that I am facing another human being who has their own perspective, and I focus attention according to the demands of the situation as I understand it, which varies as it unfolds; that is the essence of the hermeneutical circle. In particular, this means that the historical situation must be taken into account in determining how the blush appears to me. And how do I know what their specific situation is, what is causing the shame they experience? Generally I know what they tell me and what I have noticed about them, plus whatever else I glean from my knowledge of their family, friends, and other particulars. Without this context the blush in itself tells me nothing. Zahavi is aware of the importance of context, but the point is that there will be a variety of nuances associated with the blush that determine how the person is made manifest in relation to me.

We know that if I am judging or imagining while the person is blushing, this can be considered to be a form of intentionality that determines how the person shows up. If I am judging or thinking while in front of the other, then when attention is passive it will be placed in the body in support of that particular activity. That would seem to affect how "direct" the experience is. Or if I am thinking about the circumstances that have brought about the shame, my interpretation will also affect how the blush manifests to me. And in general, as noted above, the way the blush manifests depends on everything I bring to the situation, and will vary as a result. But one way in which a type of direct experience can come about is by way of active attention, as I have been arguing. This is a sort of "bare attention," in that everything I bring is at the ready (like Heidegger's sprinter in chapter 2) but held in abeyance as a space is held open for the person to manifest as blushing, and then I do indeed connect with them on a deeper level. Only when my attention is intentionally directed to the presence of the other, as it shows itself by way of *their* attention, will there be the sort of sustained direct experience that Zahavi posits.

It is odd that Zahavi rejects this type of attention in his work on mindfulness, as discussed in chapter 5, arguing that nonjudgmental awareness is not possible given the role that judgment plays in everyday activity, which is consistent with the hermeneutical view that I advance. But he misses the fact that the effort of mindfulness can hold such judging in abeyance. It can be seen as it arises, but we stay with the manifestation of the person itself and the judging remains in the background. When both engage in this manner, the overarching presence that arises offers the possibility of harmonization of the understanding that both bring to the interaction, which has significant political implications.

How Do I Know the Other Is Attending to Me?

In the second case that Zahavi considers, one knows that the other is paying attention to them. But the problem is that attention is not visible to the naked eye, so it is not possible to know what someone else is doing with their attention without inferring it from their behavior. Do I judge from their bodily orientation that they are attending to me, or from their eyes? For, as mentioned above, Zahavi (2019b, 254) discusses the role of immediate communication, where both individuals "look each other in the eyes" and are mutually aware of one another, but just looking in the eyes does not mean that each is attending to the other. Indeed, we have seen the discussion of Block (2010) in chapter 6 that attention can be directed in a covert manner, in which one cannot tell from the external orientation how it is engaged. For instance, one's eyes can be pointing straight ahead but their attention directed to one side or another. Or one may appear to be looking at you, but they are actually listening to a conversation taking place somewhere else.

Now it may be argued that in either case one is aware of being attended, although perhaps peripherally. One is somewhat aware of you, as standing in front of them, but they are primarily engaged in listening to the other conversation. But this certainly matters in the case of communal bonding, which is the subject of discussion here. I may be able to sense that you are not fully attending to me, that your mind is somewhere else, which shows how much respect you show me, but this ability depends in turn on the extent to which *I* am present *to you*. And, moreover, if you are fully engaged in attending to me with an effort of your whole being, solely for the sake of being present to another human being who is in principle worthy of respect regardless of their background or orientation, that matters enormously for the possibility of bridging the political divides that are so troublesome in today's world.

Attention can be placed anywhere in the lived body-environment, but it is typically not under control or awareness. The key question is if I am absorbed or not, for when speaking I may not be aware of you at all, or only implicitly, and I cannot know if your mind is elsewhere even though you are staring me in the face. Both need to be present to each other for them to be aware of their mutual attention, as I now show.

How Do They Know They Are Both Attending to Each Other?

In order to know how the attention of the other is oriented, we must be aware of our own embodied attention. For attention is how we are present to anything at all, and if I am unaware of my own ontological movement, I cannot know how what I bring influences how I see the other. I cannot know how the attention of the other person is deployed if I am not fully present to myself in relation to them, in which case I cannot directly experience how they themselves are brought to the fore in relating to me. For that is the only way to directly engage with their attention, which is presumably what Zahavi assumes. If he assumes we can directly experience the other person, he must also mean that we directly experience the other's attention, rather than our beliefs or inferences about it. And if we each directly experience the attention of the other, then we are mutually aware of being so engaged.

This requires active attention and its associated opening and overarching presence, which can enable such mutual awareness and bonding to occur. Under passive attention, on the other hand, the bonding is limited because it is driven by background processes, whereas under active attention the overarching presence enables both to transcend their respective backgrounds and meet in the space that opens between them. We may see flashes of connection, glancing at each other momentarily, as in when Schutz discusses the "pure We-relationship" where the "partners are aware of each other and sympathetically participate in each other's lives *for however short a time*" (1967, 164, em),[3] but a deeper bonding requires more than a momentary connection.[4]

Thus we can experience the presence of one another bodily by literally *fusing* with each other's attention, thereby overcoming Zahavi's insistence on the impossibility of fusion of individual experiential perspectives and the constitutive independence of experiential selfhood and the intersubjective (e.g., Zahavi 2021c, 10; Brinck, Reddy, and Zahavi 2017, 138). We meet in between by way of our mutual presence, which is the only way to come to such a mutual awareness of each other's attention, and that meeting must be sustained for an ontological bond to begin to form.

When we hold open such a space for the other to be made manifest, and the other does the same, mutual understanding and being together are enhanced. When we mutually attend, we have deeper insight into the being of the other who expresses themselves, who speaks from their pain. Thus, when we see the blush of the other under these conditions, it takes place in a context where we are each present together as whole human beings, ontologically bonded in that event of mutual convergence, and we each bring all we have to bear in meeting one another. In that context the blush is full of significance for each individual, and together we share the pain that each suffers in their lives. That is what empathy is.

What is key is that being face-to-face does not guarantee that we focus on that lived reality. The state of attention determines the extent to which there is an ontological connection, a bonding between individuals that constitutes their mutual understanding and that can eventually show up on the stability and efficacy of any associated institutions. We share in producing and dwelling in the spaces that come about in this manner. Thus we develop a sense of belonging and togetherness that transcends the individual contents of experience, and which is preserved bodily and linguistically. We are made manifest together at the center of attention, but the effort must be sustained.

Attention is a primordial phenomenon, and how it is understood depends on the most basic assumptions regarding human nature and all that exists. We turn now to how Zahavi deals with the question and its associated metaphysics. While he assumes intentional structures and inner time consciousness as the ground for experience in his investigations, I argue that in light of his failure to accommodate the phenomenon of mutual awareness of attention, he would benefit from a relational ontology that incorporates the hermeneutical circle of attention, language, and the body of understanding.

METAPHYSICAL PRESUPPOSITIONS

We are addressing the question of self and community. Zahavi says it is about self-understanding, relating, and belonging, but he fails to adequately incorporate attention in his analysis. Under the hermeneutical circle, on the other hand, self-understanding is how we reach out to others by way of attention. The quality of attention determines the extent of belonging and relating that takes place, where we meet in the Heideggerian clearing (see chapter 9).

Zahavi's Metaphysics

I begin with Zahavi's (2018, 63) comment that pre-reflective self-awareness can be thought of as a *phenomenal* presence, in that a mental state would not be experientially manifest without it. I have been arguing, on the other hand, that attention is an *ontological* presence, in that it is how we come into presence in the world, as whole human beings engaged in worldly activity that transcends the dichotomy between mental and physical (see chapter 3). Likewise, Zahavi's focus is on consciousness and experience, while I look at the relations that are enabled by attention, and, following Heidegger, the relation between attention and being (see chapter 9).

Now, in focusing on the posited realm of consciousness, Zahavi must explain how the mind is able to access the physical, which he does by citing Husserl as putting forward a self-transcending subject that is "per se directed toward something different than itself" (Zahavi 2003, 21). But we have seen that the Husserlian pure ego is thematically directed to such objects by way of the ego-ray of attention, or the radiating "I" in Zahavi's terms, and that other background objects are similarly accessible by a shift of attention. Thus under these conditions Zahavi implicitly assumes that attention is able to transcend the mental-physical divide, and in the present context he discusses the intentionality of the experience of others as being direct in nature and not in need of any intervening inference or analogical process (e.g., Zahavi 2019b).[5] Attention is hardly a supplement in this context, in that it is how we relate to all things at the center of our being in the world.

Zahavi cannot explain mutual awareness of each other's attention without taking account of active attention, which his metaphysics cannot accommodate. He (2021b) lays out his most fundamental assumption as the bracketing of that which cannot be made manifest in one way or another, as we are made manifest ourselves in the course of worldly engagement. This is much in concert with Heidegger's understanding of being as fundamentally involving manifestation, or rather presencing (*Anwesen*), which reflects the essential role of temporality in the manifestation process. Thus Zahavi rules out positions that assert mind-independent realities, admitting only those that are accessible in one way or another. But on the other hand, he posits structure as what is ultimate when it comes to manifestation, such as intentional structures and inner time consciousness, reasoning that under the proper methodology, such as the epoché and various reductions, such structures will come to the fore. This is in concert with the Husserlian principle of principles, under which "each intuition affording [something] in an originary way is a legitimate source of knowledge" (Husserl 2014, §24), where attention is obviously implicated. But the question is if *attention itself* can be reduced to theoretical structures, as when Zahavi speculates about a possible structure of attention (2017b, 410). This seems unlikely given Husserl's (2001, 207–21) position on the matter, where objects are constituted by the ego at the foreground, where quasi-objects that lie in await of the ego's attention are brought to the fore and thereby come into full objecthood.

I have argued that attention is a holistic phenomenon that cannot be reduced to or derived from ontic entities or structures, which by definition are abstracted from the whole. This is the essence of Heidegger's critique of Husserl, where he argues that the theoretical structures that Husserl posits are not grounded in any larger whole and are thus mere abstractions. That is in concert with the early Heidegger's inversion of the usual metaphysical order, where he posits the primacy of the practical over that of the theoretical, and which continues in other forms in later work. In that spirit I proceed with a hermeneutical circle consisting of attention, language, and the body, which are essential dimensions of human existence, each holistic in their own right and interacting in an indissoluble whole, as discussed in chapter 2.

This has significant implications for the essential philosophical questions, such as the nature of being itself, the key ontological question. I have argued, for instance, that active attention can result in time slowing down and space opening up, which enables the more profound manifestation of all things, including ourselves. This is ruled out on Zahavi's lights, where all we can hope for is the resolution of some philosophical problems and the discovery of underlying structures. But the fact that attention can enable the articulation of the "components and structures" that are implicitly contained in pre-reflective experience (Zahavi 2005, 88) means that at a minimum it plays a large role in bringing such structures to light. I am also arguing that there are reciprocal relations between any such structures, which under the hermeneutical circle are restricted to those that appear in the language and its associated meanings and institutions, and the body of understanding itself. Moreover, the nature of being is much different under the associated relational ontology that I put forward, following Heidegger, where there is a concealed or depth dimension that can show itself more or less profoundly by way of attention. Under these assumptions we truly belong here, whereas the alternative is alienation from what is ultimately an impersonally structured cosmos.

No, we belong here, and we participate in the manifestation of all things more or less fully based on the state of attention, which means that we become more or less actualized ourselves. This is because under a relational ontology, what relates us has a primacy, and that is attention. There are no freestanding ontic entities or structures, only entities in relation to each other and the whole, in which we are included. In addition, we have a key role in that we can make ontological efforts, efforts of our whole being to be more present and hence manifest more fully, while at the same time bringing other entities and, most importantly, other individuals along with us as we lead them with our presence. That is the essential difference between the two metaphysical positions under consideration here.

Attention, Language, and Relation

Zahavi seeks to solve philosophical problems, the most pressing of which is the nature of the self, which has implications for the question of the relation between self and community. I argued in chapter 6 that the minimal self cannot stand on its own without the holistic presence of attention. But Zahavi undertakes a bottom-up approach to the question, beginning with the minimal self (otherwise referred to as pre-reflective self-awareness or inner time consciousness) and adding the empirics of attention and language from the child development literature to come to a more concrete and complete notion of self.[6] Positing such structures is hardly neutral; again, this is Heidegger's critique that Husserl does not ask the question of the being of the subject, which refers, in part at least, to how the subject and its structures relate to the whole (being).[7]

Zahavi begins with pure self-awareness (the minimal, experiencing self) and adds attention and language to enable social interaction, whereas under the hermeneutical approach we see experiential presence as already bound up with attention, language, and the body. Indeed, Zahavi (2019b, 251–52) engages with Heidegger on this issue. Heidegger (as cited by Zahavi) argues that any interpersonal interaction requires prior ontological structures that enable it, which he refers to as being-with and being among others. Zahavi also discusses a similar position put forward by Schmid (2014, 11), who argues that communication is "an irreducible joint action" that presupposes a preexisting "sense of us."

Zahavi (2019b, 257) argues we can conceive of the relational world concept of Heidegger as employing a notion of "implicit we-ness," whereas he says that any more substantive group identification requires an experiential relatedness that can come about by way of dyadic interaction. He says that for Heidegger group belongingness precedes any other-experience, as in face-to-face interaction, and that there is no gap to be bridged because a basic constituent of Dasein's being-in-the-world is its being-with, where one encounters the other within a context of shared concerns and situations (251–52). He concludes:

> The we that emerges in and through concrete embodied face-to-face interaction might be developmentally and ontologically primary, but it is admittedly only one—rather ephemeral—type of we that is bound to the here and now. Far more institutionalized, anonymous and linguistically mediated forms of we also exist. Further investigations are needed in order to lay bare the processes involved in the constitution of more stable we-identities. (2015, 158)

That is, Zahavi admits the possibility of an *ontological* primacy to the implicit we-ness that is associated with Heidegger's relational world concept, which I argue can become an *explicit* we-ness depending on the state of attention, which would enable the more stable collective identities and associated institutions that he calls for.[8] But Zahavi does not consider the role of attention and its associated circle in first person experience, which he says is pre-reflective and prelinguistic (2015, 147), and then adds it in to enable social interaction. That is, he is required to introduce it to enable relation and interaction between individuals who would be otherwise cut off from one another. Thus, the choice being considered presently is between a bottom-up, formal analysis of experience together with an analysis of social development supplemented by attention, or a holistic hermeneutical circle of attention, language, and bodily understanding that is present from birth.

Attention and Structure

We have seen that Zahavi cannot accommodate mutual awareness of the living presence of attention. And there can be no minimal self without attention, for the former is abstracted from the whole human being and its holistic presence by way of the latter. That presence extends to others by way of attention and language to form the intersubjective, which enables self and community formation in turn. Thus, rather than being a supplement, attention and language are essential for world constitution, where the development of a language by way of shared attention enables the articulation of the associated bodily understanding (see figure 7.1).[9] And rather than considering experience and its structures, Heidegger thinks the relation between being

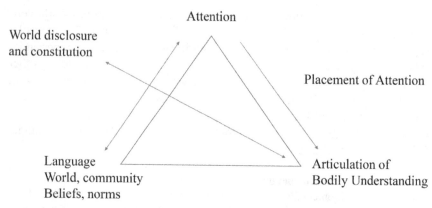

Figure 7.1. World Disclosure and Constitution

and attention, where being refers, in part at least, to the abyssal ground for the manifestation and relation of all that is.

We saw in the last chapter that under the hermeneutical circle such posited structures are subject to a profound historicity. In the circle we have the body and language as standing under (under-standing) the worldly presence of attention, and any relative invariance depends on those formations, which are physiological and intersubjective in nature. As noted above, this does bear on the question of the political, for the stability and responsiveness of these formations depends on the state of attention. Any positing of invariant structures depends on that state, for otherwise it is a case of the metaphysics of presence by Heidegger's lights, which is the traditional assumption of constant presence which he critiques (see chapter 9).

Take, for example, the state of democracy in the United States as this book is being written. The Trump administration took advantage of virtually all the weaknesses of the system, long seen as the exemplar for democracies around the world, in pursuit of the personal interests of the president. This included the fragility of the rule of law, election systems, and many norms of the presidency, where trust in the performance of government functions was put into question. Since it is not possible for all such rules to be codified in detail, and indeed because they must be interpreted in order to be applied in varying situations, Trump upended many of these conventional arrangements in his quest to remain in power. So here we see that the practical structures that stand to enable the pursuit of the common good are susceptible to being brought to light in public spaces, and when faith in those institutions is eroded, it can take years to restore them to their former efficacy. Any such conventions require reaffirmation when they are no longer in the background of public attention. This is an important instance of the primacy of attention: Any such structure is contingent upon the placement, movement, and state of attention, where the latter must be sustained for the stability and responsiveness of the institutions.

Since the placement of attention within the lived body-environment is how it acts within the hermeneutical circle, we must look there for the ground for any posited structures. But we find that relations there are much more organic and fluid than noetic and noematic structures, where the term "noetic" betrays an epistemological bias in what is an ontological matter. The body has the full range of processes that stand under our being in the world and interact in a highly intricate manner (Gendlin 2017a) that can hardly be called structural, where the latter has connotations of the physical sciences which are not applicable to the human being (e.g., Fuchs 2021). Under the hermeneutical approach it is rather the case that we seek self-understanding in relation to others and world rather than objective knowledge.

The same applies to any analysis of structures of the self. On the hermeneutical circle view the understanding body (including the understanding of language) is brought to bear in the course of engagement as befits the particular circumstances in which it is made manifest. Consider James again, where we find ourselves initially in a fully dispersed state, until "an energy is given, something—we know not what—enables us to gather ourselves together, we wink our eyes, we shake our heads, the background-ideas become effective, and the wheels of life go round again" ([1890] 1983, 382). James talks about energy, which resonates with the present discussion of "embodied resources," where a complex of bodily sensibilities is brought to bear which is constantly shifting with new experience and situations. Now, there will certainly be many habitual modes of engagement that operate in the background, which enable us to think the human being in terms of structural proclivities, but these are subject to disruption and transformation when they are brought to the foreground, as in the Chuck Knoblauch example discussed in chapter 2. Thus, even in this case of sedimented habitualities, such structures are also subject to modification when they are brought to attention (e.g., Romdenh-Romluc 2013).

Sealing the Circle

The notion that attention does not affect the composition of intentional structures that are brought to bear in various circumstances is itself a metaphysical position that does not stand up to the primacy of attention for which I argue. The key is how and where attention is placed. For instance, when one is judging, it supports *that* activity in the body, whereas when it extends to others it can open a space in which we may commune. Relations are not like physical structures, for they vary depending on the state of attention.

This has considerable implications for the stability and responsiveness of political institutions to the demands of living together in a world. The placement of attention creates the link with the lived body-environment in which we dwell, thereby supporting the development of language and its associated worlds, in particular the political institutions where we seek to work for the common good. Similar to the question of rightness considered in chapter 2, the state of the attention that is thereby placed determines how well integrated these institutions are with the lived realities of its citizens (see figure 7.2). When the movement of attention is passive, as is ordinarily the case, there is a tendency for them to be cut off from those realities and therefore to be less responsive to what people experience in the course of their lives. In the same manner, language itself can be so cut off, producing abstract discourse that is similarly unresponsive to life realities, which feeds back to the latter, resulting in disintegration and conflict in those realities themselves. But when attention is active, the tendency will be for integration, and in that case we *speak from* our lived bodies and do not speak about them from a distance. This is the key distinction that Heidegger makes between *speaking from* and *speaking about* in *Contributions to Philosophy* (GA 65: 3/5), to be considered in chapter 9.

On the Individuation of the Minimal Self

Zahavi does not have the resources to explain how each can know that the other is attending to them, but he is undoubtedly relying on an intuition here. For how is it that I can sometimes sense that your attention is not fully engaged with me, even though it is not visible to the naked eye? Does this point to something that bonds us prior to the face-to-face engagement, to our

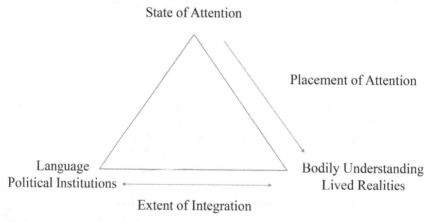

Figure 7.2. Sealing the Circle

mutual belonging together in a world? We must be brought together ontologically rather than each having an awareness of each other's attention, which maintains the separation that Zahavi posits between individuals and is problematic for the possibility of deep bonding that I put forward.

On the view here, attention is our presence in the world, what Zahavi refers to as functioning subjectivity, which cannot be seen upon reflection except by way of Heidegger's approach to attention, as discussed in chapter 5. It is a holistic phenomenon that enables us to relate in worlds that are founded by language. That is, as seen in the hermeneutical circle, attention and language are dimensions that exceed us as individuals, and we are thus related by them whether we know it or not. We can sense the attention of the other because it is the primordial bond that exists between us, offering the potential of more profound bonding by way of the effort of active attention, or mindfulness.

Attention is the core of our being in the world, where we live and meet as whole human beings to the extent to which we are present. This can be seen in the Bitbol and Petitmengin (2011) citation discussed in chapter 5, where the narrator becomes aware of Paul's diffusely sensed presence by being more present herself. That presence is brought to bear by way of attention. When we meet in this manner, our presence can merge in the space that opens, and we are made manifest together and are thus more aware of self and other. Zahavi (2017b, 412) insists on the *how* of experiencing rather than the *what*, or its content (what it's like), and in the present case, the how of experiencing is that we are made manifest together. That is an ontological togetherness rather than the epistemological "experiencing" that is the focus of the Husserlian approach Zahavi puts forward. As mentioned above, in Zahavi pre-reflective self-awareness is a phenomenal presence, which betrays its epistemological bias, whereas under the hermeneutical/Heideggerian approach it is ontological, based on what we bring to bear as whole human beings to our encounters.

Zahavi wants to argue that our presence in the course of social interaction is independent of the results of such engagement, such as the formation of self and communal understanding, but he misses the fact that language itself, which is a communal formation embodying a mutual understanding that bonds its speakers, is an essential dimension of the hermeneutical circle that is the basis for our coming into presence by way of attention. Thus when attention is understood as human presence, we see the communal and bodily individuality both playing essential roles in its movement, which in turn is the basis for the further formation of language and the body politic. So while it is true that the presence or lack thereof of social interaction may not be an ongoing determinant of my first-person experience, the fact that a shared language transcends us all indicates the intersubjective nature of our worldly presence.

Moreover, Zahavi does not consider the difference between passive and active attention, where the latter enables more explicit awareness of one's presence and action in the lived body-environment, whereas passive attention is absorbed in its objects and indeed has little or no explicit awareness of its relation to the background. This is important in contesting the claim that the experience of the minimal self is completely individuated, for (as in chapter 6) active attention enables spaces to open that enable us to be made manifest together as a *we*, where we are ontologically bonded in the course of experiencing, while individuality is preserved in individual bodies. This means that the experience we share under these conditions is *our* experience, not just mine as an individual. Moreover, attention and language are how we relate to all entities, which means that our coming into presence and thus experiencing always has an intersubjective dimension even when language is protolinguistic, as in early childhood. And while for Zahavi community is grounded in pre-reflective experience, for hermeneutics *it requires an ongoing grounding* by way of active attention.

Zahavi relies on the intuition that what I experience bodily occurs from my own individual perspective, with my own history and bodily idiosyncrasies which others do not share, but he ignores the fact that we share a world of experience together, to the extent that the shared language determines what we focus on and how we understand the situations in which we interact.

Attention as Abyssal Ground I

I am arguing that attention is an abyssal ground, in that there are no ontic structures that serve as its basis. To consider this question, let us look at Zahavi's position on attention in more detail. We have seen that for him it is the basis for the direct perception of the other, where each can monitor the attention of the other. In *Subjectivity and Selfhood*, he says it is a concept that comes from perceptual experience which does not change intentional structures, but only highlights objects that await in the background (Zahavi 2005). He later lays out this position in more detail, where, following Husserl, he distinguishes between self-awareness that is "for me" and the more explicit "I-consciousness" that comes about by way of attention (Zahavi 2017b, 409). But he fails to recognize that, given his emphasis on the correlation between subject and object, a more explicit self-awareness together with the highlighting of objects means that those objects will be made manifest as more real, or actualized. This is consistent with Husserl (2001), who says that objects in the periphery are not objects in the full sense of thematic objects for the ego, and thus attention not only provides a more explicit self-awareness but also enables the more complete manifestation of entities.[10] In the case of face-to-face relations, each of us shows up as more actualized depending on the state of attention. This is more clearly the case when we think in terms of the relational ontology which is called for under his metaphysical assumptions.

I showed in the previous chapter that the minimal self is at best a fully passive "experiencer" of undifferentiated streams of consciousness. On the other hand, Zahavi cites Husserl's notion of ego-rays of attention, or as he refers to it, a "radiating I," saying that "[t]he I lives in such cogito-acts, they are carried out by the I, and Husserl consequently describes attention as an I-ray (*Ichstrahl*)" (2017b, 409), which means that there is a sense of agency associated with it. This is a ray that extends into relation with others and the world, unlike the notion of attention as merely "structuring experience" that Zahavi (2005, chap. 4) posited previously. Moreover, he cites Henrich (1971, 20) as associating this sort of consciousness with an "active principle of organization" and speculates that attention may also have a "special kind of ownership" (Zahavi 2017b, 409–10). This would be a more profound sense of self, as gathered rather than diffused over all possible objects of experience.

The implication is that Zahavi is moving toward associating attention with self-organization, agency, mineness (or a sense of self), and a more explicit self-awareness, which is quite consistent with the position that is being put forward in this book. But he does not think in terms of attention as self-manifestation, where peripheral objects are peripheral to the center of attention and thus to the self that is thereby made manifest, which is consistent with the fact that the memory of such objects is weaker depending on how peripheral they are. When attention is thought as self-manifestation, we see that our very presence is produced in the act, and we can see how that presence can extend into the world and in relation with our fellows, which is essential for the analysis of empathy. It should also be noted that Husserl's analysis of inner time consciousness is not the only way to produce an implicit self-awareness, for the hermeneutical circle also produces such awareness without positing intentionality and consciousness by merely pointing to the lived body and its relations to all entities within the body-environment, which replicates the "aboutness" that characterizes intentionality and self-awareness by way of the body's awareness of itself.

While Zahavi can be understood as putting forward a bottom-up metaphysics, the hermeneutical circle is a holistic approach in which individuals can be more or less present to one another, and where the possibility of ontological bonding is much more prominent. Rather than being conceived in structural terms, in this sort of metaphysics we can situate attention as an abyssal ground, where there is no structure as its basis beyond its place in the hermeneutical circle. This allows for access to a depth dimension where we can bond together when the practice of mindfulness is sustained. We noted above that Zahavi (2015, 158) sees face-to-face interaction as "ephemeral" and in need of institutional grounding, but I argue that any such structures ultimately depend on the hermeneutical circle and the state of attention. Any such institutions are enabled by language in the hermeneutical circle, and thus ultimately depend on how attention is placed in the body-environment, as I have argued above. It is true that the movement of attention can indeed be ephemeral, which is ironic given its role in human spatiotemporality, but that is exactly what the practice of mindfulness is about, providing a discipline that enables the stability and responsiveness of political institutions that is desperately needed in contemporary public life.

I have shown that the efficacy of interpersonal interaction in building community depends on the state of attention of its participants and the associated possibility of ontological bonding. This in turn can enable the integration of institutions and discourse with the lived realities of its citizens and the formation of a powerful and harmonious body politic. In the next chapter, I turn to the question of political engagement and consider the role of attention there.

Chapter 8

The Power of Attention

The dysfunction in our politics is most alarming, given the planetary crisis that is upon us. We need to speak with one voice to the powerful to let them know this is not acceptable. One response presently under consideration is to encourage more public engagement in political affairs, and it is essential to understand the nature of attention to be more effective in this regard. For this purpose, I review the work of Ben Berger, who addresses the question in *Attention Deficit Democracy: The Paradox of Civic Engagement* (2011).[1] He takes an approach that in many respects looks like a version of the hermeneutical circle I have put forward in this book. Berger pays particular attention to the positions of Hannah Arendt and Alexis de Tocqueville, and sees much of value in the latter but rejects Arendt's argument for the intrinsic value of political engagement as idealistic and inconsistent. In doing so he does not consider the question of attention in Arendt, and she herself does not treat it systematically, but it is present in the phenomenological thought she brings to bear in an implicit form.[2] And the public spaces that are so important in her work are themselves grounded in mutual attention, which, as I show, argues for the intrinsic value of such engagement assuming the presence of active attention.

Berger ultimately finds that more responsive institutions are required to channel limited attentional resources in desired directions, and that political engagement requires a robust foundation in local communities that are bonded socially and morally. I take this further below, suggesting that the intentional gathering of attention, which indeed requires institutional support, can enable more creative and coordinated responses to the problems that we face today. And although the notion of limited attention certainly has validity, it misses the qualitative dimension that is associated with properly executed efforts of mindfulness.

I show that making attention explicit can advance Arendt's position and meet some of the criticisms that Berger lodges. In fact, I argue that mindfulness is intrinsically valuable in *any* mode of engagement, public or private,

173

and that mindful political engagement is particularly important. I conclude with a discussion of Arendt's notion of council democracy, which together with an institutionalized form of mindfulness can address some of the issues associated with political engagement. For we saw in chapter 7 that face-to-face interaction is not enough, and that active attention is required to form the ontological bonds that can produce stable and effective political realities in the long term.

ATTENTION DEFICIT DEMOCRACY

Berger considers the question of civic engagement, which he parses into three dimensions: social, moral, and political. This is important because he argues that social and moral engagement is required for effective political action, which resonates with the above emphasis on the role of interpersonal interaction in building community. The model of engagement that he puts forward draws largely on Tocqueville ([1835] 1969), where tastes and interests determine the movement of attention, which determines in turn the disposition of human energies.[3] That is, Berger argues for an intimate relation between attention and engagement, which is much in concert with the claim here that attention is human presence, the condition for any engagement whatsoever where one is brought bodily to bear in the present moment.

We can see the resemblance between this model and the hermeneutical circle, where tastes and energies correspond roughly to understanding and action. And indeed, given the role of tastes in engagement and the fact that they are subject to education, the efficacy of which depends in turn on the attentional deployment of the students, we can see that a circle is indeed operative here. In addition, the notion of energies corresponds roughly to my notion of resources and sensibilities, and while it is a good fit for large-scale analyses of political activity, the question of its quality is also important, as we shall see below.

Berger's model of attention is quite interesting. On the one hand it has elements of a rational choice model with tastes and interests driving attention, and of course when the choice is about attention itself, that is a new approach, although such a choice is rarely conscious. Human energy has an emotional and bodily connotation, where the usual assumption is that emotion drives attention, so there is more circularity. Here, of course, we are faced with the perennial question of the relation between the rational and the irrational, but within a hermeneutical context the approach is to consider the whole human being, where emotion provides another perspective on what matters to us most. I have argued that when attention is passive the background takes over, with emotion playing a key role, while under active attention there is the possibility of growth of the whole human being, including the transmutation of emotion to a higher state, one that would be less inclined to be taken by the emotional appeals of demagogues. We consider this in what follows.

Berger argues for more responsive institutions, but attention as human presence holds as the condition for the possibility of engagement for all actors, including those who manage our institutions, for they are subject to the same sources for self-understanding that all draw upon, which is how their attention is deployed in articulating and putting institutional values into action. Thus, institutions are only as good as the people who implement them, which depends on their attention and understanding, depending in turn on the cultural understanding that predominates. That is why calling for more responsive institutions to channel attention and energy more effectively is somewhat problematic.

Suppose, for instance, that an individualistic understanding predominates, which is much the case in the United States today (and my focus is on US politics in this work). If that is reinforced in social interaction, there is little reason to believe that robust communities will develop beyond those who agree that the world is dog-eat-dog and may the best man win. Since that understanding will be at least an influence on the actions of our leaders, this is a significant impediment to institutions that work for the good of all.

Now, the paradox of civic engagement in the subtitle of Berger's text refers to the problem that people are free to attend to what they wish when they live in democracies, but the democracies need their attention in order to be sustained. The result is that people end up attending to private pleasures or material pursuits and not political affairs, echoing Arendt on the expansion of the private realm at the expense of the political. Berger looks to Tocqueville's ([1835] 1969) study of civil associations in *Democracy in America* for guidance on this matter. Political associations by themselves can further balkanization when they focus on specific doctrines (Berger 2011, 111), and when they are insular and partisan, they do not produce moral virtues (112). Tocqueville argues that associations with no political object can build robust communities and eventually stimulate interest in political action. They can serve to stabilize society and balance the potential partisanship of political associations. Most importantly, political associations that are grounded socially in this manner can serve as *sites of resistance* to individuals or groups who seek power for their own benefit and not the common good. Such associations can unite the energies of the public, thereby producing clear goals and the instrumental benefits that can result (Berger 2011, 111). Both types of associations can serve to keep attention and energy focused on the needs of a self-governing nation, facilitating a self-interest that recognizes the importance of community rather than individualism and its potential for isolation (114). Berger advocates for small groups gathered in hierarchies, following Tocqueville, where networks of local groups move up the ladder to higher levels of political participation.

Berger highlights the problem of wandering attention and the associated inability to focus where it is needed in support of democratic institutions. This, of course, is the aim of mindfulness, to stabilize and deepen our presence, thereby bringing to bear a more holistic understanding of the demands of a situation. He emphasizes the importance of people entering into political engagement of their own free will, in contrast to some versions of civic republicanism where citizens are coerced to participate, as in the civic religion of Jean-Jacques Rousseau (Berger 2011, 127).

Berger also says that Arendt's argument for the intrinsic value of political engagement does not stand on its own. It requires complementary notions that point to the potential for autocracy in the absence of a public presence. He therefore frames the discussion in terms of two aspects of her thought: the visionary and the cautionary. I consider these dimensions from the perspective of the distinction I have been drawing between active and passive attention, and argue that the visionary view assumes the presence of active attention as enabling the clarity, unification, and resilience which are associated with it, while the cautionary view presupposes the absence of such a foundation and the associated tendency for power to accumulate with individuals or groups who take advantage of it for their own ends. The implication is that much of the value of political engagement conceived in this manner comes from the discipline of attention for its own sake. Indeed, over the course of the book I have been arguing for the features of active attention that make it intrinsically valuable. I now discuss this in more detail.

THE INTRINSIC VALUE OF MINDFULNESS

Attention is how we are made manifest as individuals and communities. We can be more or less present depending on its state, and more or less harmonized and unified in working together to articulate and actualize the common good.[4] This is consistent with a relational ontology where there are no given, fixed entities, which are rather made manifest more or less profoundly as constitutive of human realities. These are not extrinsic relations between freestanding, willing subjects, but rather intrinsic relations between individuals who are made manifest according to how the situation is understood. The quality of that understanding depends on the quality of the attention that produces our presence in the world, and, as I have been arguing, all we can do to enhance that web of relations is to stay with our ontological movement, or, alternatively, place attention intentionally in the lived body-environment.

For in this manner we act on that which enables the relations and associated entities to be made manifest in the first place.

I discuss two existential potentialities that are associated with mindfulness, which attest to its intrinsic value: (1) freedom and autonomy, and (2) self-awareness, integration, and transformation. Thus, we have free and autonomous individuals acting in the public realm, who with enhanced awareness of their presence in the lived body-environment can come to a more profound self-understanding, which can translate into more appropriate ways of being together in the world.

These features are highly idealized, especially in light of the present state of political affairs, and they are difficult to implement given the effort involved in sustaining active attention and engaging a significant proportion of the population in such an enterprise. The intent, however, is to provide the motivation to develop institutional structures for the training and ongoing support of the group practice of mindfulness in conjunction with enhanced political engagement, as proposed in the section entitled "Mindful Council Democracy" below.

Freedom and Autonomy

Attention is how we are made manifest, as our factical being is brought to bear in relation to others and the world. When it is active, it enables an overarching presence that prevents background resources from taking over its movement, rather holding them in a readiness (as in the sprinter example in chapter 2) to respond to what the situation calls for. In the course of engagement, we typically see various impulses arise that would take us away from that sort of stance. They are associated with a particular emotional valence that immerses us in the activity and distracts from the living presence in which attention is placed and from seeing the bodily manifestation of the impulses. The background comes from many sources, including cultural influences over which one has no control. Thus, we lose the ability to see the action of the background resources that support attention, ceding our very manifestation to their action, which prevents the more holistic response to the demands of the situation that a sustained attention can bring. The latter enables us to gather ourselves and thus be free from immersion in the action of those resources, particularly the emotional, and open to the presence of others for bonding.

Active attention is an autonomous act because only I am responsible for the effort. For instance, as we saw in the discussion of Zahavi in chapter 7, face-to-face interaction enables a more actualized self-manifestation in relation to others, although it can also make it difficult to ground one's movement in attention, depending on the demands of the situation. It enables self-insight and also more presence in the face of the other, for if the other is more present themselves, that can be sensed as we feel similarly inclined to meet the challenge of their penetrating gaze. But that can only last for so long, and we eventually find a way back into our own world of thoughts and feelings when we think the other is not looking or if we believe we can appear to be attentive while otherwise engaged. On the other hand, when in a therapeutic relation where grounded attention is specifically called for by the therapist, as in Focusing, that can enable a more sustained presence, but ultimately we alone are responsible for the effort. This is the autonomy that is associated with mindful, active attentiveness.

It may be argued that we are free to be immersed if we so choose, but the question is whether this is a conscious choice, for we typically fall into such states with little or no awareness. But the point is that it is possible in principle to engage in any activity while being mindfully present, so nothing is lost when one engages in such an activity in this manner except perhaps the dispersion of one's being that is ordinarily the case. In that event, we are not free of the action of the background and, indirectly, the effects of others who seek our attention for their own ends by appealing to the basest aspects of our being.

We are not free when we are taken by background impulses and are thereby immersed, for this means we see only the objects and not the movement of attention that enables their manifestation. In this way we are similar to cave dwellers who see only the images cast upon a wall, not the light that enables them to appear. This points to the relations between light metaphors and attention that abound in the literature, including Arendt and Heidegger. There is thus an illusion of control under passive attention, as we see only the objects and not the process that generates them, where the former includes the very thoughts that lead us to believe we are in control of our actions. That is, thought is itself produced by the movement of attention as it goes about its action within the hermeneutical circle, and we are rarely aware of, or in control of, that movement. The illusion arises because we identify with "the thinker," where we understand ourselves in this manner with the support of socially constructed narratives that say who we are. It is true that an action corresponds to the thought, but that is because the thought itself is understood, which shows itself in the movement of attention and the corresponding manifestation/performance.

For instance, consider again the cocktail party example from chapter 6, where we see not an instance of self-control but rather a case of competition between background processes, where the forces that are operative are not at all transparent. All we can do in the face of this is exercise presence by way of placement in the lived body-environment and be more present to the action of the embodied resources that move us. We are only "in control" if we stay with the movement of attention during the entire process, including thought and the ensuing action, as in Descartes's requirements for indubitability in *Meditations*.[5]

Thus, I can be grounded at the very site of the manifestation of such impulses by way of active attention, in which case I can withstand their effects and in so doing gain insight into their nature, which is the path to transcendence and transmutation of the whole human being, including the emotions that are so important in the realms of meaning at stake in political interaction. This is one aspect of the claim for the primacy of attention that has been put forward herein.

Self-Awareness, Integration, and Transformation

We have considered a privative sort of freedom, a freedom from the influence of background resources whose action proceeds unawares. On the positive side, when we stay with the movement of attention we are free to place it in any manner, or better yet, to let it move as it wishes based on the body's intelligence, but always under our watchful eye. In this manner a self-integration takes place, in that while we are ordinarily absorbed in activity at the center of attention, we do not see the background resources that act unbeknownst to us, but under active attention a space opens in which we can see how those resources affect us bodily. And they must do so to be able to influence the movement of attention, for we are made manifest in the lived body-environment and must be affected at that very site if they are to influence our ontological movement. Thus a self-awareness occurs in which the background influences that typically act on us unawares are now brought to light as they show up at the center of attention, and we can withstand that influence or go with it, but always knowingly, and an integration of attention and background occurs instead of the bifurcation that is typically associated with reflective activity, as discussed in chapter 5. So when Zahavi (2005) sees Heideggerian attention as another form of reflection, he misses the fact that we can be more or less present by way of attention, and that the associated effort brings more of the self to bear in an integrated fashion, rather than working behind the scenes. And indeed, Zahavi admits that this approach to attention enables Heidegger to overcome the bifurcation that is typically associated with reflection.

We thus become aware of our factical being in action, which enables transcendence and transformed modes of engagement, which enable, in turn, more profound relations with our fellows, and more intelligence to be brought to bear in fashioning creative ways of living together in the world. For in bringing to light the action of background resources at the center of attention, their influence is transcended. When attention is sustained on that action and articulated by way of language, as in therapeutic and other inter-personal interaction, there is the possibility of transformation of the associ-ated resources in light of the general principle that attention's deliverances form the background resources that are constitutive of the self that is made manifest at the center.

Thus, rather than seeking invariant structures, the approach is to enhance self-understanding in concert with others, which can lead to more profound bonding and the ability to articulate and act on visions of the common good. Each serves as a mirror for the other: understanding ourselves and bringing each to a more profound presence. Sustained active attention in public spaces thus offers the possibility of bringing forth something new (see Arendt on natality, below) in freshly responsive action to worldly circumstances in a manner that is free and autonomous. This is our responsibility, to bond together by way of attention, for otherwise we cede the power of our attention to others who do not necessarily have our best interests at heart.

I turn now to the question of political engagement and show that it is intrinsically valuable when achieved by way of mindfulness. My claim is that participation in the public articulation and implementation of the common good when accompanied by mindfulness offers the possibility of individual and communal growth and a path to making it a better world. We need the sustained presence of others to help in this regard, the sense of which reminds us that our task is to be more attentive simply for the sake of being more present, which is intrinsically valuable. This is essential to make progress in political matters, bringing all of our creative potential to bear in dealing with what have been intractable problems for much of human history. For we can be collected or scattered, harmonized or discordant, and so on, and the extent to which we are gathered and ontologically bonded depends on the state of attention, which is how we grow as members of communities and hold and deploy power—enabling us to speak truth to power when it is called for.

To make the case I consider fundamental categories in Arendt's thought and show that they ultimately derive their power from active attention. I also show that passive attention is apparent in some of the cautionary concepts that she employs to demonstrate the risks associated with failure to engage the public sphere, for it is then subject to manipulation by actors with a defi-cient understanding of the common good.

THE INTRINSIC VALUE OF MINDFUL POLITICAL ENGAGEMENT

Although attention is not thematic in Arendt's work, it is very much present in the phenomenological orientation of Heidegger and Karl Jaspers, who are significant influences. We see it in terms such as relevance, concern, interest, and, most importantly, presence, appearance, disclosure, and manifestation. Related to these are the light metaphors that abound in her work, such as visibility, shining glory, and public light, in contrast to the darkness and blindness that come about in the absence of a vital public space, which is the site of mutual manifestation, bonding, freedom, and action. And in fact the relation between public space and attention has been well noted, for instance when Taylor sees it as a "common focus through speech" (1985, 260, n. 11) and relates it to Heidegger's clearing/lighting (1995, 116–17).[6]

I discuss below how the notion of public space appears in Arendt's work, and its relation to power.[7] For her, power keeps the public space in existence (1958, 200), while the public space is how power comes about in the first place.[8] Thus we have a reciprocal relation between these essential political dimensions, both of which are grounded in attention, as I have been arguing. This means that the extent to which the intrinsic value posited by Arendt is achieved depends upon its state.

Public Space

The presence of phenomenological thought in Arendt's work and the associated manifestation by way of attention is clear in her focus on appearances in public spaces and the relation she sees to the real. The notions of disclosure and appearance are most prominent, in particular in sections 24 and 28 of *The Human Condition* (1958), entitled "The Disclosure of the Agent in Speech and Action" and "Power and the Space of Appearance," respectively. Section 24 begins with an epigraph from Dante, which says that every action primarily intends the disclosure of one's own image, and that "everything that is desires its own being, and since in action the being of the doer is somehow intensified, delight necessarily follows. . . . Thus, nothing acts unless [by acting] it makes patent its latent self" (1958, 175). We see that what is implicit is made explicit in the action itself, and that the actor's very being is intensified in so doing. This corresponds to self-manifestation by way of attention as discussed in chapter 4.

In order to appear in the public space, something must be relevant, must be appeal to our interest; in a word, it must be worthy of public attention. Only then does the public gaze create a stage on which one can be made manifest in a more actualized manner. I have argued that these spaces, which are essential to the exploration of who we are and how we should live together, are constituted by way of joint attention, or attending to matters of shared concern. Indeed, Arendt is quite clear when she says that "everything that appears in public can be seen and heard by everybody and has the widest possible publicity" and "the presence of others who see what we see and hear what we hear assures us of the reality of the world and ourselves" (1958, 50).

When discussing the relation between private and public realms, Arendt says, "There are a great many things which cannot withstand the implacable, bright light of the constant presence of others on the public scene; there, only what is considered to be *relevant, worthy* of being seen or heard, can be tolerated, so that the irrelevant becomes automatically a private matter" (1958, 51, em). The constant presence referred to here indicates the implicit assumption of active attention, as I have shown in chapter 7. We also see the joint attention which is constitutive of the public space when she says, "[T]he reality of the public realm relies on the simultaneous presence of innumerable perspectives and aspects in which the common world presents itself" and "differences of position and the resulting variety of perspectives notwithstanding, everybody is always concerned with the same object" (57–58).

When we are more present, we are actualized, as all that we can bring to bear is activated and in readiness depending on the quality of attention. There are thus ontological implications to the effort of active attention, as we participate more fully in the web of relations in which all are made manifest. This is not a psychological notion of actualization, for being actualized here means to engage, to show up more profoundly and enable others to be so manifest as we support one another in this manner.

In Arendt's terms, the reality of the public realm comes about by way of the presence of others, which produces the space for appearance in which our acts become a reality for us and the others. The assumption is that the others are indeed present, attending to the activity of the agent, rather than merely being physically there. Arendt makes this clear when she discusses how only matters relevant to all actors are considered in public spaces, which are otherwise relegated to private realms. Associated with this are concepts such as the real and actualization together with notions such as awakening and living in one world,[9] which are contrasted with the masses living in a dream world, or in an unreality where facts are not grounded in any common vision of the world.[10] My claim is that all else equal, the extent of such actualization depends on the state of attention.

Arendt also says that power requires an organization that "assures the mortal actor that his passing existence and fleeting greatness will never lack the reality that comes from being seen, being heard, and, generally, appearing before an audience of fellow men" (1958, 198). This claim for the reality of the public realm and its associated disclosure and appearance is crucial for the argument for the intrinsic value of political engagement. She does not consider, however, the associated quality of attention, which is crucial for the sort of power that is generated in these realities, as I discuss below.

The presence of attention can also be seen in Arendt's notions of natality and action, where natality means that something new is born in action. As indicated above, natality corresponds to the possibility of fresh and responsive deliverances at the center of attention when we are fully present and able to meet the moment. Better ways of being together can be put in place when all are present at the birth of such action in the public space. We also see the distinction between passive and active attention when Arendt says that action interrupts "what otherwise would have proceeded automatically and therefore predictably" (1972, 133).

Power and Attention

A power is generated by way of the gathering of attention and its associated ontological bonding. It comes about when each bonds with the other in an overarching presence, where the tendency is otherwise to be dispersed and isolated from one another. Such a power can enable resistance, making it more difficult to impose restrictions that do not have the explicit consent of the people.

Arendt says that power keeps people together (1958, 201), that a union forms by way of a gathering. We then share a world in common that is man-made, with things in between gathering us together (52) as the object of a common focus. She has the related notion of common sense and world (208), which I associate with ontological bonding and the associated hermeneutical understanding that holds us together, to the extent that the bonding is sustained. On the other hand, when it is not, civilizations can fall: "What first undermines and then kills political communities is loss of power and final impotence; and power cannot be stored up and kept in reserve for emergencies, like the instruments of violence, but exists only in its actualization" (199). Attention also cannot be stored, although its deliverances do shape the background resources that support future efforts for a time, at least, beyond which a new impetus is required.

In later work, Arendt associates power with the ability to act in concert (1972, 143), depending on the plurality that is associated with the public sphere, so we see the reciprocal relation where power keeps the public space in existence, which is in turn necessary for its formation. And we see that for Arendt, power is an end in itself, as the condition for thinking and acting, and that "government is essentially organized and institutionalized power" (150), which again attests to her position that power (as she conceives it) is intrinsically valuable.

The Politics of Attention

The politics of attention refers to politics as usual, where the craven manipulation of emotions such as fear and loneliness is enabled by the isolation and atomization that is characteristic of contemporary societies. Politicians often direct the public attention to purported "facts" that resonate with such emotions and support their accounts of the good, in what is a deviant form of hermeneutical reasoning. This is particularly onerous when we see that attention lies at the heart of our being in the world, and in light of the potential and promise that is present in its gathering. The problem lies in part with the cynical world view of such politicians, who see no greater place for us in the ultimate context and thus little value in human life, as is particularly evident in the criminal brutality of some of the worst offenders.

The appeal of those who seek power for its own sake acts on self-understanding as embodied in the background resources that move attention. There are two dimensions to resisting such appeals, corresponding to attention and understanding in the hermeneutical circle: (1) efforts of active attention where we stand our own ground, thereby seeing the action of the appeals as they affect us bodily, and (2) the formation of a shared hermeneutical truth in public communion. The antidote is thus to meet in public forums where mindfulness enables the formation of ontological bonds and trust in the testimony of others, as we seek to understand ourselves and find better ways of living together. In this way, any discourse that comes from afar that is not integrated with the living reality of the public as gathered in this manner will not resonate and thus have the power it would otherwise have enjoyed. The gathering of attention binds us and provides the power to resist such appeals and stand for the whole community in its truth.

The Power of Consent

Consistent with this approach, Arendt sees power as the consent of the people, which consists of active support and participation (1972, 85). There is a difference, however, between implicit and explicit consent, which can be seen when she says that we often accept a given state of affairs until we are led to public dissent (88). Arendt sees the latter as a version of the voluntary associations that she and Tocqueville champion, but I would argue that passive acceptance is an abdication of power, for without participation in the political process it may be too late to intervene by way of dissent. This requires an ongoing articulation of fundamental values and bonding with our fellows, which enables us to speak a shared hermeneutical truth to power. Our voices must be gathered and heard, for we need such bonding to overcome what could otherwise be a disintegration of common understanding (Arendt's common sense).

The quality of public attention is rarely considered. For instance, when leaders appeal to emotions such as fear, hatred, and anger, attention will be directed in a corresponding manner, and the public space will have an atmosphere that is conducive to action along those lines.[11] The bonds that form between individuals are based on that shared experience, which can end up in violence directed toward the purported sources of that fear and anger. Alternatively, when people gather because of concerns such as decaying infrastructure or gun violence, they will be bonded based on that participation, with shared feelings associated with doing something constructive. They form a force for change based on the experience, which can be opposed to others who see other priorities as more pressing. These oppositions are more likely to be reconciled when opposing parties are able to meet in an open forum that allows for discussion of all viewpoints, which depends on the quality of the public space in which such meetings occur.

The typical assumption is that matters of concern for the community at large are under consideration, which means that public attention will be trained on those who step into the spotlight. There will also be significant clashes, differences in point of view between the various actors that add tension to the proceedings. So the power of attention in this case is less a matter of consent, although there is common interest in the proceedings, and more due to of the state of the background resources that are brought to bear in these spaces, or the energies that are activated in Berger's (2011) terms. This is not optimal because of the lack of an overarching presence that would enable a more harmonious reconciliation of differences.

In all these cases, attention is directed in a passive manner, and the outcomes depend on the state of background resources and the associated understanding of the demands of the situation. I am not arguing that passive attention will always be detrimental to political outcomes, not only because attention is almost always passive absent an intentional effort to gather ourselves for the purpose of presence, where the latter is always marked by a self-awareness as engaged in such an effort because of the relation between attention and the manifestation of the self. There are of course many factors that influence the health of democratic institutions absent the sustained and/ or institutionalized practice of active attention, such as natural endowments of the population, culture, education, and in general the historical tradition that works in present political action. Attention will still be a major factor, but its movement will be determined by the action of background resources that are themselves shaped by the prior deliverances of attention. In this case, the projection of the past by way of the background stands in the way of more profound relations with the people and situations that show up at the center of attention.[12]

Gathering by baser forms of emotion can eventually result in violence, whereas a higher-quality atmosphere can arise in an open society with spaces for communion that are enhanced by active attention. We are then grounded in the living actuality of our presence and enjoy a resistance and autonomy rather than being taken by the powers that be. In the face of leaders who manipulate attention by way of appeal to base emotions, active attention can enable articulation of these feelings and recognition of more appropriate ways to be. My proposal is that such an atmosphere can enable a release of creative potential due to the more effective deployment of the bodily intelligence that we all share. I offer empirical support for this claim below and consider a metaphysical argument in chapter 9.

Attention as Abyssal Ground II

I have been showing how Arendt's concepts map into the set of notions I have developed regarding attention and the associated hermeneutical circle. I now argue further for their dependence on attention as the abyssal ground for interaction in political affairs, which argues for the necessity of active attention for effective action. The claim is that Arendt's notions depend on the living presence of the people by way of mutual and sustained attention. We see, for instance, the relation between appearance and reality because the attentive presence of others gives us the required objectivity, which enables the formation of shared truth and a common world. The deliverances of attention are what are real for me, which are presented to me, where I am made manifest in relation to what shows itself. It is more or less direct, depending on the quality of attention, as we have seen in the notion of bare attention.

Arendt's key claim is that all of this depends on the lived reality in which we dwell, which corresponds to the lived body-environment that appears in the hermeneutical circle. She also speaks in terms of lived flux, or living presence. For Arendt, we need the stability that comes about with the presence of citizens in public spaces, for the law is not enough (1958, 195). For instance, she says that the space of appearances (grounded in mutual attention) predates constitution and organization (199), which does not survive the dispersal of the supporting presence of its agents.

Arendt also talks about the notion of a "principle of action" and insists that it is manifest only in the course of performance ([1961] 1977a, 150–53). She says that "all political institutions are manifestations and materializations of power; they petrify and decay as soon as the living power of the people ceases to uphold them" (1972, 140). These are holistic living realities that can be more or less integrated, as in the sealing of the hermeneutical circle in chapter 7.

Arendt sees action and speech as ephemeral, which, as we have seen, calls for mindfulness. She tells us that greatness is achieved only in performance, in the activity itself, and cites Aristotle as saying that the living deed and spoken word are the greatest achievements of which human beings are capable, that it is in "the experience of this full actuality that the paradoxical 'end in itself' derives its original meaning" (1958, 206) and that "this actualization resides and comes to pass in those activities that exist only in sheer actuality" (208). Such living deeds and spoken words require the extraordinary presence of attention to be intrinsically valuable, to be ends in themselves.[13]

As noted above, Arendt mentions the requirement of the constant presence of others (1958, 51) that is necessary for the public realm to be effective.[14] But since it cannot be only a physical presence, the question again is what kind of presence it is. If it is merely a concerned presence without the autonomous and free effort of mindfulness, it is prone to dispersion once the cause of the concern is remedied. Such a constant presence can come about only by way of mindfulness, which itself requires institutional support, where all understand themselves first as being there to produce the overarching presence that can unite its members. This is possible if each fulfills the duty to make efforts of their whole being, in being as fully present as possible, as always, with the aid of their fellows who understand the intrinsic value of mindfulness and who remind us with their presence, which can be felt. Thus, attention as abyssal ground is the ground on which we stand in the course of political activity, and its state is essential for the articulation and achievement of the common good.

We have a need for ongoing participation in public life, for it offers opportunities to grow as we articulate and work to achieve the common good together. Arendt says (regarding Thomas Jefferson's position on the ward system) that "no one could be called happy without his share in public happiness, that no one could be called free without his experience in public freedom, and that no one could be called either happy or free without participating, and having a share, in public power" ([1963] 1977b, 247). With this in mind, I turn to a discussion of her notion of council democracy and its potential enhancement by way of the institutionalized practice of mindfulness.

MINDFUL COUNCIL DEMOCRACY

There are two movements afoot today: experimentation in participatory democracy and the practice of mindfulness in group settings to deal with issues such as trauma, community building, and spiritual growth. I have argued that political engagement undertaken with mindfulness is intrinsically valuable, but ordinarily (as Berger noted above) such engagement in isolation from such forms of bonding is subject to balkanization as people disperse into partisan groups. My idea is to combine the two to address the present crisis, which calls for political engagement based on a solid communal foundation in mindfulness given that face-to-face interaction is often not enough. Given the wide variety of approaches that are presently being implemented, I can only sketch some forms that such a conjunction could take.

Participatory Democracy

A recent Organisation for Economic Co-operation and Development (OECD) study (2020, 3) found that political engagement can deliver better policies, strengthen democracy, and build trust. It collected 289 case studies of citizen participation that were initiated by government bodies, and where their impacts were monitored to ensure they were taken seriously. The report focuses on deliberative democracy, where small groups of citizens work on specific problems, as opposed to participatory democracy, which involves larger numbers who can discuss less focused issues. In deliberative processes participants are selected randomly and spend a significant amount of time digesting information to enable more informed recommendations.[15]

The study (OECD 2020, 152) only briefly mentioned participatory models that involve larger proportions of the population, such as village democracy in India, democracy festivals, and twenty-first-century town meetings, but it points out that deliberative and participatory models can be combined, where there is more participation in the early stages, followed by more focused groups that follow up on the ideas that are generated.[16]

My proposal is similar to this, which is to form citizen councils as envisioned by Arendt. She says ([1963] 1977b, chap. 6) that such councils ruled in the French and Russian revolutions, when all were intently engaged in developing a fresh, new politics.[17] The approach in the present context would be to have many groups of, say, thirty randomly chosen individuals meet frequently to discuss key issues facing the community and the nation. Periodically, a representative from each group would be sent to form a new one at a higher level, and representatives from these groups would then make up a final group of, say, fifty individuals. The powers of the latter group would be up for discussion, but its authority would derive from the participation of a significant portion of the population. The other aspect is to conduct such engagement by way of institutionalized mindfulness, to which we now turn.

Relational Presencing

Partly in response to the pandemic, people have been finding community in online meetings with a variety of agendas, many of them therapeutic in nature, which are organized around the practice of mindfulness. When individuals speak, for instance, others are encouraged to listen deeply and respectfully, and the speakers themselves are asked to stay with their presence in the moment and speak from that, not just whatever comes to mind. The idea is that the more present we are, the more hospitable and compassionate the space that comes out of the gathering. Groups can range in size into the hundreds, and there are often breakout groups of three to five people where individuals can participate in more intimate face-to-face settings.[18]

Participants in these meetings often talk about "holding space," which resonates both with the discussion in chapter 6 of the opening that can occur with mindfulness and with Heidegger's notion of the clearing (see chapter 9). This means that in these meetings a space can open in which each has an opportunity to be seen and heard, which is becoming quite rare in today's fragmented world. And when we share a space like that and allow the other to speak, we can see their depth and creative potential even though we may differ significantly on the issues of concern. This means that the mood of the proceedings may begin to shift, because in the absence of such a presence the atmosphere can degenerate into antagonistic interaction, while when it is present, ontological bonding can lift the spirits of all.

I have found that when they are in these groups, people say they experience an openness and bonding with others that goes well beyond what they are accustomed to. They say it must be experienced to be appreciated and mention things like connecting at the heart level, the gift of seeing and being seen, being in the presence of humanity, and being deeply touched and vulnerable. There is something new here, something magical about what happens when we are able to listen deeply to one another.

Similar experiences have been reported in the participatory democracy groups discussed above, although they are not as intense given the absence of institutionalized mindfulness. For instance, Diamond (2019) reports that the deliberative groups discussed in Fishkin (2018) enable people to overcome the political divisions that have become so toxic in the United States. Some participants said that it was the issues that riveted their attention, not ideology. One person said, "I didn't know who was a Democrat, who was a Republican, and who an independent. People just shared their views. That made it much easier to listen and have a respectful exchange." Many people had serious policy discussions and even formed friendships across the great divides in US politics.

Mindful Political Engagement

The proposal here is to combine mindfulness and participatory democracy. There are considerable overlaps. For instance, the political situation is traumatizing to people, and the same techniques used in dealing with trauma can be useful in developing creative ways to deal with political issues. In order to deal with the most pressing issues facing the country, such as immigration, gun control, and climate change, we must eventually deal with the values questions that underlie the different positions that are taken. Taylor (2016, 251), for instance, discusses how questions of respect for the liberty of others must eventually deal with what matters most for a good life, so we must delve into realms of meaning that are bound up with bodily enacted emotional expressions that can be more or less articulated (see chapter 2).

Thus, the whole human being must be considered in the question of political engagement. It is true that researchers have found that ordinary citizens can often contribute in areas that require considerable expertise (e.g., Fishkin 2018), but for the most pressing questions, we need to develop spaces that enable expression of not just opinion but rather how we feel about the issues, how we are affected personally. Discussion in public spaces will be much more riveting when these aspects are brought into view. This is all part of forming what I have referred to as a hermeneutical truth that must be present to be able to speak with one voice in the affairs that matter to us most.

There is already some work being done along these lines. For instance, Taylor, Nanz, and Taylor say that the individuals who facilitate such gatherings need to be trained in the ability to listen deeply and understand the particulars of the situation: "It requires a certain kind of sensibility to recognize the differences, as well as the powers of articulation to find/recognize the right words, the key terms" (2020, 21).[19] Zubizarreta's essay "Listening for Aliveness" (2014) provides a detailed discussion of the role of active listening in the course of political and other organizational engagement. She also focuses on the role of the facilitator, although she notes that the same results hold for small breakout groups where active listening is encouraged. Employing Rough's (2002) method of "dynamic facilitation," facilitators understand that the core competency is the ability to listen deeply, "to *really* listen." The point is that participants can tell the difference, and it has a large impact on the outcomes that are observed. For instance, it is important in being able to draw people out, for the first statements they make often are not particularly revealing. They are more likely to be able to articulate their feelings on the issues when they sense they are being heard. Otherwise—if, for instance, the participants merely hear what they say reflected back to them, which is a common technique—they can sense the attitude of the facilitator, which affects how well they are able to contribute. They need to feel that the process is genuine, which depends on how much they feel seen and heard.

Listening is also contagious. When a facilitator listens deeply to a participant, other members of the group can sense it and a different tone in the conversation can result. Here are some remarks that were made by facilitators about the results when participants did indeed feel seen and heard, as reported by Zubizarreta:

> By the time I was done, the library people were completely flabbergasted that we had come up with so many solutions. . . . The library's bottom line was to get solutions. But they ended up with more than they had asked for, because they also ended up with customers that felt heard.

> I am continually amazed by the gold and diamonds that are in these groups. The first couple of times I tried this approach, I thought we got lucky. Eventually I said, this is not a matter of luck. This can happen almost every time. (2014)

The question is whether this can be the basis for overcoming the misinformation and manipulation that prevail in today's politics. Can the growing infrastructure of these groups serve as the foundation for a better direction? The power of the process comes from the face-to-face meetings, either in person or online, where bonds arise from the quality of presence to one another, and where each feels directly what the other is saying and experiencing. This means that each member can eventually develop trust in the group and participate in developing a shared truth, which enables the accommodation of multiple perspectives and freer discussion of the issues that divide the country. They will be better able to resist propaganda that comes from afar, relative to discussions that take place in the close proximity of the groups. This is the hope that these sorts of meetings can bring when we don't simply put people together, but do so with a commitment to being fully present to and respectful of one another.

THE NATURE OF POWER

I have argued that there is a power associated with the gathering of attention, which comes about when each bonds ontologically with the others. But the question is, what is the nature of this power and why is attention able to produce it? I have argued throughout the book that attention is human presence, which is how we are made manifest in relation to self and others, and that it together with language exceeds us as individuals; indeed, it exceeds us as a human race, not only because other animals participate in it in a limited fashion but because it enables us to relate to all that is made manifest.

I have been indicating that this is consistent with an ontology in which relations are intrinsic, not extrinsic to preexisting entities, and I propose in the next chapter that Heidegger's philosophy can be thought along these lines. This leads to the claim that attention has this power because it is related to that which enables all things to be made manifest in relation to each other, which Heidegger simply refers to as being. This is the abyssal ground for all that appears, in which we participate by way of attention, which enables it to bring us more profoundly in relation to one another and hence produce a bonding power under appropriate conditions.

For Heidegger, we belong to the *physis* of the early Greeks, the creative process that enables the manifestation of all that is, in addition to participating in the attention and language that are essential for that very manifestation. This, I would argue, is the basis for our participation in that cosmic creative process and therefore the natality that Arendt champions. It means that we belong here, that we are not the "accidents" that quasi-scientific thought posits.

This means a great deal for our fundamental attunements, which for Heidegger come out of our relation to all that is, and which in turn is the basis for any specific emotionality that may present itself. For instance, if we believe ourselves to be alienated and cut off from all that is, the implications are large for the ways in which we comport ourselves. But when we see that we belong here, that we participate in the manifestation of all that is, that can make a large difference in how we see ourselves, which shows up in the felt intuitions that guide us in everyday activity and in response to the present world crisis.

I consider the relation between attention and being in the next chapter. The implication is that mindful bonds between individuals are truly ontological, because they participate in the being of all that is.

Chapter 9

Attention as the Way to Being

Heidegger thinks on the grand scale. In this chapter I turn to a textual analysis of his work in support of the some of the positions I have advanced and discuss the implications for questions of ultimate meaning that bear on our considerations. Most importantly, I am arguing that attention as human manifestation and relation is essentially related to the manifestation and relation of all that is, which Heidegger refers to as being.[1] Some implications of the relation between attention and being are: (1) we belong here, because we are related to all that is by way of attention; (2) attention is fundamentally related to the clearing of being, and our task is to hold it open; (3) the constant presence that is often assumed would require perpetually steadfast human presence by way of the effort of mindfulness, which is not possible for human beings; (4) our fundamental attunements, which are the basis for the emotions which are so powerful in directing attention, say how we correspond (relate) to being; and (5) when being itself is made manifest it shows itself *in us* in the form of higher ways of being in the world.

For Heidegger, we ultimately have a task—to hold open a space he calls the clearing by way of acute and sustained attention. That attentiveness can enable the emergence of better versions of ourselves and the worlds in which we live. In this manner we can be more sensitive to the sublime dimensions of the cosmos, a cosmos that includes us, and I would add that Heidegger has been an important figure in movements such as radical or deep ecology for many years (e.g., Zimmerman 1994).

We ask why attention has the ability to affect us in this manner and see that it is how we participate in the manifestation and relation of all that is. This means we are part of something greater that can lift us up, and that it is possible to gain transformative insight and a more profound attunement by way of gathering attention as in mindfulness and related practices. In this manner we can blossom into something more appropriate for our nature, which means that attention is the path to better ways of living together in the historical situations in which we find ourselves.

ATTENTION IN *BEING AND TIME*

In the early work, Heidegger seeks to go beyond notions of detached consciousness that abound in the literature, which for him at the time include attention. In *Being and Time* (SZ), he introduces a new set of terms to more appropriately take account of the role of understanding and context. He does so in §28 by transforming the notion of *lumen naturale*, which is intimately related to attention in Descartes,[2] into the clearing (*die Lichtung*):

> When we talk in an ontically figurative way of the *lumen naturale* in man, we have in mind nothing other than the existential-ontological structure of this entity, that it *is* in such a way as to be its "there" [*Da*]. To say that it is "illuminated" means that *as* being-in-the-world it is cleared in itself, not through any other entity, but in such a way that it *is* itself the clearing [*die Lichtung*]. . . . By its very nature, Dasein brings its 'there' along with it. If it lacks its "there," it is not factically the entity which is essentially Dasein; indeed, it is not this entity at all. *Dasein is its disclosedness* [*Erschlossenheit*]. (SZ: 133/171)

Light metaphors are important in Heidegger, and they are also important for attention (as noted in the introduction), as in the spotlight theory of attention and the notion of foreground as the highlighting of attention. In this citation Heidegger equates the "there" (which I relate to the presence of attention), the clearing, and disclosedness. We see that Dasein is "cleared in itself, not through any other entity," which corresponds to my characterization of attention as abyssal. In later work he describes the clearing as follows:

> In the midst of beings as a whole an open place occurs. There is a clearing [*Eine Lichtung ist*]. Thought of in reference to what is, to beings, this clearing *is* in a greater degree than are beings. This open center is therefore not surrounded by what is; rather, the clearing [*lichtende*] center itself encircles all that is, like the Nothing which we scarcely know.
>
> That which is can only be, as a being, if it stands within and stands out within what is cleared [*Gelichtete*] in this clearing. Only this clearing grants and guarantees to us humans a passage to those beings that we ourselves are not, and access to the being that we ourselves are. Thanks to this clearing, beings are unconcealed in certain changing degrees (GA 5: 39–40/ PLT 51–52, em, tm).

Heidegger says that the clearing is the basis for the manifestation of entities, and it thus "is" in a greater degree than such particulars. I have been referring to this as the center of attention, where we ourselves are made manifest in relation to other manifesting entities, and where an overarching ("encircling") presence can arise by way of active attention. We also see that entities themselves can be more or less present, as I have argued.

Heidegger goes on in §34 of SZ to consider the related notions of hearing and listening: "Listening to [*Das Hören auf*] . . . is Dasein's existential way of being-open as being-with for Others. Indeed, hearing constitutes the primary and authentic way in which Dasein is open for its ownmost potentiality-for-being" (SZ: 163/206). I have been arguing that moving toward this potentiality-for-being can translate into more appropriate ways of being together in the world.

The sort of attentiveness that Heidegger calls for in *Being and Time* and later work is of an extraordinary nature, which I refer to as an ontological effort that calls on one's whole being. As J. Glenn Gray puts it in the introduction to *What Is Called Thinking?* (GA 8), "Thinking is not so much an act as a way of living or dwelling. . . . It is a gathering and focusing of our whole selves on what lies before us and a taking to heart and mind these particular things in order to discover in them their essential nature and truth." On the other hand, the themes of dispersion, distraction, and immersion (*zerstreuen* and *aufgehen*) are also quite prominent in *Being and Time*. Dasein's state is characterized in terms of lostness in the "they" in contrast to the gathering, the standing on one's own of authenticity. For example:

> Everyday Dasein has been dispersed into the many kinds of things which daily "come to pass." . . . So if it wants to come to itself, it must first *pull itself together* [*zussamenholen*] from the dispersion and disconnectedness of the very things that have "come to pass." . . . It asks rather in which of its own kinds of being Dasein *loses itself in such a manner that it must, as it were, only subsequently pull itself together out of its dispersal*. . . . The Self's resoluteness [*Entschlossenheit*] against the inconstancy of distraction, is in itself a steadiness [*Ständigkeit*] *which has been stretched along*. . . . In such constancy [*Ständigkeit*] Dasein is indeed in a moment of vision [*Augenblick*] for what is world-historical in its current Situation. (SZ: 390–91/441–42)

We see here the theme of constancy in relation to the authentic temporality of the moment of vision, which relation to attention is developed in the later Heidegger. Although attention in the form of *Achtsamkeit* and *Aufmerksamkeit* does not appear thematically in this text, McNeill (1999, 121; translating *Gewärtigen* [awaiting] as attending) says that attention is how Dasein is open for the presencing of beings.[3] Indeed, there is support for a relation between attention and waiting in the later Heidegger, for instance, in *Country Path Conversations*: "In waiting [*warten*], the human-being becomes gathered in attentiveness [*Achtsamkeit*] to that in which he belongs, yet without letting himself get carried away into and absorbed in it" (GA 77: 226/147).[4] McNeill argues that attention understood in the sense of tarrying and dwelling enables the authentic temporality that characterizes the moment of vision. Here the human being attends the presencing of beings in such a way as to accompany them in their presencing, to let them be, to let them come to presence. Such attending in the sense of tarrying is a slowing down, a stilling that is to be contrasted with the flitting about of curiosity (1999, 190). Thus McNeill argues that attention understood as "waiting-toward" is essential for authentic presencing itself, and we see how attending in this manner affects the temporality of manifesting entities, including ourselves.

The Metaphysics of Constant Presence

For Heidegger, the being of the early Greeks is presencing (*Anwesen*), where entities emerge from concealment into unconcealment, linger a while, and then withdraw into concealment. At the same time, presencing is a gathering and an ordering, a unifying—that is, for Heidegger being and Logos are the same. It is important to note, however, that presence as *Gegenwart* is also very important for him, because this refers to the understanding of being (*Vorhandenheit*, presence at hand) that comes about in the history of metaphysics as a fall from the originary Greek inception. Heidegger devotes much effort to explaining how this fall into the oblivion of being comes about. What is key to emphasize is that the first notion of presencing is dynamic, in that being understood in this manner is not a highest genus or a collection of preexisting objects but is rather an emergence out of concealment. Moreover, the articulations that define the boundaries (*perata*, limits) and relations between entities are also not given as preexisting but rather are subject to conflict, struggle, and the effort of various entities, including human beings. Thus the notion of being as presencing is to be contrasted with the assumption of constant presence where all is perpetually unconcealed, which I have referred to as a metaphysics of constant presence. In the section entitled "Being as Presencing" below, I argue that Heidegger's understanding of being as presencing goes beyond this interpretation of the Greeks.

ATTENTION IN THE LATER HEIDEGGER

A number of enigmatic statements linking attention to the way to being appear in Heidegger's corpus, such as: "Underway, then—we must give particularly close attention [*achten*] to that stretch of way [*Wegstelle*] on which we are putting our feet. We meant to be attentive [*acht zu haben*] to it from the first lecture on" (GA 8: 50/46).[5] This statement illustrates the importance of attention (*Achtsamkeit, Aufmerksamkeit*) and its movement in Heidegger's later thought; indeed, it is the essence of human presencing, and as such is intimately related to being as presencing. He says as much in translating

Parmenides: "For the same: taking-heed-of [*In-die-Acht-nehmen*] is also the presencing of what is present [*Anwesen des Anwesenden*]" (GA 8: 245/241, tm). As essentially related to being, attention is the abyssal ground for all modes of human engagement, be they walking, talking, reflecting, and so on. Its movement is the very movement of our being, which is how we participate in the being of all that is.

Awareness of this movement is how we move toward the showing of being itself, by way of an effort of acute and sustained attention. Such an effort must be aware of its own movement, for the effort comes out of the movement of attention itself, and one must *stay with* that movement to be able to sustain it. One must thus stay with the very act of attending, the ground of worldly engagement, in order to approach being, but paradoxically, the very self that would stay with its own movement is itself made manifest in that movement. Such a paradox at the heart of attention corresponds to the paradox of being itself.[6]

It can be verified phenomenologically that when we are acutely attentive in this manner, we become more present, we "come together"—we are more gathered, more integrated. Such a gathering (*Sammlung*) is not a "mental" phenomenon but is rather an event in the world, for it is how we participate in being, which can also be conceived as a collecting or gathering. By way of this effort we are on the way to being, moving beyond the superficial meanings that typically govern this ontological movement.

We can understand being in this context as the self-withdrawing presencing and gathering of beings. What is key is that for Heidegger, we may participate more or less fully in this gathering, for it is not a collection of objects, or a highest genus, but rather *essentially involves a force* that is characterized in terms of the standing and holding (*stehen und halten*) that holds beings in readiness, a stillness in which things are held in a tension.[7] Attention involves exactly this sort of effort. The implication is that to better understand the meaning of being, we can look to attention and see what the associated effort is: It is a staying-with, a with-standing, a holding in readiness, a tarrying. We can gain insight into being, and participate in it directly, by engaging in this sort of ontological effort.

Attention and Thinking

In *What Is Called Thinking?* Heidegger says that the common meanings and prejudices that capture attention prevent us from going deeper toward being.[8] The movement of attention depends on the understanding and its associated terms, so when all things are reduced to a common denominator (GA 8: 220/216) attention follows that path. Only the effort of acute and sustained attention enables us to break out of the circle and go deeper into the nature of the things themselves, to hear them speak: "Language likes to let our speech drift away into the more obvious meanings of words. It is as though man *had to make an effort* [*Mühe*] to live properly with language. It is as though such a dwelling is prone to succumb to the danger of commonness" (GA 8: 122/118–19, em). This means that attention (synonymous here with dwelling) is confined to the surface of things because it is captured by the superficial meanings which in turn reflect the shallowness of our own dwelling.[9] The only hope to be able to "reach what *is*" (70/66), to move toward the being of beings, lies in acute and sustained attention. It is listening to what is unspoken that enables us to go deeper than the common meanings. Heidegger also tells us that the title of this work can be thought as *What Calls for Thinking?*, which is that there *is* anything at all, that anything is made manifest in this cosmos, including ourselves. This is the call, or appeal of being, to which we can be more or less related in our very presence in the world by way of profound listening.

In this text Heidegger argues that thinking is attention (*noein*) in conjunction with the gathering of being (*legein*). We do not gather anything ourselves, but only hold open and thus let the presencing of entities occur in an appropriate (*ereignet*) manner. That is, we are characterized by a fundamental passivity that corresponds to my notion of passive attention, and the holding open is active attention in my terms. He begins by saying that in order to be capable of thinking, we first need to be ready, gathered in our whole being so we are oriented to the task at hand. This is enabled by the staying-with of attention, which gathers us in correspondence and thus attunement to the gathering of being. Much of *What Is Called Thinking?* is devoted to spelling out this relationship as the essence of thinking.

Heidegger's focus is on fragment 6 of Parmenides, which is typically translated: One should both say (*legein*) and think (*noein*) that being is (171/168). His central claim is that the nature of thinking lies in the conjunction of *legein* (laying and gathering) and *noein* (attention), which is in turn oriented to the being of beings.[10] The being of beings calls for the effort, but whether the effort actually occurs, whether the call is heard, is indeterminate. This is why Heidegger calls for attention, for listening to what calls for thinking: "Hence our need and necessity first of all to hear [*hören*] the appeal of what is most thought-provoking [being]. But if we are to perceive what gives us thought, we must for our part get underway to learn thinking. . . . What we can do in our present case, or anyway can learn, is to listen closely [*genau hinzuhören*]" (GA 8: 28/25, tm). We must learn to listen to the appeal of what calls for thinking to be able to get underway, which learning requires attention itself.

Heidegger first considers the nature of *legein*, the gathering of being. For this purpose he directs the reader to the essay "Logos," where he considers fragment B50 of Heraclitus, which is can be translated as "When you have listened not to me but to the Meaning [*Sinn*], it is wise within the same Meaning to say: *One* is All" (GA 7: 213/ EGT 59). Heidegger discusses the relation between laying and a gathering that is more than a mere amassing, but is rather a collecting, a bringing together (GA 7: 215/ EGT 61).[11] This enables the presencing (*Anwesen*) of that which lies before us into unconcealment (217/63). While letting is the essence of *legein*, Heidegger further distinguishes between *legein* in general and mortal *legein*, which is called *homologein*. The product of the primal gathering of being is collected and brought forward by human effort (225/70).[12] Thus we see the foregrounding that is associated with attention appear here in the context of human participation in the gathering of being. There is a sense in which the presencing of beings is not complete unless there is proper hearing.

We belong to being by participating in the gathering and preserving of what comes into presence, which corresponds to my version of the hermeneutical circle, where the deliverances of attention are preserved in language and understanding. By way of attention we are essentially related to the site of presencing (the clearing), where entities come to the fore in their being. The extent to which we belong (*gehören*) to the primal gathering depends on the extent to which we listen (*hören*) profoundly, rather than being lost in the appearances themselves. We are called to listen and thus be gathered in a manner that is similar to the primal gathering itself, except that *we do not assemble anything ourselves*, for that is the action of being; rather, we are to let lie and *speak from* whatever is presented to us by way of the primal gathering of Logos.[13] This points to the fundamental passivity of our being, where the ontological action of active attention enables being to "act" through us.

Turning back to *What Is Called Thinking?*, Heidegger now translates *noein* as *In-die-Acht-nehmen*, or "taking heed of." He begins by thinking of *noein* in terms of *vernehmen* (perceive) and other variants with a root of *nehmen*, such as *aufnehmen* (receive), but says that it should not be thought of as passive acceptance (GA 8:205/203) but rather must include an active dimension, such as undertaking (*vor-nehmen*) something. But how is such an undertaking taken up? "We take heed of it [*Wir nehmen es in Acht*]. What is taken heed of, however, is to be left exactly as it is. This taking heed does not make over what it takes. Taking heed is: keeping at attention [*in der Acht behalten*]" (206/203, tm). Heidegger concludes, "We translate *noein* with 'taking heed of'[*in die Acht nehmen*]" (211/207, tm). He sees *noein* as attention, but an attention that looks ahead, that perceives beforehand. At the same time, it lets what lies before us, as it is presented to us, be present in our safekeeping by way of the associated *legein* (gathering of being).

Heidegger says that the reason *legein* is mentioned first in the fragment is that *legein* provides *noein* with something to attend to (as lying before us), and that once something is heeded it is again gathered and safeguarded. He explains how each enters into the other, how they are reciprocally related: On the one hand, *legein*, the letting lie before us, "unfolds of its own accord" into the *noein* (GA 8: 212/208). This means that *noein* participates in the letting of *legein*, which is a letting lie before that is *tacitly disposed* to *noein*.[14] It must be noted, however, that the letting is not limited to that which comes about due to mortal *noein*, for as in the essay "Logos," mortal *legein* is understood to be *homologein* relative to *legein* in general. This is key for Heidegger's assertion of the primacy of *legein* relative to *noein*, as it provides a letting lie before us in advance of the taking heed.[15]

On the other hand, we can also see how attention enables a gathering itself: "When we take heed of [*in die Acht nehmen*] what lies before us, we attend [*achten*] to its lying. In attending we collect ourselves in relation to what lies before us, and gather what we have taken heed of. Where to? Where else but to itself, so that it may be made manifest, as it of itself lies here before us" (GA 8: 212/209, tm). Thus, attention enables a gathering of ourselves and what we have taken heed of; that is, it enables the manifestation of the self in relation to the entities with which we engage, as I have argued above. Heidegger concludes that *legein* and *noein* are in a conjunction that achieves "what later . . . is specifically called *aletheia*: to disclose and keep [*halten*] disclosed what is unconcealed" (213/209), and thus we see how attention enables participation in the presencing of entities. But this conjunction does not rest in itself; rather, it is oriented toward what calls for thinking, which is the twofold of being and beings. "The twofold [*eon emmenai*] must first lie before us openly and be taken heed of [*in die Acht genommen*]," for this is what it calls for (227/223).[16] This is the way to being, as we see in the concluding segment of *What Is Called Thinking?*

The Way to Being

After noting that Parmenides often speaks simply of *noein* instead of the conjunction of *legein* and *noein*, Heidegger says that *noein* (*In-die-Acht-nehmen*) is thinking only to the extent that it is focused on *eon*, which is the twofold (or duality) of being and beings. He says that the essential nature of *noein* consists in remaining focused on *eon*, the presencing of what is present, which *in turn* "keeps and guards *noein* within itself as what belongs to it" (GA 8: 245/241–42). Thus we see again a reciprocal relation between attention and being. But why does presencing/being need human attention? For this purpose I turn to undelivered material that was later revised and published as "Moira" in *Early Greek Thinking* (GA 7/ EGT).

In this essay Heidegger inquires into the relation between thinking and being, and we see that attention itself comes into presence because it is called for by the being of beings. That is, it is on the way to being: "Thinking comes to presence [*anwest*] because of the still unspoken duality. The presencing [*An-wesen*] of thinking is on the way to the duality of being and beings. The duality presences [*anwest*] in taking-heed-of [*In-die-Acht-Nehmen*]." (GA 7: 248/ EGT 88–89). Thus it is in the very presencing of attention as called for by the being of beings that attention belongs to being, which is itself a presencing. What is of interest here is that *the twofold itself* comes to presence in the taking-heed-of [*In-die-Acht-nehmen*]. That is, instead of our being absorbed in the beings which come into presence, the very presencing (the being) of beings *itself comes into view* when the call of the twofold is heeded. This is something that the twofold demands (248/89), but Heidegger says we are far from experiencing the twofold itself in an essential way, far from thinking.

Heidegger now notes that for the Greeks, the essence of saying lies in *legein*, in which *noein* is grounded, as we have seen above. This means that *noein* is essentially something said, where saying means to bring forward into view (GA 7: 248–49/ EGT 89–90). This bringing forward into view *completes* (*vollbringt*) *the gathering* that is called for by *eon*, which is why *eon* needs efforts of human attention that are directed in the appropriate manner (250/91). He concludes: "We have to learn to think the essence of language from the saying, and to think saying as letting-lie-before (*logos*) and as bringing-forward-into-view (*phasis*)" (250/91). This intricate relation between attention and language is quite prominent in the hermeneutical circle that has been developed herein.

Thus the question that Heidegger poses is: Do we heed, do we *stay with* (remain present to) the event of presencing itself, or are we immersed (*aufgehen*) in the objects that arise in the process, thereby being absent to their very manifestation? This determines the extent to which we participate in being, for by attending to its presencing we take part in its work. For instance, discussing fragment B16 of Heraclitus, he says, "[W]e must heed [*achten*] something else: *physis* and *kruptesthai*, rising (self-revealing) and concealing" (GA 7: 277/ EGT 113). We are called on to let entities stand forth more appropriately in the clearing, with implications for more harmonious interaction in human worlds, as they emerge from the primal unfolding of being. For this purpose attention must be paid to the primal presencing itself and not be taken by the entities that arise; this is how we participate in the work of being. It requires an extraordinary effort of attention, because, as Heidegger puts it, "What essentially unfolds in nearness is too close for our customary mode of representational thought" (GA 7: 287/ EGT 121).[17]

Being calls for the movement of attention, and we must stay with that movement to be able to approach it—for that is how it shows itself. That is, Heidegger calls on us to stay with (attend to) the way, with the movement of attention itself, because being itself comes to presence in this taking-heed-of (GA 7: 247/ EGT 88). Instead of being immersed in the beings that come into presence, the very presencing itself comes into view when we stay with that movement, which is how the call of being is explicitly heeded. Thus, staying with the movement of attention is the way to being.

The key to staying with our ontological movement lies in knowing directly (not by way of reflection) that one is present, embodied, and engaged in a particular activity. For as the essence of human presencing, attention is how one is so engaged. One must stay with that engagement, gathering oneself as presently embodied and thereby being grounded in this manner. By staying with that embodied grounding, one is on the way to higher ways of being, which is how being shows itself.

Thus, being shows itself in qualitatively higher ways of being in the particular historical context in which we find ourselves, which is the only way we can know what being is. For we speak from our being, and we cannot speak from what we are not. Being showing itself is an event (*Ereignis*) that shows itself in us, in higher ways of being in the world. The possibility of elevation is essential to the notion of being, as gathering and dispersal are intrinsic to the ways in which beings can be made manifest. In attention terms, this corresponds to the distinction between active and passive, where active attention is gathered and passive attention is dispersed and distracted.

PARTICIPATION IN BEING

The notion of *Ereignis* and its relation to the notion of authenticity from *Being and Time* can be understood by way of the notion of belonging to or participating in being. This points to the performative dimension of Heidegger's thought, in that he insists it is necessary to participate in the subject matter in question, which enables us to *speak from* being related to the thing itself and not merely about it. This is evident, for instance, on the opening page of *Contributions to Philosophy: (Of the Event)*:

> The issue is no longer to be "about" something, to present something objective, but to be appropriated over [*übereignet*] to the appropriating event [*Er-eignis*]. That is equivalent to an essential transformation of the human being: from rational animal to Da-sein. The fitting rubric is therefore *Of the Event*. That is not to be understood in the sense of a report about it. Instead it means that a belonging [*gehören*] to being and to the "word" of being, a belonging in thinking and saying, is something appropriated by the event. (GA 65: 3/5)

That is, appropriation (*Eignung*) and *Ereignis* (the Event) are later versions of authenticity (*Eigentlicht*), where the early transcendental structures are replaced by the human relation to being, so instead of the rational animal, we speak of Da-sein (the later version of Dasein). So we are not speaking about being from a distance, but since we are profoundly related to it, since we belong (*gehören*) to it to the extent that we listen (*hören*) to it, we speak *of* it, we speak *from* our relation to it. This is a participation in the very event of being in the cosmos, from our correspondence to being (see below).

The limits of representation is a major theme in Heidegger. We are not to represent freestanding objective realities, but rather must belong, must participate in the events of interest. How do we participate and thus come to knowledge of the sort that Heidegger calls for? As Heidegger puts in *Origin of the Work of Art*, "Do we know, which means do we give heed to [*achten*], the nature of the origin" (GA 5: 66/ PLT 75)? Knowing here is not representational but is rather a being related by way of attention. We participate, we engage by way of the presence of attention; that is what is called for in order to belong to being.

The idea is that we can only know what being is by belonging (*gehören*) to it, by listening (*hören*). It is thus no accident that *hören* and *gehören* are related. In the citation above (GA 65: 3/5), it appears we have little choice in the matter, and that is true if we think of choice in traditional terms, but here the question is if we exercise presence or not. That seems to be up to us in a sense, in that *human cooperation* is called for (GA 65: 248/195) in the grounding of the clearing. Similarly, we can only know what Dasein is if we take the *leap* out of the ordinary to that higher ground (GA 65:297/234).

For instance, Heidegger says that any attempt to explain the essential occurrence (*Wesung*) of being must fail. We cannot take a perspective from outside of being and distance ourselves from it, for we belong to it essentially (241/190). He says the same about attention in *The Event*, that "[h]eedfulness [*Aufmerksamkeit*]—as inceptual thinking . . . is outside of all 'reflexion' and every 'systematics' and 'science'" (GA 71: 289/251).

Heidegger discusses how being is not to be understood on the old model of becoming, or in terms of life or motion: "This interpretation speaks of the event as an object instead of letting its essential occurrence (and only this) speak for itself such that thinking would remain a thinking of being which does not talk about being but, instead, says being in a saying that belongs to what is opened up in the saying" (GA 65: 472/371). We must let the things speak for themselves, enabling a saying that belongs to what is thereby opened up. In turn, this sort of speaking induces an appropriate response in those who can hear what is spoken. In this way participation is related to the theme of formal indication (see Hatab 2017; 2019), where language evokes the appropriate response, thereby enabling participation.

Correspondence and Attunement

Although it is operative in *Contributions to Philosophy*, the notion of correspondence (*Entsprechen*) is not particularly prominent in that text. We can see
it in this citation from *Identity and Difference*: "But man's distinctive feature
lies in this, that he, as the being who thinks, is open to being, face to face with
being; thus man remains referred to being and so answers to it. Man *is* essentially this relationship of responding [*Bezug der Entsprechung*] to being, and
he is only this" (GA 11: 39/ ID 31). Correspondence describes *how we are* in
relation to being, how we are attuned and belong to the relational context for
all that is. As such, it must include attention as the basis for human relation
and participation in the whole. Entities do not exist outside of this web of
relations, coming into their own only within relational contexts.[18]

The key notion here is that "[n]o being, not even that being (namely, the
human being) which draws its historical essence from the relation of being
to itself, can ever effect and determine being. Instead, the historical human
being must correspond (*entsprechen*) to being" (GA 71: 87/73). The idea is
that individual entities do not stand on their own outside of the relational
context, and as such cannot effect change that is independent of it. Rather,
they enter into relation and speak and act out of the holistic context in which
they always already belong. This corresponds to my claim that our essential
responsibility is to be mindful, to stay with the movement of attention as it
occurs within the lived body-environment, and to thereby let our action emanate out of being profoundly related to that larger context, which can enable
change in that relational world context itself.

The relation between the gathering of attention and correspondence is
evident in a citation from *What Is Called Thinking?*: "Man learns when he
brings everything he does into correspondence [*Entsprechung*] with whatever
essentials are addressed to [*zugesprochen*] him at any given moment. We
learn to think by attending [*achten*] to what there is to think about" (GA 8:
5–6/4, tm). Attending gathers us in relation to the essentials which arise out of
being. It enables us to correspond in our being (our disposition or attunement)
to those essentials. Heidegger provides an example of an apprentice cabinet-
maker who is learning his craft and indicates that cabinetmaking, poetry, and
thinking all require the relatedness to being-essentials that is associated with
correspondence (GA 8: 17/14–15).

We are discussing the response to the appeal of being, which shows itself in
the lack that we feel in our depths, a metaphysical hunger for what we know
implicitly that we can be. Heidegger says that far from being "incomprehen-
sible and alien to thinking," the call must be thought and is "waiting for a
thinking that corresponds to it" (GA 8: 168/165). The inceptual thinking that
occurs at pivotal epochs in the history of being is characterized by thinkers

who experience and respond to the call (171/167). Discussing a saying of Parmenides, Heidegger says that the way to understanding the call to which Parmenides was responding is to undergo it ourselves, by giving "attention [*achten*] directly to what is recounted here" (179/175).

I now turn to the 1955 lecture *What Is Philosophy?*, where Heidegger discusses how listening (*hören*) to a Greek word "with a Greek ear" enables one to follow (*folgen*) its speaking (*legein*), which is its direct presentation: "Through the audible Greek word we are directly in the presence of the thing itself, not first in the presence of a mere word sign" (GA 11: 9/ WP 45). Following is closely related to corresponding, since in listening we stay with the speaking of the word. In this text Heidegger also says that *homologein*, where humans speak the way the Logos speaks, is therefore in correspondence (*entsprechen*) with the Logos (GA 11: 14/ WP 47). He claims that the answer to the question "What is philosophy?" is "the cor-respondence [*Entsprechung*] which responds [*entspricht*] to the being of beings. . . . Everything first depends upon our attaining a cor-respondence before we set up a theory about it" (GA 11: 19/ WP 69)

Thus the source of philosophical thought is the direct relation with the *Sache selbst*. But the question arises, how are we to attain such a correspondence? He now makes the key point that the manner in which we intentionally enter into such relation is contingent upon the effort of *Achtsamkeit:*

> To be sure, although we do remain always and everywhere in correspondence to the being of beings, we, nevertheless, rarely pay attention [*achten*] to the appeal of being. The correspondence to the being of beings, does, to be sure, always remain our abode. But only at times does it become an unfolding attitude specifically adopted by us. Only when this happens do we really [*eigentlich*] correspond to that which concerns philosophy which is on the way towards the being of beings. Philosophy is the correspondence to the being of beings, but not until, and only when, the correspondence is actually fulfilled [*vollzieht*] and thereby unfolds itself and expands this unfoldment. (GA 11: 20–21/ WP 73–75, tm)

Heidegger goes on to discuss how disposition (attunement) is determined in correspondence: "It is rather solely a question of pointing out that every precision of language is grounded in a disposition of correspondence, of correspondence, I say [*sage ich*], in heeding [*Achten*] the appeal" (GA 11: 21–22/ WP 79). Thus we see again the intimate relation between correspondence and *Achtsamkeit*, in that attention is essential for the responsiveness which in turn enables the various dispositions. Heidegger focuses on astonishment for the early Greeks, which he says is a "disposition in which and for which the being of beings unfolds. Astonishment is the tuning within which the Greek philosophers were granted the correspondence to the being of beings"

(23/85). Thus, attentiveness enables dispositions that correspond to being, thereby enabling a proper relation to and participation in being that is essential for philosophical activity. He concludes that philosophy is "the expressly adopted and unfolding correspondence which corresponds to the appeal of the being of beings" (91).

It is important to note that the possibility of such higher-quality dispositions has implications far beyond that of philosophy, for our very being in the world and relation to others depends on the same sorts of dispositions. The more gathered we are by way of *Achtsamkeit*, the more well disposed and harmonious our relations with others, as I have been arguing.

BEING AS PRESENCING

I have argued that attention (human presencing) is how we participate in being as presencing (*Anwesen*), which is the key to speaking from it. It may be argued, however, that an important source for the claims put forward herein is Heidegger's interpretation of the Greeks. For instance, I have pointed to his translation of Parmenides in *What Is Called Thinking?*—"For the same: taking-heed-of [*In-die-Acht-nehmen*] is also the presencing of what is present [*Anwesen des Anwesenden*]" (GA 8: 245/241, tm)—as arguing for the essential relation between attention and being. The problem is that Heidegger is elsewhere critical of the notion of *Anwesen*, preferring *Wesen* in what may be presumed to represent his own thought on the subject, rather than what may merely be a sympathetic retrieval of the Greeks. For instance, the very same *What Is Called Thinking?* is cited by some scholars as indicating the *limitations* of thinking being in terms of *Anwesen*: "We would fall prey to an error if we wanted to believe that the being of beings signified only, and for all times, the presencing of what presences" (GA 8: 239/235, tm).

In order to better understand what Heidegger is getting at in this citation, we must consider the immediate context in which it appears, which is the eleventh lecture in part II of *What Is Called Thinking?* Heidegger says there that in translating the saying of Parmenides, we must stay within the matter itself to be able to speak from it: "Such translation [*über*setzen] is possible only if we transpose ourselves [*über*setzen] into what speaks from these words. And this transposition can succeed only by a leap, the leap of a single vision [*einzigen Blickes*] which sees [*erblickt*] what the words *eon emmenai* say, heard [*gehört*] with Greek ears" (GA 8: 236/232). Staying within the matter means that we dwell therein by way of hearing, seeing (*blicken*), or attending in general. Heidegger says that any proposition coming out of such an effort requires an ongoing return to the matter itself, which in turn enables more speaking from. What is decisive is the looking (*Hinblicken*), for the mere repetition of the statement cannot compel such a seeing: "At best, it can offer a token of what a seeing look [*Blicken*], renewed again and again, would presumably show more clearly [*deutlicher*]" (GA 8: 237/233).

Heidegger now puts forward the "questioning statement [*ein fragendes Sagen*]" that the expression *eon emmenai* (the twofold of being and beings) names the presencing of what presences (*Anwesen des Anwesenden*). The statement cannot be taken as a settled matter that holds for all epochs, for we must always stay with the matter itself, listening and speaking from that staying-with. But at the same time, he goes on to argue vigorously for how the statement applies *to us*, in our historical situation. For while the notion of being seems quite vague, "The word 'present [*anwesen*]' speaks at once more clearly: something present [*Anwesendes*], that is, present to us [*uns Gegenwärtiges*]. Presencing and presence [*Anwesen und Anwesenheit*] means: what is with us [*Gegenwart*]. And that means: to endure in the encounter [*Entgegenweilen*]" (GA 8:237/233–34, tm). Heidegger is highlighting the fact that we are talking about something presenting itself to us, being made manifest to us. He says that if the being-here of what is present did not prevail (*walten*), beings could not appear as objects, and Kant would not have been able to write *The Critique of Pure Reason*. Likewise, the functioning of modern technology also depends on that being (GA 8: 238/234), and he concludes that "It may thus be of some importance whether we hear [*hören*] what the decisive rubric of Western-European thinking, *eon*, says—or whether we fail to hear it" (GA 8: 238/234–35), since it determines our relation to the nature of technology. He continues:

> The first service one can render is to give thought to the being of beings, and that is first of all to pay it heed [*in die Acht nimmt*]. A remote preparation therefore is the attempt to give heed [*achten*], in questioning, to what the word *eon* says. The word says: the presencing of what is present [*Anwesen des Anwesenden*]. What it says speaks in our speech long before thinking gives attention [*beachtet*] and a name of its own to it. (GA 8: 238–39/235, tm)

The Greek word for being, *eon*, says presencing, which continues to speak *in our speech* long before we think and name it.[19] Such thinking takes long preparation, which in this case consists of disciplined attention to the essential matter that addresses us.[20] When we do so, it is brought to words in a historical context that consists of what has already been made manifest and expressed in the language.

It is at this point in the lecture that we come to the statement cited above, which begins with Heidegger saying that Greek thinking arises in a context where being already reigns as presencing, which is why the Greeks are called to attend (*in-die-Acht-nehmen*) the *Anwesen des Anwesenden*.[21] Even under these circumstances, however, there is no guarantee that the unspoken will be brought into words "with all possible clarity [*Klarheit*] and in every possible respect," which points to the above stated requirement that such clarity requires the continued renewal of a seeing look (*Blicken*). Moreover, there is no guarantee that the expression of the thought will elicit "That [*Jenes*]" which constitutes it, and therefore that being means, for all time, the presencing of what is present. This again hearkens back to the thought that mere repetition of any such statement cannot compel the associated seeing—a seeing that is required to call forth the matter itself, from which all such statements ultimately speak. There is no guarantee that in all possible epochs the matter will address us in this manner and that we will be able to speak from it in this way. But the fact is that being as presencing matters very much *to us*, in the flesh, as it were, as Heidegger continues to argue. "Of course, the essential nature of presencing [*das Wesen des Anwesen*] alone gives us enough to think about. And even this—what the presencing of that which is present [*Anwesen des Anwesenden*] might mean in its Greek sense has not been adequately traced in our inquiry" (GA 8: 239/235–36, tm).

In order to trace that meaning, Heidegger notes that the Old High German *wesan* means enduring staying (*bleibendes Weilen*), and he asks why we translate the Greek *einai* and *eon* as being present (*an-wesen*), where "the German preposition '*an*' means originally '*auf*' and '*in*' at the same time" (GA 8: 240/ untranslated). This leads to a major theme, thinking the hyphenated *an-wesen* in the context of the reciprocal relation between thinking and being, where the latter comes toward us and concerns us (*angehen*) in its essential unfolding, and thus presences (*an-wesen*) in relation to us.[22] Heidegger discusses this earlier, in the third lecture in part II, when he considers the relation between memory, thanking, and thinking:

> "Memory" . . . designates the whole disposition [*Gemüt*] in the sense of a steadfast intimate concentration [*steten innigen Versammlung*] upon the things that essentially speak to us [*wesenhaft zuspricht*] in every thoughtful meditation. Originally, "memory" means as much as devotion [*An-dacht*]: a constant concentrated staying with something [*das unablässige, gesammelte Bleiben bei*]—not just with something that has passed, but in the same way with what is present and with what may come. What is past, present, and to come appears in the oneness of its own essencing *toward* [An-*wesen*]. (GA 8: 144/140, tm)

We see a broader notion of presencing here that includes past, present, and future, together with a gathering of oneself in relation to that which addresses us in this manner, a devotion (*An-dacht*), a constant concentrated abiding. We are thus approached by what makes itself manifest, and memory here means gathering oneself in a way that suggests the steadfast presencing of *In-die-Acht-nehmen* that is so important in this text.

Heidegger discusses further that which touches and concerns us, in a graphic depiction of the relation between mortals and being:

> The *thanc*, the heart's core, is the gathering of all that concerns [*angeht*] us, all that we care for [*anlangt*], all that touches [*liegt*] us insofar as we are, as human beings. What touches us in the sense that it defines and determines our nature, what we care for, we might call abutment [*Anliegen*]. Residents [*Anlieger*] are those whose properties [*Anwesen*] lie [*liegt*] on a road or on a river. We use "abutment [*Anliegen*]" in the sense of "presence [*An-wesen*]". . . . The thing that touches us [*anliegt*] . . . is gathered *toward* us beforehand [*im voraus* auf *uns* zu *versammelt*]. In a certain manner, though not exclusively, *we ourselves are that gathering*. (GA 8: 149–50/144, tm, em)

The presencing of being is a matter of the utmost concern to us in that it determines our very nature. Thus we see the intimate relation between the gathering and reaching out of being and our own coming into presence, which resonates with the discussion above of the laying (*Liegen*) of *legein* and its relation to *noein* as attention. The focus is on the heart of the relation between mortals and being. There is nothing closer, for this is the near (*Nähe*; GA 79: 77/73), where we always already dwell. It is simply a matter of gathering ourselves in that dwelling place and letting being show itself there.

To argue further that this represents the mature thought of Heidegger, I now discuss the 1962 "Time and Being" (GA 14).[23] The essay begins with a discussion of the necessity of listening, and provides a "hint [*Wink*]" on how to do so: "The point is not to listen to a series of propositions, but rather to follow the movement of showing [*zeigen*]" (GA 14: 5–6/ TB 2). Thus, staying with the movement of what shows itself is essential, rather than being restricted to propositions that ultimately arise out of what is made manifest in this manner.

In this text Heidegger highlights the indeterminacy of the notion of being, which is consistent with Capobianco's position that the many names for being refer to different aspects or dimensions that show themselves: "Being itself: the unifying one and only, temporal-spatial *emerging or appropriating of beings into presence*—but also the giving, granting, freeing, letting of beings—as long as we understand by 'letting' this 'enabling' (*Ermöchlichung*) and 'empowering' (*Ermächtigung*) movement into (and out of) presence" (2014, 25).[24] And Heidegger provides textual support here:

> We can also note historically the abundance of transformations of presencing [*Anwesen*] by pointing out that presencing shows itself as the *hen*, the unifying unique One, as the *logos*, the gathering that preserves the All, as *idea, ousia,*

energeia, substantia, actualitas, perceptio, monad, as objectivity, as the being
posited of self-positing in the sense of the will of reason, of love, of the spirit, of
power, as the will to will in the eternal recurrence of the same. (GA 14: 11/ TB 7)

Notice that Heidegger discusses how *presencing* shows itself in an abundance
of transformations, which means that it is common to all of them. And as
noted above in the discussion of *What Is Called Thinking?*, he says here that
we cannot help but think being in terms of *Anwesen*: "An attempt to think
upon the abundance of being's transformations secures its first foothold—
which also shows the way—when we think being in the sense of presencing
[*Anwesen*]. (I mean think, not just parrot the words and act as if the interpretation of Being as presencing were a matter of course.)" (GA 14: 10/ TB
6). Thus presencing is *the first foothold on the way to being*, which must be
returned to again and again. For being shows itself when it approaches by
way of presencing, in which we come into presence ourselves, as Heidegger
argues further:

What is present concerns us [*geht uns an*], the present, that is: what, lasting,
comes toward us [*entgegenweilen*], as human beings. . . . man, who is concerned with and approached by presence [*der von Anwesenheit Angegangene*],
who, through being thus approached, is himself present [*Anwesende*] in his own
way for all present and absent beings [*zu allem An-und Abwesenden*]. (GA 14:
16/ TB 12).[25]

Thus we see again that human beings are made manifest in their own way
through being approached in this manner.[26]

Heidegger goes on to offer an enhanced notion of presencing that plays
a large role in the relation between thinking and being, time and being,
and being and appropriation. Presencing is considered to be a reaching
(*erreichend*), an extending (*reichend*) that approaches humanity, and it is
further assumed that being is presencing; time is the manifold presencing of
past, present, and future (all of which concern and approach human beings);
and appropriation (*Ereignis*) determines both being and time in their belonging together (GA 14: 24/ TB 19). However, he cannot conclude that being is
a species of appropriation or vice versa, because these would be metaphysical statements that quickly run into difficulties (GA 14: 26–27/ TB 21–22).
The task is rather to stay with our own movement in correspondence with the
sendings of being. Only then can we speak from what appeals to us as we
follow this path, just as Heidegger claims to do, and only then can we verify
the truth of which he speaks. We must stay within these thought paths to be
able to speak from them, for they are otherwise ungrounded, meaningless
statements. This is why the Capobianco position seems quite reasonable, that

various dimensions of the matter present themselves to be thought, dimensions that are made manifest when we are able to take heed of them.[27]

Heidegger speaks of other features of appropriation, such as withdrawal and, most importantly for our purposes, the relation between human being and appropriation/being. Thus the question of being does not end with appropriation, but rather circles back to the relation between the human being and being, where being shows itself in the human being who comes into presence by way of extraordinary attentiveness. We always come back to being as presencing, the first foothold, how we come into being ourselves, thereby enabling the speaking from being itself. All we have is what speaks when we are addressed by the *An-wesen* of being. We must listen deeply and speak from what emerges in that listening.

> We always say *too little* of "being itself" when, in saying "being," we omit its essential presencing [*An-wesen*] *in the direction of* the human essence and thereby fail to see that this essence itself is part of "being." . . . Presencing ("being") is, as presencing, on each and every occasion a presencing directed toward the human essence, insofar as presencing is a call [*Geheiß*] that on each occasion calls upon the human essence. The human essence as such is a hearing [*hörend*], because the essence of human beings belongs [*gehört*] to the calling of this call, to the approach of presencing [*ins An-wesen*]. (GA 9: 407–408/ PM 308)

Attention is human presencing, the essencing of the human being, which is always already oriented to the presencing of being. But extraordinary attentiveness is called for in the present circumstances, for "the essence of technology cannot be led to a transformation (*Wandel*) of its destiny without the assistance of the human essence" (GA 79: 69/65), which in turn requires that the human essence become attentive (*achtsam*) to the essence of technology (GA 79: 70/66). The implication is that for all the focus on Heidegger's failings as a human being, his philosophy provides one of the more uplifting visions of what it is to be human, in that the very attention that quietly operates at our core is the way to participate in the transformation of our relation to being itself. Perhaps this is why Heidegger concludes "Moira" as follows: "The dialogue with Parmenides never comes to an end . . . because what is said there continually deserves more thought. This unending dialogue is no failing. It is a sign of the boundlessness which, in and for remembrance, nourishes the possibility of a transformation [*Verwandlung*] of destiny" (GA 7: 260–61/ EGT 100–101).[28]

CONCLUDING REMARKS

I have shown that for Heidegger, the human being is subject to the appeal of being, which can enable a more profound relation and higher attunement to the gathering of all that is made manifest. This supports the claim that active attention enables a more harmonious deployment of resources and an ontological bonding to speak truth to power. I have argued that attention has this power because it participates in being, in the manifestation of all that is. But the question may arise as to the feasibility of such harmonious states of affairs, given the historical state of the world. What is the nature of being that would enable it? After all, could it not be just an impersonal process that has nothing to do with a higher potential for humanity? We see no evidence of such possibilities in the natural world, as living things simply go through determined life cycles. Why would that not be the case for humanity?

I can only sketch a response here. One is that humanity is of a higher order, where the imperative is that we grow as human beings, which is different than the flowering of trees, for instance, in that it depends on us to make appropriate, conscious efforts. But the real question is, what is it about the appeal of being that would make our noncompliance with it show up in the lack that we feel at our core, an attunement in which we feel something is missing in our lives? And if being is merely impersonal, how do we have the capacity to gather our attention as we do in the practice of mindfulness? Is it just an evolutionary outcome? I would argue that this position would be an instance of the predominant metaphysics that rules out any intrinsic meaning for the human being. Heidegger himself argues vehemently against it when he says that we belong to being, in that we participate in its presencing. So what does that mean? How does participating in the manifestation of all that is translate into actual possibilities for humanity?

We have seen that we can be more or less present and gathered, which is the basis for the harmonization that can come about by way of mindfulness. I have argued for our fundamental passivity and for the gathering of active attention that enables an opening to that which exceeds us. We have seen that for Heidegger that opening is our most fundamental task, and that any creative potential and harmonization of the human being issues forth from the relation to being that is thereby enabled.

I have pointed to the importance of emotion in the deployment of attention and shown that for Heidegger our fundamental attunements correspond to our relation to being. What this says is that the question of ultimate context matters to us, which shows up in those attunements. That is, as intelligent beings we wonder about our place in the cosmos, and the question of ultimate meaning is always present in how we are disposed in the course of worldly activity. The question then becomes, how is it that we exist? What does our presence say about the ultimate context? That is, we must stand in wonder not only regarding the presence of all that is, but regarding our very existence as miraculous creatures who inquire into the question of our presence in a cosmos itself. So how is it that we exist in the face of such fundamental passivity and openness to that which exceeds us? What is the nature of being that it has the power to affect us in this way?

This leads to an important theme in Heidegger's work, which is that of the holy, or divine dimension. The thought is that the appeal of being calls for ontological effort, the impulse for which ultimately issues from the divine. I have been arguing that this effort is best rendered as an acute and sustained attentiveness, a *staying-with*, a readiness, waiting, watchfulness, or mindfulness (*Achtsamkeit*). This puts Heidegger squarely within the contemplative traditions, both East and West, where such practices have been in place for thousands of years. But he does not approach it in a traditional manner, instead looking at it phenomenologically and inquiring into the conditions under which the divine may be made manifest. Rather than positing features of the divine in the abstract, the approach is to speak from the manifestation, whether it shows itself as present or absent. He finds that we are called on to prepare a concrete site for divine manifestation, and that such an event can show itself in great works of art, and in our very presence in the world (see Berger 2022). He comes to the astonishing idea of (what I refer to as) world resacralization, which means that the glory of the divine can reappear in the life of the people if they work to preserve its manifestation in the things of this world, in which they themselves are included. This means that we can aspire for our lives themselves to be works of art that manifest the divine presence, as long as we persist in the effort to stay acutely present.

We are left with the mystery of our own existence. But ultimately there is no doubt that we have the power of attention, which enables us to inquire into these matters, as long as we are acutely present as we stay with this, our own ontological movement. We can engage in this practice and simply stay open to what may show itself in ourselves and others. For instance, I have been arguing that mindfulness offers the possibility to harmonize the manifestation and action of individuals and communities. I would like to tell of a personal experience which illustrates the effect of such efforts on musical harmony.

The Magic Baton

I am an amateur singer, and I participate in some chorales with very fine conductors. One, Eric Dale Knapp, is particularly accomplished. When preparing for concerts he often tells singers to pay attention to his baton, because "that is where the magic happens," for when they are able to focus on the baton, they sing in unison. That is the power of attention, for when singers pay attention to how the conductor guides them, the efforts of what would otherwise be disjointed individuals become one. That is how the magic happens, for when they are unified in this manner something new and fresh is born. For Knapp this is not theoretical, because he speaks from years of experience and can tell when the magic is there and when it is not. It depends on whether his singers are harmonized by way of jointly attending to the baton.

Attending to the baton transforms the singers from isolated individuals into a group that is more harmonized. They are made whole as all of their musicality is marshaled in the act of singing, and they become more than they could be in the absence of such an effort. The group is also transformed, for it now consists of transformed individuals who are united under the guidance of the conductor, and magic happens at the level of the entire company. Their unique talents and backgrounds merge into a single, harmonized group that is unified by way of the vision that the conductor seeks to impart. That vision is far more than what appears on the printed page, for the wisdom the conductor brings to the creative process is imparted by way of the gestures and guidance that he offers, all of which show themselves during the performance as centered on the baton.

The conductor is the gateway to the audience. He hears what the singers are as a whole, and his vision and effort form the vehicle by way of which their musicality is expressed. It is essential to understand that the audience is aware of the extent to which they are unified—the extent to which they are one musical group that is integrated by way of the baton. The audience knows the difference, even if they are not explicitly aware of it and even if they have little or no musical background. When the magic happens, the audience feels it and responds, even if they don't know why, and they walk away enriched when the group is unified in this manner. That is why it is crucial for the singers to pay attention to the conductor's gestures throughout the performance, for in this way musical works are produced that enrich the communities in which they live.

This is their duty to the community, and to the world of music at large, to enhance the art that is given to them. By working in this manner they enable the conductor to impart his vision, and as that develops, he sees more that is possible given the talents at hand. For they all bring unique gifts to the process that can be sensed as the conductor sees what sort of work is being produced. This enables his appreciation of the work, and vision for what can be achieved, to develop in the course of rehearsal. So it is the singers' duty to themselves, the conductor, the audience, and the art of music itself to get command of the music so they can attend to the baton and produce works that are original to them, which may then be recognized as gifts to the world.

Similarly, we need some magic in our politics. My proposal is that the power of harmonized voices can change the course of history. That is the promise of mindfulness.

Notes

INTRODUCTION

1. The argument is not that attention is unitary in an ontic sense. It can be dispersed and distracted, in which case it is not unitary, but there is the possibility of ontological effort where we gather ourselves as a whole, in which case it is a unifying phenomenon. This is the characteristic of attention that, in my view, cognitive science (except perhaps for the mindfulness literature) does not recognize because of its metaphysical commitments.

2. The notion of active attention is drawn in part from Heidegger's early notion of authenticity and the later *Inständigkeit* (steadfastness) and *Achtsamkeit* (mindfulness). I conceive of mindfulness as necessarily involving acute and sustained attentiveness, which is the litmus test in determining how fully engaged one is in the process, rendering it thereby an ontological effort of the whole human being.

3. The phenomenon of attention appears in philosophical discourse as early as Aristotle, who associates it with selectivity and clarity, and it is also quite prominent in René Descartes. In "Rules for the Direction of the Mind" Descartes ([1701] 1985) observes (Rule 9): "If one tries to look at many objects at one glance, one sees none of them distinctly. Likewise, if one is inclined to attend to many things at the same time in a single act of thought, one does so with a confused mind. Yet craftsmen who engage in delicate operations, and are used to fixing their eyes on a single point, acquire through practice the ability to make perfect distinctions between things, however minute and delicate. The same is true of those who never let their thinking be distracted by many different objects at the same time, but always devote their whole attention to the simplest and easiest of matters: they become perspicacious" (33). For Descartes, of course, clarity and distinctness are the hallmarks of knowledge. The implicit assumption is that attention enables access to the most fundamental entities: In Rule 6 we are to "attend to what is most simple in each series of things" (21), and in Rule 8 we are to stop if "we come across something which our intellect is unable to intuit sufficiently well" (28). Similarly, in Rule 12 we are to intuit each simple nature separately "with steadfast mental gaze" (48). "[E]ach of us, according to the light of his own mind, must attentively intuit only those things which are distinguished from

all others" (49). See Hatfield (1998) for a discussion of the premodern treatment of attention and Crary (2001) for the modern period.

4. Attention also appears in the form of circumspection (*Umsicht*) in §32. The circle also appears in Taylor's (2016) discussion of Johann Gottfried Herder's work on the origin of language, where the space of reflection in which things are named is explicitly thought in terms of attention, and there is a sense of rightness in such naming that is thought in terms of bodily understanding (or resonance). It is interesting that Heidegger (GA 85) first explicitly considers attention (in the form of *Aufmerksamkeit*) in his own lecture course on Herder in 1939. I draw on Taylor's work in chapter 2 on the hermeneutical circle.

5. See Marino (2019) for an inspiring essay on the importance of attention (in the form of listening) in the course of daily life.

6. Cited in Arvidson (2006).

7. The relation between attention and presence sheds light on the findings in cognitive science that attention is essential for memory, for one must be present to be able to remember that one was there, together with the details of the experience, such as how one was occupied. The relation between attention, volition, and control also becomes clearer when it is recognized that one must be present, one must *stay with* relevant activities to be "in control" and pursue an intention.

8. The notions of full and active attention can be thought of as regulative ideals that cannot be indefinitely sustained by finite creatures such as ourselves. While full attention can be produced by the demands of a situation, active attention, on the other hand, is an effort to be present simply for its own sake. See chapter 8 on the intrinsic value of mindfulness.

9. James calls this "active or voluntary attention" and says, "We get it whenever we *resist the attractions* of more potent stimuli and keep our mind occupied with some object that is naturally unimpressive . . . or resolutely hold fast to a thought so discordant with our impulses that, if left unaided, would quickly yield place to images of an exciting and impassioned kind" ([1890] 1983, 397). Recognizing the difficulty of such an effort, James says it cannot be sustained for more than a few seconds at a time, after which there is an inevitable turn to activities with more intrinsic interest. The notion of active attention is essential in this book for the construction of the argument and verification of its key assumptions, and, I argue, for the practice of phenomenology in general.

10. I consider Heidegger's position with regard to this question more fully in chapter 9.

11. As James puts it in *Talks to Teachers*, "Our acts of voluntary attention, brief and fitful as they are, are nevertheless momentous and critical, determining us, as they do, to higher or lower destinies" ([1899] 1981, 127).

12. "The world of the waking is one and common, but the sleeping turn aside each into their private world" (Heraclitus, DK B89).

13. See also Thompson's (2015) related notion of selves that come to the fore in this manner.

14. See also Montemayor and Haladjian (2015), North (2012), Prinz (2012), and Dallmayr (2014) for other recent works on the philosophy of attention.

15. See also Mole (2017) on spotlight theories in particular and for a broad review of the attention literature.

16. See also Romdenh-Romluc (2013) for the relation between attention and agency.

17. Mindfulness is often defined as paying attention to the present moment. It is the focus of considerable scholarly interest today, as in Brown and Ryan (2003), Chiesa, Calati and Serretti (2011), Felder et al. (2014), Kee and Wang (2008), Keng, Smoski, Robins (2011), and Schmalzl et al. (2018). See also Casey (2007), Depraz (2014), and Thompson (2015). For a discussion of its roots in spiritual disciplines see Kabat-Zinn (1994).

18. We also see the relation between engagement and presence in Ganeri: "Engagement is the world's pressing itself upon the mind, having an impact, bringing the mind . . . 'into touch' with the world, being open and in a condition of ongoing sensitive contact. Presence, a basic form of engagement, is enabled by any of the five sense modalities, and is already minded: not a *mere* bodily state or motor instruction, it refers to the minded condition of being *in touch* with the world that a body's presence in the world sustains" (2017, 68).

19. As he puts it, "consciously attending to something in part consists in consciously experiencing what is unattended in characteristic peripheral ways" (Watzl 2011, 155). For Watzl, an essential part of what it is to attend to something is that the experience is at the center of consciousness. He provides examples involving visual, auditory, and interoceptive modes of engagement. For instance, on a subway the structure varies according to whether one looks at a newspaper or a fellow passenger. If one focuses on one the other is peripheral. When listening to a jazz band, the experience varies according to whether one focuses on the saxophone or the piano.

20. See also Arvidson (2006), who discusses Husserl and Gurwitsch in this regard.

21. See also McGilchrist (2019) on attention as an ontological phenomenon.

22. Chapter 9 draws on Berger (2016, 2020, and 2022).

CHAPTER 1

1. The definition of the physical is considered in chapter 3.

2. Nagel admits the possibility of a more radical approach when he says, "I am certain that my own attempt to explore alternatives is far too unimaginative. An understanding of the universe as basically prone to generate life and mind will probably require a much more radical departure from the familiar forms of naturalistic explanation that I am at present able to conceive" (2012, 127).

3. In a discussion of first-person phenomenological methods, Thompson says, "The relevance of these practices to neurophenomenology derives from the capacity for sustained attentiveness to experience they systematically cultivate. This capacity enables tacit and prereflective aspects of experience, which typically are either inaccessible or reconstructed after the fact according to various biases, to become subjectively accessible and describable in more accurate ways" (2007, 339).

4. See Reddy (2011) for a discussion of the experience of attention within the context of early child development.

5. Clarity of intuition is also a theme that is associated with attention and apodicticity in Descartes: "[I]ntuition is the indubitable conception of a clear and attentive mind which proceeds solely from the light of reason" (Descartes [1701] 1985, 14).

6. There are a variety of ways to demarcate this field; Gurwitsch (1964), for example, distinguishes between theme (focal center), context (periphery of objects relevant to the theme), and margin (ultimate horizon). See also Watzl (2017) and Arvidson (2006) on how attention structures experience as foreground and background.

7. Attention enables distancing from immersion in the immediate and the production of phenomenological descriptions of experience. It is little wonder that it is quite prominent in discussions of the implementation of phenomenological method, which can be seen, for instance, in Steinbock's discussion of "phenomenological reflective attentiveness" (2004, 39–40). As Vermersch puts it, "attention is the primary instrument of the phenomenological exploration of lived experience" (2004, 78, n.7). Depraz also says, "Attentional activity is another name, far more concrete, of the real *praxis* of intentionality, the reduction, and genetic constitution" (2004, 7). Attention is also quite prominent in Ihde's (1986) *Experimental Phenomenology*, where he aims to show how phenomenology is actually done. We can see an example in Gallagher's discussion of the phenomenology of proprioception:

> But let's consider the phenomenology more closely. When I shift my attention away from the book to my fingers, then that very act of attention brings my body into an objective presence, as something perceptually identifiable. This works equally well for visual or proprioceptive attention. In the latter case, however, this shift of attention, would generate an involuted, proprioceptive awareness of my fingers that originally plays no part in the perception of the book. Indeed, it interrupts that perception. When my attention is shifted toward my body, I do in fact identify my body as the object of my perception as, for example, I attend to the relative spatial position of my fingers. But when my attention is directed at the book, my awareness of my body is precisely not an *identifying* awareness of it *as an object*, that is, it is not a perceptual awareness. As I keep track of the book, I do not have to keep track of my hands. (2003, 57)

How could such an analysis come about except by way of attending in the manners that are described?

8. This passage occurs in a section on the "natural attitude," before the move to the phenomenological attitude, but it nevertheless speaks to the freedom of movement of attention that holds under all assumptions.

9. I know of little work that connects the phenomenon of attention with the notion of extended mind. There is the statement of Rowlands (2010, 76), that if Heidegger's notion of "being-in-the-world" is taken seriously, the extended mind thesis follows immediately, and Berger (2016, 2020) relates attention to being-in-the-world. Heidegger is also cited in Clark's (1997) *Being There*. Perhaps this indicates the extent to which attention is taken for granted in philosophical discourse, which further

argues for its importance. Although Gallagher has written on joint attention in early childhood development (e.g., Gallagher and Hutto 2008), to my knowledge he has not written on the relation between attention and the extended mind. In the following examples of the extended phenomenon, I employ attention where it is appropriate, assuming that it is equivalent to operative intentionality that is thematic.

10. See Gallagher (1986) for a discussion of the notion of incorporation in Merleau-Ponty.

11. Although Fuchs and De Jaegher (2009) do not explicitly mention attention in these examples, it figures quite prominently in their article in a manner similar to its employment herein, especially when they discuss "mutual incorporation." The relation between incorporation and attention is clear when they say, "If you remain focused on the side you are standing on or only have eyes for the gap, you fall in" (473), and the relation between incorporation and the center of attention is evident in the case of fascination: "The object or person by whom we are fascinated becomes the external source of the vectors or field forces that command our body. In other words, the center of the 'operative intentionality' of our body shifts towards that of the other" (474).

12. As discussed above, consciousness can be viewed as a broader notion than attention, where the latter is the foreground for consciousness, and the former includes the background. When attention is entirely diffuse, however, cases where consciousness can be said to exist without such a central tendency cannot be ruled out.

13. This argument is augmented below in the section entitled "The Subject of Pain" to respond to more sophisticated versions of representationalism.

14. Or vital area, in Merleau-Ponty.

15. This will become the public space that is so important in political realities, as discussed in chapter 8. It is true that such an intermodal space can be peripheral when, for instance, I am immersed in thought, but the quality of such coordination will be reduced depending on how removed it is from the center.

16. Introspection will tend to be more "glance-like" rather than acute and sustained, as required in active attention (or phenomenological reflection). The question of indubitability and attention is addressed further in chapter 4, and the relation between introspection and phenomenological reflection is considered in chapter 5.

17. I treat "subjectivity" and "selfhood" synonymously over the course of the text.

18. See Schwitzgebel (2007) for a discussion of the relation between attention and the experience of one's feet.

19. Crane goes on: "A full account of this phenomenon needs to probe more deeply into the relationship between the experience of one's body in sensation, in kinaesthesia and proprioception, and the awareness of one's body as a unique and unified object of one's bodily awareness. The account would also need to link bodily awareness with one's sense of one's body in agency. I do not give such an account in this essay; but I note here the need for further investigation" (136). I aim to contribute to such an account in this discussion.

20. This is consistent with Leibniz's treatment of apperception, which term he coined: "When we are not alerted, so to speak, to pay heed to certain of our own present perceptions, we allow them to slip by unconsidered and even unnoticed. But if

someone alerts us to them straight away, and makes us take note, for instance, of some noise which we have just heard, then we remember it and are aware of [apperceive] just having had some sense of it" ([1765] 1996, 54).

21. Watzl (2011) discusses the case where one has a pain when listening to a jazz band, so the choice is between auditory and interoceptive modalities. For instance, one could focus on the pain and the band would be in the background. There is a structure to the experience that depends on how attention is deployed, where one is centered.

22. See Bitbol (2018) on panpsychism, where it is assumed that the physical is given as independent and then infused with consciousness to explain how the mind fits in.

23. As mentioned in the introduction, Depraz, Varela, and Vermersch (2003) call for staying with the movement of attention without being absorbed in the content that arises, which itself can only occur by way of acute and sustained attentiveness. Thus active attention can transcend the content that Crane takes to be the sole relation to the subject.

CHAPTER 2

1. As we shall see in chapter 3, this puts significant limits on the sorts of claims that can be made regarding the status of categories such as the mental and the physical.

2. The modalities are constituted in the course of engagement, and any future engagement is approached on the basis of the historically constituted modes of engagement and the understanding that is made manifest in them. Attention enables access by way of the specific modalities, which results in a revised understanding of the situation that leads to the further deployment of attention.

3. See Hatab (2017, 2019) on indicative concepts.

4. A bibliography as of 2007 is available at http://www.focusing.org/gendlin/gol _primary_bibliography.htm.

5. The Focusing Institute, http://www.focusing.org.

6. Gendlin says, "Humans have the capacity to perceive patterns not as things but *just as patterns.* . . . Animal perception is only 'of' objects. The human perception *of* separable patterns *of* objects involves a doubled 'of,' an essentially human development" (2009, 343).

7. Gendlin is best known for this notion of the felt sense. See Kleinberg-Levin (2007) for a collection of essays on Gendlin's work in which the felt sense is an important theme.

8. It may be argued that all of this knowledge resides in representations in the brain, but it can be verified phenomenologically that implicit knowledge is accessible by way of attention, and Hendricks (2009) shows that the capacity for such access is measurable. The bodily sentience is always there, and one can attend to it directly producing a felt sense of the situation. This is contrary to Dreyfus (2005), who assumes that the body is always in the background, which functioning is disrupted when attended to.

9. This is consistent with the thought of Allport (2011), mentioned in the introduction, where attention is the outcome of the whole body process.

10. The active/passive attention distinction should not be conceived as bimodal, although there will be more bodily self-awareness when attention is active.

11. E.g., MacLean et al. (2009).

12. Schatzki says that "Dreyfus nowhere, curiously, addresses the role of perceptual *attention* in nondeliberate action" (2000, 38).

13. This is reminiscent of Mole's (2011) definition of attention as the full devotion of available resources to the task, as discussed in the introduction.

14. The gathering of the runner and the tension in which he is held in readiness (or the lack thereof) characterizes the being of the runner. This is a being gathered up into standing still, an "ingathering" that gathers the runner in his being. He is thus disposed to the upcoming activity, as his whole being is oriented to the task—that is how he is made manifest, how he comes into presence. Attention is what *holds the runner in readiness* in this manner, in his orientation toward worldly engagement, and as such it is the basis for the organization of his being in the world. The rest and repose that holds these orientations comes about by way of attention; it is the stabilizing force that is the basis for how he is made manifest in the present circumstance. The theme of holding (*Halten*) in Heidegger is considered further in chapter 9 below.

15. The efficacy of this technique has been well documented (e.g., Hendricks 2009).

16. This dialectic can be seen in Fuchs and DeJaegher, who argue that the generation of language and "participatory sense-making" takes place at the center of gravity of mutual interaction. They write:

> When two individuals interact in this way, the coordination of their body movements, utterances, gestures, gazes, etc. can gain such momentum that it overrides the individual intentions, and common sense-making emerges. This process has been described at the systems level as the social interaction gaining an autonomy of its own (De Jaegher and Di Paolo 2007). Phenomenologically speaking, this may be experienced as the process gaining its own "centre of gravity": The "in-between" becomes the source of the operative intentionality of both partners. (2009, 476)

17. Gendlin (2017b, chap. 6) discusses how patterns, situations, and bodies are inherently linked. For instance, new language symbols develop to manage a new distinction between situations. Our bodies produce language directly from being in situations, which results in large shifts in how the body feels the situation. For Gendlin, we feel the situation and how we are changing it. In this manner, language develops and differentiates situations and the distinctly human world.

18. Taylor (2016) argues that rightness is assumed by figures such as Condillac, enabled as it is by a background understanding which is built into each linguistic sign.

19. Rouse (2013) says that "we should think of conceptual understanding as itself involving practical-perceptual skills in ways that build upon Dreyfus's account"

(255). He considers our ability to speak as such an example, which poses a problem for Dreyfus's insistence on the nonconceptual nature of such skills.

20. For more on the relation between body and language, see the journal *Biosemiotics*, Cowley et al. (2010), and De Jesus (2016), and also the emerging field of ecolinguistics (Li, Steffensen, and Huang, 2020).

21. Language and understanding in their conjunction are brought to bear in activity at the center of attention. The understanding of language that is brought to bear is the power to arrange words in phrases that fit the situation based on the deliverances of attention.

22. As discussed by Fuchs and DeJaegher (2009, 478), "Six- to eight-week olds already engage in these conversations with their mothers by smiling and vocalising. The dyad exhibits a finely tuned coordination of movements, rhythmic synchrony and mirroring of affective expressions that has often been compared to a couple dance (Gopnik and Meltzoff 1997, 131). Infant and caregiver also follow a turn-taking pattern, shifting the roles of agent and recipient in a non-random sequence (Jasnow and Feldstein 1986)."

23. See Fried (2021, 2024) on the related notion of a polemical ethics.

CHAPTER 3

1. In practice, physicists often act as if they are idealists, in that elegance in mathematics is often taken to provide the ultimate comfort that the theory is going in the right direction. It is interesting that most of the mathematics applied in physics developed in the course of actual engagement in solving physical problems, which relation to worldly engagement goes a long way toward explaining why the application is so successful. The one theory that came out of pure mathematics that led to string theory has been criticized for not being falsifiable, which demonstrates the lack of integration with real-world physical phenomena.

2. See Gendlin (2017a) on the related notion of crossing in the implicit body, discussed in chapter 2.

3. Similarly, string theory hypothesizes that the position, mass, and momentum of elementary entities come about by way of excitations of underlying fields (Healey 2016, 3).

4. The classical notion of causality is also brought into question in quantum physics due to the entanglement phenomenon.

5. One way to deal with this is to define global physicalism to mean that if two ways the whole world might be agree in all physical respects, then they agree in all other respects as well, but this does not support the mechanistic view in the same way that local physicalism does.

6. It is interesting that there is a developing phenomenology in physics that considers the relation between theoretical structures and experimental results that may or may not validate them.

7. The literature on structuralism recognizes this, e.g., Schmidt (2014).

8. Similarly, planets are only what they are as existing within a law-governed cosmos.

9. See O'Shaughnessy (1995) on the movement of attention within and without the lived body. I would add that the modality does not determine which is public or private. For instance, one can listen to the sense of the body and then shift attention to an external sound, as readers can check for themselves.

10. See also Colombetti (2011) on the bodily experience of emotions in chapter 4.

11. For Descartes, the intensive dimension appears in terms of the fixing of attention, concentrating the mind, and clear and distinct intuition. His Rule 3, for instance, suggests that we "investigate what we can clearly and evidently intuit" ([1701] 1985, 13), where intuition is defined as "the indubitable conception of a clear and attentive mind" (14). Rule 5 calls for "concentrating our mind's eye" on properly ordered objects of inquiry (20), and Rule 9 says, "We must concentrate our mind's eye totally upon the most insignificant and easiest of matters, and dwell on them long enough to acquire the habit of intuiting the truth distinctly and clearly" (33).

CHAPTER 4

1. E.g., Brough (2016) and Mensch (2009).

2. By the state of attention, I mean the extent of active attention, as defined above.

3. It may also be argued that the assumption that attention is typically passive ignores the fact that we generally believe that we are in control of ourselves in the course of daily life. Cognitive science recognizes this in the notion of endogenous and exogenous attention, where the former stands for movements that arise from internal processes such as thought, and the latter means that attention responds to stimuli that arise from external sources. This fails to recognize, however, that such internal processes are themselves typically absorbed and unaware of their very movement, which is that of attention itself, for it is how the self manifests itself in a variety of modes of engagement.

4. In Heideggerian terms, this means that the clearing of being comes to the fore (see chapter 9). See also the notion of witness consciousness in eastern thought, as in Albahari (2009) and Henry and Thompson (2013).

5. I am assuming here something like the pre-reflective awareness that Zahavi (e.g., 1999) puts forward in his works.

6. Emotion is paradigmatic in this regard, in that it can be particularly powerful in orienting the self in various manners.

7. The term "emotional hijacking" is used in the literature on emotional intelligence in this regard, e.g., Goleman (2006).

8. See chapter 9 for further discussion of the metaphysics of constant presence.

9. Moreover, Steinbock (2004) says that while such reflection goes on, we must keep an eye on ongoing experience, for we are still living, experiencing beings, thereby imposing still more attentional demands on the phenomenologist. If one were to engage in reflection on a full-time basis, there would be no ongoing experience at all for one to reflect on except that of reflection itself, so one must stay in the natural

attitude, keeping "one eye on the world" in the manner of positing beliefs about the reality of the world in order to have material to reflect upon.

10. Under passive attention, the form varies according to the nature of the engagement, while under active attention it is free to vary quite widely. Husserl recognizes this variation in form in *Ideas I*: "This function of the wandering focus, expanding and contracting in range, signifies a *sui generis dimension of correlative noetic and noematic* modifications, the systematic and essential investigation of which belongs among the basic tasks of universal phenomenology" (2014, 184).

11. Husserl recognizes this changing modal configuration: "Taking place in the life of consciousness is a constant transformation of the modalities of execution; foreground lived-experiences, egoic acts, lose this form of execution and then take on the altered form and *vice versa*" (2001, 20). Given that he likens the ego-pole to object poles in Husserl (1950, §31), this would suggest that he considers the ego as the rule governed basis for deployment of the modalities, but this ignores the possibility of active attention, which is fully indeterminate.

12. Thereby supporting the thesis that attention enables the extension of the embodied modes to the general lived body-environment.

13. The predominance of habitual behavior in engaged activity is well recognized in Husserl, but I am arguing that this sort of passivity extends to many functions of the ego, such as judgment and willing, which are typically considered to be active. The key test for active attention is explicit self-awareness, which shows itself in the form of awareness of being embodied and placed in a lived body-environment.

14. The absorption also means that he is not executing any reductions, given that they require additional attention.

15. As will be discussed in chapter 9, Heidegger refers to this opening as the *clearing*, which enables things to be accessible (SZ, 133/171).

16. See Edie (1987) on the James-Husserl relation.

17. This similar to Husserlian reduction except that rather than bracketing the natural attitude by way of an intellectual and hence partial effort, active attention affects the whole human being by momentarily stilling the action of the modes and staying ready and receptive for what is to be made manifest. In this regard, Depraz says, "Attentional activity is another name, far more concrete, of the real *praxis* of intentionality, the reduction, and genetic constitution" (2004, 7).

18. It is also possible that the center of attention can be placed between the body and any encountered entities, which is considered in chapter 6.

19. Colombetti also distinguishes between the foreground and reflection. She notes that background processes are pre-reflective but argues that emotional processes that are foregrounded are also pre-reflective. Both the background and foreground can be "lived through," whereas reflection is always after the fact. It should be noted, however, that although the contents of reflection are retrospective, the event of reflection itself is lived in the foreground and can be experienced as such.

20. Zahavi (1999) gestures in this direction when he writes, in a section entitled "The ego as a principle of focus,"

Ultimately, an adequate investigation of egological consciousness would have to undertake a much more detailed taxonomy, since the precise character of the ego-involvement differs from act-type to act-type. The ego is present in voluntary acts in a different way than in involuntary acts, just as one must distinguish the egological character of experiences where I am formally present, such as attentive perceptions or recollections; experiences where I am emotionally engaged and responding with feelings of joy, indignation, or hatred; and acts for which I am responsible and of which I am the author. The ego is present in different ways when I scrutinize a menu written in French, when I am hit by a snowball, and when I decide to climb up a rock face. (148).

I am emphasizing that the presence of the ego and attention are one and the same.

21. Taylor has called for "perpetual revaluation of our most basic understandings with a stance of attention . . . and with a readiness to receive any gestalt shift in our view of the situation. . . . [I]t is to look again at our most fundamental formulations, and at what they were meant to articulate, in a stance of openness, where we are ready to accept any categorical change, however radical, which might emerge. . . . I am trying to see reality afresh and form more adequate categories to describe it. To do this I am trying to open myself, use all of my deepest, unstructured sense of things in order to come to a new clarity. . . . [I]t engages my whole self in a way that judging by a yardstick does not." (1985, 40–42).

22. The question arises as to whether the body itself can be viewed as a center of experience, but that is the case only when attention is on the sensation of the body itself. Then indeed the body rises to prominence, a prominence that depends upon the deployment of attention.

23. The paradox of how the self is able to actualize/affect itself will continue to characterize the effort. After the initial impulse, the shift in focus means that the originating activity subsides and a new configuration of the self comes to the fore—which may render the original impulse to attend ineffectual. Thus the question is how to sustain the effort under such circumstances when the initial impulse to be present in this manner is no longer there.

24. One could in principle do both, attend to the hand and doubt that one is doing so by expanding the center of attention to support both activities, but the doubt would be enacted by way of attention, and one would see that it was false.

CHAPTER 5

1. Although the chapter purports to consider the relation between attention and phenomenological reflection, it may not be obvious to the reader how attention relates to Heidegger. Zahavi nowhere cites any references to attention in Heidegger's work, and in fact since he restricts his study to the early Heidegger, such references are difficult to come by, because Heidegger does not take up the question of attention until the turn of the 1940s. Prior to that he deliberately avoids the use of the attention terms that Husserl employs (such as *Aufmerksamkeit* and *Achtsamkeit*) because of the associated ontological assumptions. But we can infer that attention is implicitly present in Heidegger's approach, and indeed there are numerous terms that substitute for

various aspects of the phenomenon during different phases of his work (see Berger 2016, 2020).

2. Zahavi goes on to say that this should not be taken too literally, for these are all parts of oneself, so we have a self-awareness that is characterized by an internal division that enables the "I: to become thematic: "Becoming a theme to oneself is a matter of becoming divided from oneself. Reflective self-awareness involves a form of alienation. It is characterized by a type of *self-fragmentation* that we do not encounter on the level of pre-reflective self-awareness" (2005, 91).

3. Chapter 16 of Ganeri (2017) posits an empirical, functioning self, or a core self that consists of those aspects that have been made more central in the course of attending. It is not "a mere collection," but is rather "those specific elements which attention centralized."

4. E.g., Zahavi (2017a, 12–15; 2011), Petitmengin, Remillieux, and Valenzuela-Moguillansky (2018), Petitmengin (2009), and Petitmengin and Bitbol (2009). Many of Petitmengin's papers in this debate have been coauthored with Bitbol.

5. Vermersch (2011), for instance, says that Husserl is "a great unrecognized psychologist" (22).

6. This is undoubtedly a reference to the Eugene Gendlin's *felt sense* (e.g., Kleinberg-Levin 1997), which Petitmengin often cites.

7. It is indeed interesting that while Zahavi says that psychology has a number of implicit metaphysical presuppositions, the problem of attention is not taken for granted in that discipline—theorists never fail to wonder, for instance, how William James could have said (famously) that "everyone knows what attention is."

8. It is no accident that Petitmengin often cites Gendlin in her articles, although she rarely explicitly discusses his relevance.

9. Now, we may understand the bottle to have certain properties beyond those that are presently perceived, but that sort of understanding presents itself in the manifestation itself. All that we understand about the bottle is present in the way it manifests itself to us in various ways over the course of time. On the hermeneutical circle view attention can be understood as a form of apperception, in which the object as presently understood comes into presence, is made manifest accordingly. But what is key here is that any such properties must have previously been made manifest in some form or other for the bottle to be understood in such a manner.

10. There are Heideggerian influences in Petitmengin's work, as evident in the work of her colleague Bitbol (e.g., Vörös and Bitbol 2017), which considers the work of Varela and its affinities with Heidegger.

CHAPTER 6

1. See the related literature on place, e.g., Casey (1997, 2009), Malpas (2018), and Benjamin (2011). Malpas in particular is strongly influenced by Heidegger. Attention does not play much of a role in this literature, but see the unpublished essay by Malpas (2022), "Presence and Human Presence."

2. The notion of gathering (*Sammlung*) is quite important in Heidegger, as discussed in chapter 9.

3. As Augustine puts it in *Confessions*, "None can deny that present time lacks any extension because it passes in a flash. Yet attention is continuous, and it is through this that what will be present progresses towards being absent" ([1660] 1998, XI. xxviii [37]).

4. We will see in chapter 7 that for Zahavi we can experience others experiencing various states, but we do not experience the state itself.

5. Zahavi also talks sometimes about the subjective feel of an experience, which resonates with the bodily intelligence or felt intuition that has been considered herein, but we have seen that it is intimately bound up with the action of attention and language within the hermeneutical circle, not a stand-alone "minimal" self.

6. That is the ground for experience and any differences there may be between us, and we have to ask if it is possible for plural attention to move somewhat in unison, indeed, to share the same space. In that case a fusion of perspectives could occur at the ground of experience itself, which would seem to be contrary to Zahavi's insistence that first-person experience is inaccessible, or that it is accessible only as the experience of another person rather than occurring within a shared ontological space which preserves any individual differences due to body, history, etc. This will be the subject of chapter 7.

7. See also the discussion in chapter 4 regarding the unrealistic demands on the attention of the phenomenologist, as stated in Steinbock (2004).

8. Husserl thinks in terms of memory as immediate retention in the constitution of the present moment.

9. We have also seen that for Bitbol and Petitmengin it is possible to experience the presence of others, which has implications for intersubjective relations, the subject of chapter 7.

10. These are events in which, in Heideggerian terms, we hold open the clearing in which entities are made manifest, as discussed in chapter 9.

11. Heidegger talks in terms of captivating (*Entrückung*) and transporting (*Berückung*) in GA 65.

12. O'Shaughnessy (1995, 175) says that proprioception is attentively recessive. It is atypical to involute attention away from ordinary objects, and to actively turn it to some body part like an arm. This is typically purely inquisitive, where the body falls out of natural obscurity into the full light of awareness.

13. See Hatab (2017, 2019) on meaning and absorption.

14. This relation is essential for the coming discussion of political fragmentation and dispersion, the subject of chapters 7 and 8.

15. In a discussion of first-person phenomenological methods, Thompson says, "The relevance of these practices to neurophenomenology derives from the capacity for sustained attentiveness to experience [that] they systematically cultivate. This capacity enables tacit and prereflective aspects of experience, which typically are either inaccessible or reconstructed after the fact according to various biases, to become subjectively accessible and describable in more accurate ways" (2007, 339).

See also Strawson, who claims that "the subject of awareness can be fully thetically aware of itself as it is in the present moment of awareness," and goes on to argue:

> It certainly seems right to say that the awareness of oneself can in this case be fully *express*, no less express than any awareness of anything is when one's awareness of it is thetic, even though there is in this case no sort of posing or positing or positioning of oneself for inspection of the sort that may seem to be built into the meaning of the word "thetic." I think, in fact, that it can also be said to be *thetic*, taking the core meaning of "thetic" to be just: genuinely in attention, and rejecting the idea that attention requires articulation or construc-tion of such a kind that the subject is bound to present to itself in a posed or set-up way given which one can't be said to be aware of it as it is at that moment. (2011, 294)

16. Indeed, Held argues that the thickness of the present moment depends on the state of attention:

> Husserl anchors his phenomenology of time in an analysis concerning time-consciousness of a particular present. By taking sensory perception of a presently encountered object as the paradigmatic example, he makes his ground-breaking discovery, which was partly anticipated by Augustine and William James, about the concretely experienced now being not a limit without exten-sion, but rather a field of presence: the consciousness of the present expands through "protention" and "retention" to an extent which depends on the degree of focused attention. (2007, 328–29)

17. See Nikulin (2022) on boredom, especially on Heidegger's treatment (20–52).
18. See also Wittmann (2015), Wittmann et al. (2015), Droit-Volet and Dambrun (2019), Singh and Srinivasan (2019), and Kramer, Weger, and Sharma (2013).
19. This also applies to gathering multiple individuals, and it produces the same sort of harmonization; see chapter 8.
20. E.g., see the recency effect in cognitive psychology, such as Jahnke (1965).
21. The "cocktail party effect" was noted in an important early work on attention (Cherry 1953).

CHAPTER 7

1. "Now the fact that I look upon you as a fellow man does not mean that I am also a fellow man for you, unless you are aware of me. And, of course, it is quite possible that you may not be paying any attention to me at all" (Schutz 1967, 164).
2. "Every interaction is, therefore, based on an action of affecting another within a social situation. The object of the action is to lead the partner to have conscious expe-riences of a desired sort" (Schutz 1967, 159). See also the joint attention literature (e.g., Eilan et al. 2005) where this is a typical stage in child development.

3. See also Casey (2007), who considers the question of the glance in depth.

4. This citation from Schutz also touches on the sympathetic or emotional dimension, which is largely absent from Zahavi's analysis, that of the feeling for the other that can arise when each is present to the other. We can see this in Condon et al. (2013), who find under experimental conditions that meditators offer their seats to suffering individuals more frequently than nonmeditators. Although Zahavi (2019b, 251; 2015, 150) talks about proceeding empathically, the effort required to do so is not discussed. This is our most primordial responsibility, the work of attention (Jacobs 2022).

5. It is true that Zahavi employs a broader definition of experience that includes peripheral objects, but in considering our empathic relation to others it must be thematic.

6. This is similar to the approach that Zahavi (1999, chap. 8) takes in discussing the nature of the ego in Husserl, where there are three stages: inner time consciousness, attention, and act transcendence.

7. I address this question in chapter 9, where I show that, for Heidegger, attention, or human being/presencing, and being are essentially related.

8. Moreover, Zahavi and Rochat (2015) also provide support for the claim made in chapter 2 that the hermeneutical circle is present soon after birth, and thus for its *developmental* primacy. Indeed, Zahavi spends a good deal of time discussing the role of joint attention (in secondary intersubjectivity) in child development, even going so far as to point to the importance of primary intersubjectivity (otherwise known as mutual attention), where each is the object of attention of the other. In addition, he also provides support for the notion that attention is present from birth when he says, "It is now well established that we are not born in a blooming, buzzing, confusion, in some state of undifferentiated fusion with the environment, as proposed by William James over a century ago. . . . " (Zahavi and Rochat 2015, 546). So we see Zahavi cite the famous passage (James [1890] 1983, 462) that is associated with James's explanation of the role of attention. For James there is no attention without something that stands out from a background of other potential objects, so from this perspective he is indicating that a proto-attention is present from birth. Zahavi also writes: "Infants at birth open their eyes and orient their gazes toward faces, preferring face to nonface objects. . . . By 6–8 weeks . . . the gaze becomes unmistakably shared and mutual, inaugurating a proto-conversational space of social exchanges made of turn taking and a novel sensitivity" (Zahavi and Rochat 2015, 547–48).

9. Consider, for example, the world of professional baseball, which consists of the players who engage in the sport, the fans who watch the games and follow the results, those who administer the infrastructure, the gamblers, those who play fantasy baseball, etc. The people who live in this world share experience by way of attention and language, and they are (implicitly or explicitly) aware that other people are so engaged. The knowledge that there are many people who attend to the activity of professional baseball is world constitutive, for this world is what it is because everyone knows that there are multitudes of others who watch the games, either in person or by way of the various media. They each understand themselves to be interested in baseball, and they understand that others also identify themselves as such. On the

basis of this understanding, they attend to and thus share experiences of games and associated events, converse about them, and develop a language that is specific to the world of baseball, with terms such as whip, can of corn, chin music, pickle, dinger, and the Mendoza line. Of course, the world of baseball has its sub-worlds, consisting of the fans of particular teams, the players themselves, the gamblers, and the fantasy players, all of whom pay attention to the games from their particular perspectives, with ever finer divisions and associated centers of attention, shared experience, and terminology. But all of these worlds have one thing in common: If their members were to shift their attention elsewhere, the worlds would disappear. For example, if all baseball fans suddenly stopped watching baseball due to a change in understanding and redirected their attention to other sports, the world of professional baseball would vanish. The evaporation of revenue from game attendance and other sources would mean that the players would suddenly find themselves unemployed, and the world of professional baseball would no longer exist. Even if the players decided to persist in the activity, it would not be on a professional basis, and the nature of the world would be completely different without the millions of fans and other associated personnel. The world and its associated terms would descend into oblivion without the shared attention of the multitudes.

10. See also Heidegger on this in chapter 9.

CHAPTER 8

1. All references to Berger in this chapter refer to Ben Berger (2011).

2. See Loidolt (2019) on phenomenological influences in Arendt's thought. See also Topolski (2015) on relational themes in her work.

3. See also Jones (1994), Jones and Baumgartner (2005), and Baumgartner and Jones (2015) for an information-processing approach to the role of attention in politics.

4. There is a considerable literature on the psychological, health, and performance benefits of mindfulness. See, for instance, Brown, Creswell, and Ryan (2016); Treleaven (2018); Siegel (2007); and the Springer journal *Mindfulness*.

5. E.g., "I cannot fix my mental vision continually on the same thing, so as to keep perceiving it clearly " (Descartes [1641] 1984, 48).

6. See also Bellah et al., who conclude *The Good Society* with a chapter entitled "Democracy Means Paying Attention" and say, "When we are giving our full attention to something, when we are really attending, we are calling on all our resources of intelligence, feeling, and moral sensitivity" (1991, 254); and Bernstein, who says in a discussion of Dewey that "[d]emocracy is a 'way of life,' an ethical ideal that demands *active* and *constant* attention" (2005, 25).

7. See Polt (2019) for a critical review of Heidegger's approach to the political and the relation between Heidegger and Arendt in this context.

8. See Allen: "Power is a function of collective action; it emerges out of the kinds of actions that we engage in with others when we strive to achieve common ends. However, while power is the result of action (specifically, collective action), it is also,

in turn, a condition for the possibility of action. . . . For Arendt, power is generated continually through action in the public space, which space power in turn both constitutes and preserves" (2002, 138).

9. Arendt (1958, 199) cites Heraclitus DK B89 in this regard: "The world of the waking is one and common, but the sleeping turn aside each into their private world." See also Plotinus: "One must come to the sight with a seeing power made akin and like to what is seen. No eye ever saw the sun without becoming sun-like, nor can a soul see beauty without becoming beautiful" (1991, I.6.9).

10. This can be seen in the following citations from Arendt (1958): The public space, or the space of appearances is not an actuality, only a potentiality when we gather together (199), where we can be seen and heard (50). "The *polis,* properly speaking, is not the city-state in its physical location; it is the organization of the people as it arises out of acting and speaking together, and its true space lies between people living together for this purpose, no matter where they happen to be" (198). She also says, "This space does not always exist, and although all men are capable of deed and word, most of them—like the slave, the foreigner, and the barbarian in antiquity, like the laborer or craftsman prior to the modern age, the jobholder or businessman in our world—do not live in it" (199), which is consistent with the notion that presence is not constant and the associated need for actualization. And in this regard, Arendt says, "But for all its intangibility, this in-between is no less real than the world of things we visibly have in common" (183), which indicates the importance of relationality for Arendt.

11. See the literature on emotional atmosphere, e.g., Pallasmaa (2015), Trigg (2020, 2021), and Krueger (2021).

12. Is the distinction between active and passive attention black and white? As noted above, there is an undeniable marker associated with active attention, and that is the explicit self-awareness that is associated with it, not necessarily in linguistic terms but rather in one's bodily experience in the present moment. Attention can otherwise of course be more or less intense and will vary qualitatively, but this depends on background resources and how they are brought to bear in the course of engagement.

13. We see the presence of performance in the hermeneutic circle (as specified herein) because understanding is performative in nature.

14. See also: "[O]nly action is entirely dependent upon the constant presence of others" (Arendt 1958, 23) and "Their reality depends entirely upon human plurality, upon the constant presence of others who can see and hear and therefore testify to their existence" (95).

15. It should also be noted, of course, that juries made up of ordinary citizens have been a bulwark of the administration of justice for many years. See Forsyth and Morgan ([1875] 1996) on the history of trial by jury.

16. See also Fishkin (2018) and Alexander (2022) for more on deliberative democracy, and databases such as AmericaSpeaks (http://www.americaspeaks.org) and Participedia (https://participedia.net).

17. See also Muldoon (2018) on council democracy.

18. See Aristegui (2021), Monteiro (2020), and Adriansen and Krohn (2014) for relational presencing in therapeutic settings.

19. See also Block (2008) on community building where active listening (e.g., Rogers 1975, Rogers and Farson 2021) is an important skill.

CHAPTER 9

1. Although the term "being" appears in various forms in Heidegger's corpus, such as beyng and Being, I use being throughout the book.

2. "[I]ntuition is the indubitable conception of a clear and attentive mind which proceeds solely from the light of reason" (Descartes [1701] 1985, 14); "[r]ather, each of us, according to the light of his own mind, must attentively intuit only those things which are distinguished from all others" (49), "free from errors which may obscure our natural light and make us less capable of heeding reason" (16), and "[i]f one concentrates carefully, all this is quite evident by the natural light" ([1641] 1984, 32).

3. This is not an instance of the metaphysics of presence, for I have argued throughout that we can be more or less present in the course of relating to manifesting entities, which differs from an assumption of constant presence. It should also be noted that *Aufmerksamkeit* does appear once in *Being and Time* in a thematic manner at (SZ: 354/406).

4. See also: "Yet if you consider that in Logos, as the gathering toward the originally all-unifying One, something like attentiveness [*Achtsamkeit*] prevails, and if you begin to ask yourself whether attentiveness is not in fact the same as the constant waiting [*Warten*] on that which we named the pure coming, then perhaps one day you will sense that . . . the essence of the human as the being that waits is experienced" (GA 77: 225/146).

5. See also: "Nevertheless, if we are to remain underway we must first of all and constantly give attention [*beachten*] to the way [*Weg*]. The movement, step by step, is what is essential here" (GA 8: 174/170).

"When thinking is addressed by an issue and then goes after this, it can happen that it changes along the way. Thus it is advisable in what follows to attend *achten*] more to the *path* and less to the content. To duly linger upon the content would already block the progress of the lecture for us" (GA 79: 115/108).

"We would be advised, therefore, above all to pay heed [*achten*] to the way, and not to get stuck on isolated sentences and topics" (GA 7: 7/ QCT 3).

6. Heidegger discusses the paradoxical nature of being in *Basic Concepts* (GA 51).

7. In developing this view, Heidegger draws on his interpretation of the Greek experience of presencing. As he puts it in *Introduction to Metaphysics*, "Being means: standing [*stehen*] in the light, appearing, stepping into unconcealment" (GA 40: 147/154). He describes it as "what emerges from itself . . . , the unfolding that opens itself up, the coming-into-appearance in such unfolding, and holding [*Halten*] itself and persisting [*Verbleiben*] in appearance—in short, the emerging-abiding sway" (GA 40: 16/15–16).

8. "What we encounter at first is never what is near, but always only what is common. It possesses the unearthly power to break us of the habit of abiding in what is

essential, often so definitively that we never come to abide [*Wohnen*] anywhere" (GA 8: 134/129).

9. This theme appears several other times in the text. For instance, Heidegger says that ideas as commonly formed provide only "the appearances of surfaces and fore-ground facets" (GA 8: 87/82), that only a readiness to listen "allows us to surmount the boundaries in which all customary views are confined, and to reach a more open territory" (15/13), and that "the tendencies of the age always remain only in the foreground of what is" (59/55). Even the thought of Nietzsche himself "speaks only in the foreground, so long as we understand it exclusively in terms of the language of traditional thinking, instead of listening for what remains unspoken in it" (59/55). But we ordinarily do not wish to waste time tarrying (*aufhalten*) over the sense of individual words (132/127), and indeed it is very difficult for us to pay heed (*achten*) to what the words say (135/130).

10. See Dahlstrom (2017, 518), who sees the related notion of *Aufenthalt*, rendered here as staying-with or taking hold (which also involves being taking hold of us), as quite prominent in Heidegger's initial interpretation of Parmenides.

11. "Gathering is never just driving together and piling up. It maintains [*behält*] in a belonging-together that which contends and strives in confrontation. It does not allow it to decay into mere dispersion and what is simply cast down" (GA 40: 142/149).

12. "Logos needs *homologein* if present beings are to appear and shine in presenc-ing" (GA 7: 231/75).

13. "As such, the proper hearing of mortals is in a certain way the Same as the Logos. At the same time, however, precisely as *homologein* [mortal gathering] it is not the Same at all. . . . [It] only lays or lets lie whatever is already . . . gathered together and lying before us; this lying never springs from the *homologein* but rather rests in the Laying that gathers, i.e., in the Logos" (GA 7: 222/ EGT 67).

14. "For instance, when we let the sea lie before us as it lies, we, in *legein*, are already engaged in holding in attention [*in der Acht zu halten*] what lies before us. We have already taken heed of [*in die Acht genommen*] what lies before us. *Legein* is tacitly disposed to *noein*" (GA 8: 212/209, tm).

15. Thus providing support for Richard Capobianco's thesis of the primacy of being in *Heidegger's Way of Being* (2014).

16. "The attempt to hear what is expressed in the Greek words *eon emmenai*, is nothing less than the attempt to attend [*achten*] to That which calls on us to think. To the extent to which we make the effort to take heed of it [*Achtsamkeit*], we are ask-ing . . . What is That which calls on us to think, by so disposing the conjunction of *legein* and *noein* that it relates to It?" (GA 8: 234/231, tm)

17. Heidegger often describes being as that which is so near that we miss it, even though it is our essential dwelling place. As he puts it in "Letter on Humanism": "He at first fails to recognize the nearest and attaches himself to the next nearest. He even thinks that this is the nearest. But nearer than the nearest, than beings, and at the same time for ordinary thinking farther than the farthest is nearness itself: the truth of being" (GA 9: 332/253).

18. See, for example, *Introduction to Metaphysics*: "Gathering is never just driving together and piling up. It maintains in a belonging-together that which contends and

strives in confrontation. It does not allow it to decay into mere dispersion and what is simply cast down. As maintaining, *logos* has the character of pervasive sway, of *phusis*. It does not dissolve what it pervades into an empty lack of opposites; instead, by unifying what contends, the gathering maintains it in the highest acuteness of its tension" (GA 40: 142/149).

19. See also: "But what gives us the right to characterize being as presencing? This question comes too late. For this character of being has long since been decided without our contribution, let alone our merit. Thus we are bound to the characterization of being as presencing. It derives its binding force from the beginning of the unconcealment of being as something that can be said, that is, can be thought. Ever since the beginning of Western thinking with the Greeks, all saying of 'being' and 'is' is held in remembrance of the determination of being as presencing which is binding for thinking" (GA 14: 10–11/ TB 6–7).

20. See also: "The attention [*Achten*] we have given to what those words tell us has in advance prepared us to receive from their speaking a directive which carries us closer to the substance expressed in those words" (GA 8: 145/142).

21. See also: "When Plato represents being as idea and as the koinonia of the Ideas, when Aristotle represents it as energeia, Kant as position, Hegel as the absolute concept, Nietzsche as the will to power, these are not doctrines advanced by chance, but rather words of being as answers to a claim which speaks in the sending concealing itself, in the 'there is, it gives, being'" (GA 14: 13/ TB 9).

22. See also: "Withdrawal is an event [*Ereignis*]. In fact, what withdraws may even concern [*angehen*] and claim man more essentially than anything present [*Anwesende*] that strikes and touches him. . . . The event [*Ereignis*] of withdrawal could be what is most present [*Gegenwärtigste*] in all our present, and so infinitely exceed the actuality of everything actual" (GA 8: 10–11/9).

23. In addition to "Time and Being," I provide similar citations from "The Thing" and "The Principle of Identity" (*Bremen and Freiburg Lectures*, GA 79). It is interesting that all of these essays contain methodological statements regarding the role of attention. "Time and Being" and "The Principle of Identity" begin with such statements, and "The Thing" concludes with two important statements regarding *Wachsamkeit*, one of which is associated with attention (*achten*, GA 7 version epilogue). This highlights the essential role attention plays in thinking being, in that we must speak from the essential belongingness that comes to the fore by way of such an ontological effort.

24. See also Capobianco (2010, 4).

25. See "The Principle of Identity": "And being? Let us think being according to its inceptual sense as presencing [*An-wesen*]. Being does not presence for the human incidentally or as an exception. Rather, being essences and endures only in that it concernfully approaches [*an-geht*] the human. For it is the human, open for being, who first lets this arrive [*ankommen*] as presencing" (GA 79: 121/114). We also see in "The Thing" that the thing concernfully approaches (*angeht*) the human being (GA 79: 13/12).

26. This also recalls the notion that we do not gather anything ourselves but are rather more or less open for the letting of being. See also: "Man: standing within the

approach of presence, but in such a way that he receives as a gift the presencing that It gives by perceiving what appears in letting presence. If man were not the constant receiver of the gift given by the 'It gives presence,' if that which is extended in the gift did not reach man, then not only would being remain concealed in the absence of this gift, not only closed off, but man would remain excluded from the scope of: It gives being. Man would not be man" (GA 14: 16/ TB 12).

27. More insight is provided in the accompanying "Summary of a Seminar," where in comparing the statement "For the It which gives here is Being itself" (from "Letter on Humanism," GA 9: 334/254–55) with "Being vanishes in Appropriation" (cited above, GA 14: 27/ TB 22), Heidegger says that both statements "name the same matter with differing emphasis" (GA 14: 52/43). The various names for being are not ranked in order of originality but are rather "stages on a way back" (55/45). Heidegger also refers to "the entry [*Einkehr*] of thinking into Appropriation" (GA 14: 50/41), and "preparing the entry into Appropriation" (51/42), both of which mean that we must inhabit and speak from appropriation to avoid falling into ungrounded metaphysical statements. See also: "The awakening to appropriation must be experienced, it cannot be proven" (63/53).

28. See Kleinberg-Levin (2020, 2021) for a review of these fundamental notions in Heidegger, and Kleinberg-Levin (2016; 2023, chap. 5) for the role of attention in Heidegger's thought.

References

Adams, Fred, and Ken Aizawa. 2001. "The Bounds of Cognition." *Philosophical Psychology* 14: 43–64.

Albahari, M. 2009. "Witness Consciousness: Its Definition, Appearance, and Reality." *Journal of Consciousness Studies* 16, no. 1: 62–84.

Alexander, Jon. 2022. *Citizens: Why the Key to Fixing Everything Is All of Us.* Kingston upon Thames, UK: Canbury.

Allen, Amy. 2002. "Power, Subjectivity, and Agency: Between Arendt and Foucault." International Journal of Philosophical Studies 10, no. 2: 131–149.

Allport, Alan. 2011. "Attention and Integration." In *Attention: Philosophical and Psychological Essays*, edited by Christopher Mole, Declan Smithies, and Wayne Wu, 24–59. New York: Oxford University Press.

Adriansen, Hanne and Simon Krohn. 2014. "Mindfulness for Group Facilitation: An Example of Eastern Philosophy in Western Organizations." *Group Facilitation: A Research and Applications Journal* 13: 15–35.

Arendt, Hannah. 1958. *The Human Condition.* Chicago: University of Chicago Press.

———. (1961) 1977a. *Between Past and Future: Six Exercises in Political Thought.* New York: Penguin.

———. (1963) 1977b. *On Revolution.* New York: Penguin.

———. 1972. *Crises of the Republic.* New York: Harcourt Brace Jovanovich.

Aristegui, Roberto. ed. 2021. *Relational Mindfulness: Fundamentals and Applications.* Dordrecht: Springer.

Arvidson, Sven. 2006. *The Sphere of Attention.* Dordrecht: Springer.

Augustine of Hippo, Saint. (1660) 1998. *The Confessions of Saint Augustine.* Translated by Henry Chadwick. New York: Oxford University Press.

Barrett, Lisa Feldman, Batja Mesquita, Kevin N. Ochsner, and James J. Gross. 2007. "The Experience of Emotion." *Annual Review of Psychology* 58: 373–403.

Baumgartner, Frank R., and Brian D. Jones. 2015. *The Politics of Information: Problem Definition and the Course of Public Policy in America.* Chicago: University of Chicago Press.

Bayne, Tim, and Michelle Montague, eds. 2011. *Cognitive Phenomenology.* New York: Oxford University Press.

Bell, John. 1987. *Speakable and Unspeakable in Quantum Mechanics*. Cambridge: Cambridge University Press.

Bellah, Robert, Richard Madsen, William Sullivan, Ann Swidler, and Steven Tipton. 1991. *The Good Society*. New York: Knopf.

Benjamin, Andrew. 2011. *Place, Commonality and Judgment: Continental Philosophy and the Ancient Greeks*. London: Continuum.

———. 2015. *Towards a Relational Ontology: Philosophy's Other Possibility*. Albany: State University of New York Press.

Benovsky, Jiri. 2010. "Relational and Substantival Ontologies, and the Nature and the Role of Primitives in Ontological Theories." *Erkenntnis* 73, no. 1: 101–21.

Berger, Ben. 2011. *Attention Deficit Democracy: The Paradox of Civic Engagement*. Princeton, NJ: Princeton University Press.

Berger, Lawrence A. 2015. "Being There: Heidegger on Why Our Presence Matters." *New York Times, The Stone*, March 30, 2015. Reprinted in *Modern Ethics in 77 Arguments: A Stone Reader*, edited by Peter Catapano and Simon Critchley, 22–27. New York: Liveright Publishing, 2017.

———. 2016. "Dasein as Attention: The Metaphysics of the Effort of Presence." PhD diss., New School for Social Research.

———. 2020. "Attention as the Way to Being." *Gatherings: The Heidegger Circle Annual* 10: 111–56.

———. 2022. "The Divine as the Origin of the Work of Art." In *Heidegger and the Holy*, edited by Richard Capobianco, 45–61. Lanham, MD: Rowman and Littlefield.

Bernstein, Richard J. 2005. *The Abuse of Evil: The Corruption of Politics and Religion since 9/11*. Malden, MA: Polity Press.

Bitbol, Michel. 2008. "Consciousness, Situations, and the Measurement Problem of Quantum Mechanics." *Neuroquantology* 6: 203–13.

———. 2018. "Beyond Panpsychism: The Radicality of Phenomenology." In *Self, Culture and Consciousness: Interdisciplinary Convergences on Knowing and Being*, edited by Sangeetha Menon, Nithin Nagaraj, and V. V. Binoy, 337–56. Berlin: Springer.

———. 2019. "Two Aspects of Śūnyatā in Quantum Physics: Relativity of Properties and Quantum Non-Separability." In *Quantum Reality and Theory of Śūnya*, edited by Siddheshwar Rameshwar Bhatt, 93–118. Berlin: Springer.

Bitbol, Michel, and Claire Petitmengin. 2011. "On Pure Reflection: A Reply to Dan Zahavi." *Journal of Consciousness Studies* 182: 24–37.

———. 2013a. "A Defense of Introspection from Within." *Constructivist Foundations* 8: 269–79.

———. 2013b. "On the Possibility and Reality of Introspection." *Kairos, Revista de Filosofia & Ciência* 6: 173–98.

Block, Ned. 2010. "Attention and Mental Paint." *Philosophical Issues* 20: 23–63.

Block, Peter. 2008. *Community: The Structure of Belonging*. Oakland, CA: Berrett-Koehler.

Brinck, Ingar, Vasudevi Reddy, and Dan Zahavi. 2017. "The Primacy of the 'We'?" In *Embodiment, Enaction, and Culture: Investigating the Constitution of the Shared*

World, edited by Christian Tewes, Christoph Durt, and Thomas Fuchs, 131–48. Cambridge, MA: MIT Press.

Broad, C. D. 1952. "Some Elementary Reflexions on Sense-Perception." *Philosophy* 27, no. 100: 3–17.

Broadbent, Donald Eric. 1958. *Perception and Communication*. London: Pergamon Press.

Brough, John B. 2016. "Some Reflections on Time and the Ego in Husserl's Late Texts on Time-Consciousness." *Quaestiones Disputatae* 7, no. 1 (Fall): 89–108.

Brown, Kirk Warren, J. David Creswell, and Richard M. Ryan, eds. 2016. *Handbook of Mindfulness: Theory, Research, and Practice*. New York: Guilford Press.

Brown, Kirk Warren, and Richard M. Ryan. 2003. "The Benefits of Being Present: Mindfulness and its Role in Psychological Well-Being." *Journal of Personality and Social Psychology* 84: 822–48.

Campbell, John. 2002. *Reference and Consciousness*. New York: Oxford University Press.

———. 2011. "An Object-Dependent Perspective on Joint Attention." In *Joint Attention: New Developments*, edited by Axel Seeman, 415–30. Cambridge, MA: MIT Press.

Capobianco, Richard. 2010. *Engaging Heidegger*. Toronto: University of Toronto Press.

———. 2014. *Heidegger's Way of Being*. Toronto: University of Toronto Press.

———. 2022a. *Heidegger's Being: The Shimmering Unfolding*. Toronto: University of Toronto Press.

Capobianco, Richard, ed. 2022b. *Heidegger and the Holy*. Lanham, MD: Rowman and Littlefield.

Casey, Edward S. 1997. *The Fate of Place: A Philosophical History*. Berkeley: University of California Press.

———. 2007. *The World at a Glance*. Bloomington: Indiana University Press.

———. 2009. *Getting Back in Place: Toward a Renewed Understanding of the Place-World*. Bloomington: Indiana University Press.

Cherry, E. Colin. 1953. "Some Experiments on the Recognition of Speech, with One and with Two Ears." *Journal of Acoustic Society of America* 255: 975–79.

Chiesa, Alberto, Raffaella Calati, and Alessandro Serretti. 2011. "Does Mindfulness Training Improve Cognitive Abilities? A Systematic Review of Neuropsychological Findings." *Clinical Psychology Review* 31: 449–64.

Chun, Marvin M., Julie D. Golomb, and Nicholas B. Turk-Browne. 2011. "A Taxonomy of External and Internal Attention." *Annual Review of Psychology* 62: 73–101.

Clark, Andy. 1997. *Being There: Putting Brain, Body, and World Together Again*. Cambridge, MA: MIT Press.

———. 2009. "Spreading the Joy? Why the Machinery of Consciousness Is (Probably) Still in the Head." *Mind* 118: 963–93.

Clark, Andy, and David Chalmers. 1998. "The Extended Mind." *Analysis* 58, no. 1: 7–19.

Colombetti, Gianna. 2011. "Varieties of Pre-Reflective Self-Awareness: Foreground and Background Bodily Feelings in Emotion Experience." *Inquiry* 543: 293–313.

———. 2014. *The Feeling Body: Affective Science Meets the Enactive Mind.* Cambridge, MA: MIT Press.

Condon, Paul, Gaëlle Desbordes, Willa B. Miller, and David DeSteno. 2013. "Meditation Increases Compassionate Responses to Suffering." *Psychological Science* 24, no. 10: 2125–27.

Cowan, Nelson. 2008. *Attention and Memory: An Integrated Framework.* New York: Oxford University Press.

Cowley, Stephen J., João C. Major, Sune V. Steffensen, and Alfredo Dinis, eds. 2010. *Signifying Bodies: Biosemiosis, Interaction and Health.* Braga, Portugal: Faculty of Philosophy of Braga Portuguese Catholic University.

Crane, Tim. 2014. "The Intentional Structure of Consciousness." In *Aspects of Psychologism.* Cambridge, MA: Harvard University Press, 124–48.

Crary, Jonathan. 2001. *Suspensions of Perception: Attention, Spectacle, and Modern Culture.* Cambridge, MA: MIT Press.

Dahlstrom, Daniel. 2014. "Heidegger's Initial Interpretation of Parmenides: An Excursus in the 1922 Lectures on Aristotelian Texts." *Review of Metaphysics* 70: 507–27.

Dallmayr, Fred. 2014. *Mindfulness and Letting Be: On Engaged Thinking and Acting.* New York: Lexington Books.

De Jaegher, Hanna, and Enrique Di Paolo. 2007. "Participatory Sense-Making: An Enactive Approach to Social Cognition." *Phenomenology and the Cognitive Sciences* 6: 485–507.

De Jesus, Paulo. 2016. "From Enactive Phenomenology to Biosemiotic Enactivism." *Adaptive Behavior* 24, no. 2: 130–46.

Depraz, Natalie. 2004. "Where Is the Phenomenology of Attention That Husserl Intended to Perform? A Transcendental Pragmatic-Oriented Description of Attention." *Continental Philosophy Review* 37: 5–20.

———. 2014. *Attention et Vigilance: A la Croisée de la Phénoménologie et des Sciences Cognitives.* Paris: Presses Universitaires de France.

———. 2019. "Epoché in Light of Samatha-Vipassanā Meditation: Chögyam Trungpa's Buddhist Teaching Facing Husserl's Phenomenology." *Journal of Consciousness Studies* 26, no. 7–8: 49–69.

Depraz, Natalie, Francisco Varela, and Pierre Vermersch. 2003. *On Becoming Aware: A Pragmatics of Experiencing.* Amsterdam: John Benjamins.

Descartes, Rene. (1701) 1985. "Rules for the Direction of the Mind." In *The Philosophical Writings of Descartes, Vol. I*, edited by John Cottingham, Robert Stoothoff, and Dugald Murdoch, 7–78. Cambridge: Cambridge University Press.

———. (1641) 1984. "Meditations on First Philosophy." In *The Philosophical Writings of Descartes, Vol. II*, edited by John Cottingham, Robert Stoothoff, and Dugald Murdoch, 1–62. Cambridge: Cambridge University Press.

Diamond, Larry. 2019. "What I Learned from Listening to Americans Deliberate." *American Interest*, September 27, 2019. https://www.the-american-interest.com /2019/09/27/what-i-learned-from-listening-to-americans-deliberate/

Dretske, Fred I. 1995. *Naturalizing the Mind.* Cambridge, MA: MIT Press.

Dreyfus, Hubert. 2005. "Overcoming the Myth of the Mental: How Philosophers Can Profit from the Phenomenology of Everyday Expertise." APA Pacific Division Presidential Address 2005. *Proceedings and Addresses of the American Philosophical Association* 792: 47–65.

Droit-Volet, Sylvie, and Michaël Dambrun. 2019. "Awareness of the Passage of Time and Self-Consciousness: What Do Meditators Report?" *PsyCh Journal* 8: 51–65.

Edie, James. 1987. *William James and Phenomenology.* Bloomington: Indiana University Press.

Eilan, Naomi. 2005. "Joint Attention, Communication, and Mind." In *Joint Attention: Communication and Other Minds,* edited by Naomi Eilan, Christoph Hoerl, Teresa McCormack, and Johannes Roessler, 1–33. New York: Oxford University Press.

Eilan, Naomi, Christoph Hoerl, Teresa McCormack, and Johannes Roessler, eds. 2005. *Joint Attention: Communication and Other Minds.* New York: Oxford University Press.

Ellis, Ralph. 2005. *Curious Emotions: Roots of Consciousness and Personality in Motivated Action.* Amsterdam: John Benjamins.

Esfeld, Michael. 1999. "Physicalism and Ontological Holism." *Metaphilosophy* 304: 319–37.

Eysenck, Michael W. 1982. *Attention and Arousal: Cognition and Performance.* Heidelberg: Springer.

Faye, Jan. 2019. "Copenhagen Interpretation of Quantum Mechanics." *Stanford Encyclopedia of Philosophy,* edited by Edward N. Zalta (Spring 2019 Edition). https://plato.stanford.edu/archives/spr2019/entries/qm-copenhagen/.

Felder, Andrew J., Halle M. Aten, Julie A. Neudeck, Jennifer Shiomi-Chen, and Brent Dean Robbins. 2014. "Mindfulness at the Heart of Existential-Phenomenology and Humanistic Psychology: A Century of Contemplation and Elaboration." *Humanistic Psychologist* 421: 6–23.

Fink, Eugen. 1992. *Natur, Freiheit, Welt.* Würzburg: Königshausen und Neumann.

Fishkin, James S. 2018. *Democracy When the People Are Thinking: Revitalizing Our Politics through Public Deliberation.* Oxford: Oxford University Press.

Forsyth, William, and Appleton Morgan. (1875) 1996. *History of Trial by Jury.* New York: J. Cockcroft.

Fried, Gregory. 2000. *Heidegger's Polemos: From Being to Politics.* Cambridge, MA: MIT Press.

———. 2021. *Towards a Polemical Ethics: Between Heidegger and Plato.* Lanham, MD: Rowman and Littlefield.

———. 2024. *Enacting a Polemical Ethics: Through the Lens of Frederick Douglass.* Lanham, MD: Rowman and Littlefield.

Fuchs, Thomas. 2018. *The Ecology of the Brain: The Phenomenology and Biology of the Embodied Mind.* New York: Oxford University Press.

———. 2021. *In Defense of the Human Being.* New York: Oxford University Press.

Fuchs, Thomas, and Hanne De Jaegher. 2009. "Enactive Intersubjectivity: Participatory Sense-Making and Mutual Incorporation." *Phenomenology and the Cognitive Sciences* 8: 465–86.

Gallagher, Shawn. 2003. "Bodily Self-Awareness and Object Perception." *Theoria et Historia Sceintiarum: International Journal for Interdisciplinary Studies* 71: 53–68.

———. 2017. *Enactivist Interventions: Rethinking the Mind.* New York: Oxford University Press.

Gallagher, Shawn, and Dan Hutto. 2008. "Understanding Others through Primary Interaction." In *The Shared Mind: Perspectives on Intersubjectivity*, edited by Jordan Zlatev, Timothy P. Racine, Chris Sinha, and Esa Itkonen, 17–38. Amsterdam: John Benjamins.

Ganeri, Jonardon. 2017. *Attention, Not Self.* New York: Oxford University Press.

Gendlin, Eugene T. (1962) 1997. *Experiencing and the Creation of Meaning: A Philosophical and Psychological Approach to the Subjective.* Evanston, IL: Northwestern University Press.

———. 1991. "Thinking beyond Patterns: Body, Language, and Situations." In *The Presence of Feeling in Thought*, ed. B. den Ouden and M. Moen, 25–151. New York: Peter Lang.

———. 2009. "What First and Third Person Processes Really Are." *Journal of Consciousness Studies* 16: 332–62.

———. 2017a. *A Process Model.* Evanston, IL: Northwestern University Press.

———. 2017b. *Saying What We Mean: Implicit Precision and the Responsive Order*, edited by Edward S. Casey and Donata M. Schoeller. Evanston, IL: Northwestern University Press.

Gergen, Kenneth J. 2009. *Relational Being: Beyond Self and Community.* New York: Oxford University Press.

Goleman, Daniel. 2006. *Emotional Intelligence.* New York: Bantam.

Gopnik, Alison, and Andrew N. Meltzoff. 1997. *Words, Thoughts, and Theories.* Cambridge, MA: MIT Press.

Guignon, Charles. 2001. "Being as Appearing: Retrieving the Greek Experience of *Phusis*." In *A Companion to Heidegger's Introduction to Metaphysics*, edited by Richard Polt and Gregory Fried, 34–56. New Haven, CT: Yale University Press.

Gurwitsch, Aron. 1964. *The Field of Consciousness.* Pittsburgh: Duquesne University Press.

Hadot, Pierre. 1995. *Philosophy as a Way of Life.* Malden, MA: Blackwell.

Hatab, Lawrence J. 2017. *Proto-Phenomenology and the Nature of Language: Dwelling in Speech I.* London: Rowman and Littlefield International.

———. 2019. *Proto-Phenomenology, Language Acquisition, Orality, and Literacy: Dwelling in Speech II.* London: Rowman and Littlefield International.

Hatfield, Gary. 1998. "Attention in Early Scientific Psychology." In *Visual Attention*, vol. 8, Vancouver Studies in Cognitive Science, edited by Richard D. Wright, 3–25. New York: Oxford University Press.

Healey, Richard A. 2016. "Holism and Nonseparability in Physics." *Stanford Encyclopedia of Philosophy Spring 2016 Edition*, edited by Edward N. Zalta (Spring 2016 Edition). https://plato.stanford.edu/archives/spr2016/entries/physics-holism/.

Heelan, Patrick Aidan. 2016. *The Observable: Heisenberg's Philosophy of Quantum Mechanics*. New York: Peter Lang.

Held, Klaus. 2007. "Phenomenology of 'Authentic Time' in Husserl and Heidegger." *International Journal of Philosophical Studies* 15, no. 3: 327–47.

Hendricks, Marion. 2009. "Experiencing Level: An Instance of Developing a Variable from a First Person Process So It Can Be Reliably Measured and Taught." *Journal of Consciousness Studies* 16, no. 10–12: 129–55.

Henrich, Dieter. 1971. "Self-Consciousness, a Critical Introduction to a Theory." *Man and World* 4: 3–28.

Henry, Aaron, and Evan Thompson. 2013. "Witnessing from Here: Self-Awareness from a Bodily versus Embodied Perspective." In *The Oxford Handbook of the Self*, edited by Shaun Gallagher, 228–49. New York: Oxford University Press.

Heraclitus. DK B89. In *The Fragments of Heraclitus*, translated by John Burnet. Fragments of Heraclitus - Wikisource, the free online library.

Herrmann, F. W. von. 2000. *Hermeneutics and Reflection: Heidegger and Husserl on the Concept of Phenomenology*. Translated by Kenneth Maly. Toronto: University of Toronto Press.

Horgan, F., and M. Potrc. 2008. *Austere Realism: Contextual Semantics Meets Minimal Ontology*. Cambridge, MA: MIT Press.

Husserl, Edmund. 1950. *Cartesian Meditations: An Introduction to Phenomenology*. Translated by Dorian Cairns. Dordrecht: Kluwer Academic.

———. 1989. *Ideas Pertaining to a Pure Phenomenology and Phenomenological Philosophy. Second Book: Studies in the Phenomenology of Constitution*. Translated by R. Rojcewicz and A. Schuwer. Dordrecht: Kluwer. Referred to as *Ideas II*.

———. 1991. *On the Phenomenology of the Consciousness of Internal Time*. Translated by John Brough. Dordrecht: Kluwer Academic.

———. 2001. *Analyses concerning Passive and Active Synthesis: Lectures on Transcendental Logic*. Translated by Anthony Steinbock. Dordrecht: Kluwer Academic.

———. 2014. *Ideas for a Pure Phenomenology and Phenomenological Philosophy. First Book: General Introduction to Pure Phenomenology*. Translated by Daniel O. Dahlstrom. Indianapolis: Hackett. Referred to as *Ideas I*.

Ihde, Don. 1986. *Experimental Phenomenology: An Introduction*. Albany: State University of New York Press.

Jacobs, Hanne. 2022. "A Phenomenology of the Work of Attention." *Journal of Speculative Philosophy* 36, no. 2: 264–76.

Jahnke, John C. 1965. "Primacy and Recency Effects in Serial-Position Curves of Immediate Recall." *Journal of Experimental Psychology* 70: 130–32.

James, William. (1899) 1981. *Talks to Teachers*. New York: Norton.

———. (1890) 1983. *The Principles of Psychology*. Cambridge, MA: Harvard University Press.

Jasnow, Michael, and Stanley Feldstein. 1986. "Adult-Like Temporal Characteristics of Mother-Infant Vocal Interactions." *Child Development* 57: 754–61.

Jennings, Carolyn Dicey. 2012. "The Subject of Attention." *Synthese* 189: 535–54.

———. 2020. *The Attending Mind*. Cambridge: Cambridge University Press.

Jones, Bryan D. 1994. *Reconceiving Decision-Making in Democratic Politics: Attention, Choice, and Public Policy.* Chicago: University of Chicago Press.

Jones Brian D., and Frank R. Baumgartner. 2005. *The Politics of Attention: How Government Prioritizes Problems.* Chicago: University of Chicago Press.

Kabat-Zinn, Jon. 1994. *Wherever You Go, There You Are: Mindfulness Meditation in Everyday Life.* New York: Hyperion.

———. 2005. *Coming to Our Senses: Healing Ourselves and the World through Mindfulness.* New York: Hyperion.

Kahneman, Daniel. 1973. *Attention and Effort.* Englewood Cliffs, NJ: Prentice-Hall.

Kant, Immanuel. (1766) 1990. *Dreams of a Spirit Seer.* Translated by E. F. Goerwitz. London: Swan Sonnenschein.

———. (1787) 1965. *Critique of Pure Reason.* Translated by N. Kemp Smith. New York: St. Martin's Press.

Kee, Ying Hwa, and C.K. John Wang. 2008. "Relationships between Mindfulness, Flow Dispositions and Mental Skills Adoption: A Cluster Analytic Approach." *Psychology of Sport and Exercise* 9: 393–411.

Keng, Shian-Ling, Moria J. Smoski, and Clive J. Robins. 2011. "Effects of Mindfulness on Psychological Health: A Review of Empirical Studies." *Clinical Psychology Review* 31: 1041–56.

Kleinberg-Levin, David, ed. 1997. *Language beyond Postmodernism: Saying and Thinking in Gendlin's Philosophy.* Studies in Phenomenology and Existential Philosophy. Evanston, IL: Northwestern University Press.

———. 2016. "Abyssal Tonalities: Heidegger's Language of Hearkening." In *Hermeneutical Heidegger*, 222–61. Evanston, IL: Northwestern University Press.

———. 2020. *Heidegger's Phenomenology of Perception: An Introduction.* Vol. I. London: Rowman and Littlefield.

———. 2021. *Heidegger's Phenomenology of Perception: Learning to See and Hear Hermeneutically.* Vol. II. Lanham, MD: Rowman and Littlefield.

———. 2023. *Critical Studies on Heidegger: The Emerging Body of Understanding.* Albany: State University of New York Press.

Kramer, Robin S. S., Ulrich W. Weger, and Dinkar Sharma. 2013. "The Effect of Mindfulness Meditation on Time Perception." *Consciousness and Cognition* 22: 846–52.

Krueger, Joel. 2021. "Agency and Atmospheres of Inclusion and Exclusion." In *Atmospheres and Shared Emotions*, edited by Dylan Trigg, 111–31. New York: Routledge.

Kupper, Nina, Jos W. Widdershoven, and Susanne S. Pedersen. 2012. "Cognitive/Affective and Somatic/Affective Symptom Dimensions of Depression are Associated with Current and Future Inflammation in Heart Failure Patients." *Journal of Affective Disorders* 136: 567–76.

Kuravsky, Erik. 2022. "Attentiveness as an Ontological Practice in Mamardashvili and Heidegger." *InCircolo* 13: 90–110.

Langland-Hassan, Peter, and Agustin Vicente, eds. 2018. *Inner Speech: New Voices.* New York: Oxford University Press.

Leibniz, Gottfried. (1765) 1996. *New Essays on Human Understanding.* Translated by Peter Remnant and Jonathan Francis Bennett. Cambridge: Cambridge University Press.

Lerman, Sheera F., Zvia Rudich, and Golan Shahar. 2010. "Distinguishing Affective and Somatic Dimensions of Pain and Depression: A Confirmatory Factor Analytic Study." *Journal of Clinical Psychology* 66: 456–65.

Li, Jia, Sune Vork Steffensen, and Guowen Huang. 2020. "Rethinking Ecolinguistics From a Distributed Language Perspective." *Language Sciences* 80: 1–12.

Loidolt, Sophie. 2019. *Phenomenology of Plurality: Hannah Arendt on Political Intersubjectivity.* New York: Routledge.

Mackenzie, Catriona. 2019. "Feminist Innovation in Philosophy: Relational Autonomy and Social Justice." *Women's Studies International Forum* 72: 144–51.

MacLean, Katherine A., Stephen R. Aichele, David A. Bridwell, George R. Mangun, Ewa Wojciulik, and Clifford D. Saron. 2009. "Interactions between Endogenous and Exogenous Attention during Vigilance." *Attention, Perception and Psychophysics* 71, no. 5 (July): 1042–58.

Malpas, Jeff. 2018. *Place and Experience.* 2nd edition. New York: Routledge.

———. 2022. "Presence and Human Presence." https://www.academia.edu/31324336/Presence_and_Human_Presence.

Marino, Gordon. 2019. "Are You Listening?" *New York Times, The Stone,* December 17, 2019.

McGilchrist, Iain. 2019. *The Master and His Emissary: The Divided Brain and the Making of the Western World.* New Haven, CT: Yale University Press.

McNeill, William. 1999. *The Glance of the Eye: Heidegger Aristotle, and the Ends of Theory.* Albany: State University of New York Press.

Meindl, Patricia, and Dan Zahavi. 2023. "From Communication to Communalization: A Husserlian Account." *Continental Philosophy Review.* https://doi.org/10.1007/s11007-023-09601-7.

Mensch, James. 2009. "The Phenomenological Status of the Ego." *Idealistic Studies* 39, 1–3: 1–9.

Merleau-Ponty, Maurice. 1964. *Signs.* Evanston, IL: Northwestern University Press.

———. (1945) 2002. *Phenomenology of Perception.* Translated by C. Smith. London: Routledge Classics.

Mole, Christopher. 2011. *Attention Is Cognitive Unison: An Essay in Philosophical Psychology.* New York: Oxford University Press.

———. 2017. "Attention." *Stanford Encyclopedia of Philosophy,* edited by Edward N. Zalta (Fall 2017 Edition). https://plato.stanford.edu/archives/fall2017/entries/attention/.

Monteiro, Lynnette. 2020. "Mindfulness as Relational: Participants' Experience of Mindfulness-Based Programs Are Critical to Fidelity Assessments." *Global Advances in Health and Medicine* 9. https://doi.org/10.1177/2164956120940280.

Montero, Barbara. 2005. "What Is the Physical?" *The Oxford Handbook of Philosophy of Mind,* edited by Brian P. McLaughlin, Angsar Beckermann, and Sven Walter, 173–88. New York: Oxford University Press.

Montemayor, Carlos, and Harry Haroutioun Haladjian. 2015. *Consciousness, Attention, and Conscious Attention*. Cambridge, MA: MIT Press.

Morley, James. 2008. "Embodied Consciousness in Tantric Yoga and the Phenomenology of Merleau-Ponty." *Religion and the Arts* 12: 144–63.

Muldoon, James, ed. 2018. *Council Democracy: Towards a Democratic Socialist Politics*. New York: Routledge.

Nagel, Thomas. 2012. *Mind and Cosmos: Why the Materialist Neo-Darwinian Conception of Nature Is Almost Certainly False*. New York: Oxford University Press.

Natorp, Paul. 1912. *Allgemeine Psychologie*. Tubingen: J. C. B. Mohr.

Neisser, Ulrich, 1976. *Cognition and Reality*. San Francisco: W. H. Freeman.

Ney, Alissa. 2010. "Introduction." In *The Wave Function: Essays on the Metaphysics of Quantum Mechanics*, edited by Alissa Ney and David Z. Albert, 1–51. New York: Oxford University Press.

Nikulin, Dmitri. 2022. *Critique of Bored Reason: On the Confinement of the Modern Condition*. New York: Columbia University Press.

North, Paul. 2012. *The Problem of Distraction*. Stanford, CA: Stanford University Press.

O'Regan, Kevin, and Alva Nöe. 2001. "A Sensorimotor Account of Vision and Visual Consciousness." *Behavioral and Brain Sciences* 23: 939–73.

Organisation for Economic Co-operation and Development. 2020. *Innovative Citizen Participation and New Democratic Institutions: Catching the Deliberative Wave*, Paris: OECD Publishing. https://doi.org/10.1787/339306da-en.

O'Shaughnessy, Brian. 1995. "Proprioception and the Body Image." In *The Body and the Self*, edited by Jose Luis Bermudez, Anthony Marcel, and Naomi Eilan, 175–203. Cambridge, MA: MIT Press.

Pallasmaa, Juhani. 2015. "Place and Atmosphere." In *The Intelligence of Place: Topographies and Poetics*, edited by Jeff Malpas, 129–56. London: Bloomsbury Academic.

Paolini Paoletti, Michele. 2018. "Structures as Relations." *Synthese* 198: 2671–90.

Parker, Suzanne, Benjamin Nelson, Elissa Epel, and Daniel Siegel. 2016. "The Science of Presence: A Central Mediator of the Interpersonal Benefits of Mindfulness." In *Handbook of Mindfulness: Theory, Research, and Practice*, edited by Kirk Warren Brown, J. David Creswell, and Richard M. Ryan, 225–44. New York: Guilford Press.

Pashler, Harold E. 1998. *The Psychology of Attention*. Cambridge, MA: MIT Press.

Perrone-Bertolottia, M., L. Rapin, J.-P. Lachaux, M. Baciu, and H. Loevenbruck. 2014. "What Is That Little Voice Inside My Head? Inner Speech Phenomenology, Its Role in Cognitive Performance, and Its Relation to Self-Monitoring." *Behavioural Brain Research* 261: 220–39.

Petitmengin, Claire. 2009. "Editorial Introduction." *Journal of Consciousness Studies* 16, no. 10–12: 7–19.

Petitmengin, Claire, and Michel Bitbol. 2009. "The Validity of First-Person Descriptions as Authenticity and Coherence." *Journal of Consciousness Studies* 16, no. 10–12: 363–404.

Petitmengin, Claire, Anne Remillieux, and Camila Valenzuela-Moguillansky. 2018. "Discovering the Structures of Lived Experience: Towards a Micro-Phenomenological Analysis Method." *Phenomenology and the Cognitive Sciences* 18: 691–730.

Plotinus. 1991. *The Enneads*. Translated by Stephen MacKenna, edited by John Dillon. London: Penguin Books.

Polkinghorne, John, ed. 2010. *The Trinity and an Entangled World: Relationality in Physical Science and Theology*. Grand Rapids, MI: Eerdmans.

Polt, Richard. 2019. *Time and Trauma: Thinking through Heidegger in the Thirties*. London: Rowman and Littlefield.

Posner, Michael. I., and Steven E. Petersen. 1990. "The Attention System of the Human Brain." *Annual Review of Neuroscience* 13: 25–42.

Prinz, Jesse. 2012. *The Conscious Brain*. New York: Oxford University Press.

Putnam, Hilary. 1975. "What Is Mathematical Truth?" In Hilary Putnam, *Mathematics, Matter and Method*, Collected Papers Vol. 2. Cambridge: Cambridge University Press.

Ratcliffe, Matthew. 2012. "The Phenomenology of Mood and the Meaning of Life." In *The Oxford Handbook of Philosophy of Emotion*, edited by Peter Goldie, 349–72. New York: Oxford University Press.

Reddy, Vasuvi. 2005. "Before the 'Third Element': Understanding Attention to Self." In *Joint Attention: Communication and Other Minds*, edited by Naomi Eilan, C. Hoerl, T. McCormack, and J. Roessler, 85–109. New York: Oxford University Press.

———. 2011. "A Gaze at Grips with Me." In *Joint Attention: New Developments*, edited by Axel Seemann, 137–58. Cambridge, MA: MIT Press.

Roessler, Johannes. 1999. "Perception, Introspection and Attention." *European Journal of Philosophy* 71: 47–64.

Rogers, Carl. 1975. "Empathic: An Unappreciated Way of Being." *Counseling Psychologist* 5, no. 2: 2–10.

Rogers, Carl, and Richard Farson. 2021. *Active Listening*. Augusta, GA: Mockingbird Press.

Romdenh-Romluc, Komarine. 2013. "Habit and Attention." In *The Phenomenology of Embodied Subjectivity*, edited by Rasmus Thybo Jensen and Dermot Moran, 3–20. New York: Springer.

Rough, J. 2002. *Society's Breakthrough: Releasing Essential Wisdom and Virtue in All the People*. Bloomington, IN: 1stBooks Library. http://1stbooks.com.

Rouse, Joseph. 2013. "What is Conceptually Articulated Understanding?" In *Mind, Reason, and Being-in-the-World: The McDowell-Dreyfus Debate*, edited by Joseph K. Schear, 250–71. New York: Routledge.

Rovelli, Carlo. 1996. "Relational Quantum Mechanics." *International Journal of Theoretical Physics* 35: 1637–78.

Rowlands, Mark. 2010. *The New Science of the Mind: From Extended Mind to Embodied Phenomenology*. Cambridge, MA: MIT Press.

Santos, Gil C. 2015. "Ontological Emergence: How Is That Possible? Towards a New Relational Ontology." *Foundations of Science* 20: 429–46.

Schatzki, Theodore R. 2000. "Coping with Others with Folk Psychology." In *Heidegger, Coping, and Cognitive Science, Volume 2*, edited by Mark Wrathall and Jeff E. Malpas, 29–51. Cambridge, MA: MIT Press.

Scheler, Max. 2008. *The Nature of Sympathy*. London: Transaction Publishers.

Schmalzl, Laura, Chivon Powers, Anthony P. Zanesco, Neil Yetz, Erik J. Groessl, and Clifford D. Saron. 2018. "The Effect of Movement-Focused and Breath-Focused Yoga Practice on Stress Parameters and Sustained Attention: A Randomized Controlled Pilot Study." *Consciousness and Cognition* 65: 109–25.

Schmid, Hans Bernhard. 2014. "The Feeling of Being a Group: Corporate Emotions and Collective Consciousness." In *Collective Emotions*, 3–16. New York: Oxford University Press.

Schmidt, Heinz-Juergen. 2014. "Structuralism in Physics." *Stanford Encyclopedia of Philosophy*, edited by Edward N. Zalta (Winter 2014 Edition). http://plato.stanford.edu/archives/win2014/entries/physics-structuralism/.

Schumm, Bruce. 2004. *Deep Down Things: The Breathtaking Beauty of Physics*. Baltimore: Johns Hopkins University Press.

Schutz, Alfred. 1967. *The Phenomenology of the Social World*. Evanston, IL: Northwestern University Press.

Schwitzgebel, Eric. 2007. "Do You Have Constant Tactile Experience of Your Feet in Your Shoes? Or Is Experience Limited to What's in Attention?" *Journal of Consciousness Studies* 143: 5–35.

Searle, John. 2015. *Seeing Things as They Are: A Theory of Perception*. New York: Oxford University Press.

Seemann, Axel. 2011a. "Joint Attention: Towards a Relational Account." In *Joint Attention: New Developments*, edited by Axel Seemann, 183–202. Cambridge, MA: MIT Press

Seemann, Axel, ed. 2011b. *Joint Attention: New Developments*. Cambridge, MA: MIT Press.

Siegel, Daniel J. 2007. *The Mindful Brain: Reflection and Attunement in the Cultivation of Well-Being*. New York: W. W. Norton.

Singh, Amrendra, and Narayanan Srinivasan. 2019. "Concentrative (Sahaj Samadhi) Meditation Expands Subjective Time." *PsyCh Journal* 8: 28–35.

Steinbock, Anthony. 2004. "Affection and Attention: On the Phenomenology of Becoming Aware." *Continental Philosophy Review* 371: 21–43.

Steiner, David M., and Krzysztof L. Helminski. 1998. "The Politics of Relationality: From the Postmodern to Post-Ontology." *Philosophy and Social Criticism* 244: 1–21.

Stoljar, Natalie. 2018. "Feminist Perspectives on Autonomy." *Stanford Encyclopedia of Philosophy*, edited by Edward N. Zalta (Winter 2018 Edition). https://plato.stanford.edu/archives/win2018/entries/feminism-autonomy/.

Strawson, Galen. 2011. "Radical Self-Awareness." In *Self, No Self: Perspectives from Analytical, Phenomenological, and Indian Traditions*, edited by Mark Siderits, Evan Thompson, and Dan Zahavi, 274–307. New York: Oxford University Press.

Sturm, Douglas. 1998. *Solidarity and Suffering: Toward a Politics of Relationality*. Albany: State University of New York Press.

Taylor, Charles. 1985. *Human Agency and Language: Philosophical Papers 1.* Cambridge: Cambridge University Press.

———. 1995. "Heidegger, Language, and Ecology." In *Philosophical Arguments,* 100–126. Cambridge, MA: Harvard University Press.

———. 2016. *The Language Animal: The Full Shape of the Human Linguistic Capacity.* Cambridge, MA: Belknap Press.

Taylor, Charles, Patrizia Nanz, and Madeleine Beaubien Taylor. 2020. *Reconstructing Democracy: How Citizens Are Building from the Ground Up.* Cambridge, MA: Harvard University Press.

Teller, Paul. 1986. "Relational Holism and Quantum Mechanics." *British Journal for the Philosophy of Science* 37: 71–81.

Thompson, Evan. 2007. *Mind in Life: Biology, Phenomenology, and the Sciences of Mind.* Cambridge, MA: Belknap Press.

———. 2011. "Living Ways of Sense Making." *Philosophy Today* (SPEP Supplement): 114–23.

———. 2015. *Waking, Dreaming, Being: Self and Consciousness in Neuroscience, Meditation, and Philosophy.* New York: Columbia University Press.

Tocqueville, Alexis de. (1835) 1969. *Democracy in America.* Translated by George Lawrence, edited by Jacob Peter Mayer. New York: Harper Perennial Modern Classics.

Topolski, Anya. 2015. *Arendt, Levinas and a Politics of Relationality.* London: Rowman and Littlefield International.

Trigg, Dylan. 2020. "The Role of Atmosphere in Shared Emotion." *Emotion, Space and Society* 35. https://doi.org/10.1016/j.emospa.2020.100658.

Trigg, Dylan, ed. 2021. *Atmospheres and Shared Emotions.* New York: Routledge.

Treisman, Anne. 1988. "Features and Objects: The Fourteenth Bartlett Memorial Lecture." *Journal of Experimental Psychology* 402: 201–37.

———. 1996. "The Binding Problem." *Current Opinion in Neurobiology* 6, no. 2:171–78.

Treleaven, David A. 2018. *Trauma-Sensitive Mindfulness: Practices for Safe and Transformative Healing.* New York: W. W. Norton.

Trevarthen, Colwyn. 1979. "Communication and Cooperation in Early Infancy: A Description of Primary Intersubjectivity." In *Before Speech,* edited by Margaret Bullowa. Cambridge: Cambridge University Press.

———. 1993. "The Self Born in Intersubjectivity." In *The Perceived Self: Ecological and Interpersonal Sources of Self-Knowledge,* edited by Ulrich Neisser, 121–73. Cambridge: Cambridge University Press.

———. 2002. "Making Sense of Infants Making Sense." *Intellectica* 341: 161–88.

Tse, Peter U. 2010. "Attention Underlies Subjective Temporal Expansion." In *Attention and Time,* edited by Anna C. Nobre and Jennifer T. Coull, 137–50. New York: Oxford University Press.

Varela, Francisco J., Evan Thompson, and Eleanor Rosch. 2017. *The Embodied Mind, Revised Edition: Cognitive Science and Human Experience,* 2nd ed. Cambridge, MA: MIT Press.

Vermersch, Pierre. 2004. "Attention between Phenomenology and Experimental Psychology." *Continental Philosophy Review* 37: 45–81.

———. 2011. "Husserl the Great Unrecognized Psychologist! A Reply to Zahavi." Journal of Consciousness Studies 18, no. 2: 20–23.

Vörös, Sebastjan, and Michel Bitbol. 2017. "Enacting Enaction: A Dialectic between Knowing and Being." *Constructivist Foundations* 13: 31–58.

Watzl, Sebastian. 2011. "Attention as Structuring of the Stream of Consciousness." In *Attention: Philosophical and Psychological Essays* edited by Christopher Mole, Declan Smithies, and Wayne Wu, 145–73. New York: Oxford University Press.

———. 2017. *Structuring Mind: The Nature of Attention and How it Shapes Consciousness.* New York: Oxford University Press.

Weizsäcker, Viktor von. 1940. *Der Gestaltkreis. Theorie der Einheit von Wahrnehmung und Bewegung.* Stuttgart: Thieme.

Wilczek, Frank. 2008. *The Lightness of Being: Mass, Ether, and the Unification of Force.* New York: Basic Books.

Wittmann, Marc. 2015. "Modulations of the Experience of Self and Time." *Consciousness and Cognition* 38: 172–81.

Wittmann, Marc, Simone Otten, Eva Schötz, Anna Sarikaya, Hanna Lehnen, Han-Gue Jo, Niko Kohls, Stefan Schmidt, and Karin Meissner. 2015. "Subjective Expansion of Time in Meditators." *Frontiers in Psychology* 5 (January): 1–9.

Wittmann, Marc, and Stefan Schmidt. 2014. "Mindfulness Meditation and the Experience of Time." In *Meditation—Neuroscientific Approaches and Philosophical Implications*, Studies in Neuroscience, Consciousness and Spirituality 2, edited by Stefan Schmidt and Harald Walach, 199–209. Cham, Switzerland: Springer International.

Wood, David. 2019. *Reoccupy Earth: Notes Toward an Other Beginning.* New York: Fordham University Press.

Wright, Richard, and Lawrence M. Ward. 2008. *Orienting of Attention.* New York: Oxford University Press.

Wu, Wayne. 2014. *Attention.* New York: Routledge.

Yantis, Steven. 2013. *Sensation and Perception.* New York: Macmillan International Higher Education.

Zahavi, Dan. 1996. *Husserl und Die Transzendentale Intersubjektivität: Eine Antwort auf die sprachpragmatische Kritik.* Dordrecht: Kluwer Academic.

———. 1999. *Self-Awareness and Alterity: A Phenomenological Investigation.* Studies in Phenomenology and Existential Philosophy. Evanston, IL: Northwestern University Press.

———. 2002. "Merleau-Ponty on Husserl: A Reappraisal." In *Merleau-Ponty's Reading of Husserl*, edited by Ted Toadvine and Lester Embree, 3–29. Dordrecht: Kluwer Academic.

———. 2003. *Husserl's Phenomenology.* Stanford, CA: Stanford University Press.

———. 2005. *Subjectivity and Selfhood: Investigating the First Person Perspective.* Cambridge, MA: MIT Press.

———. 2010a. "Empathy, Embodiment and Interpersonal Understanding: From Lipps to Schutz." *Inquiry* 53, no. 3 (June): 285–306.

———. 2010b. "Inner (Time-) Consciousness." In *On Time—New Contributions to the Husserlian Phenomenology of Time. Phaenomenologica 197*, edited by Dieter Lohmar and Ichiro Yamaguchi, 319–39. Dordrecht: Springer.

———. 2011. "Varieties of Reflection." *Journal of Consciousness Studies* 182: 9–19.

———. 2013. "Mindedness, Mindlessness, and First-Person Authority." In *Mind, Reason, and Being-in-the-World: The McDowell-Dreyfus Debate*, edited by Jonathan Schear, 320–43. London: Routledge.

———. 2015. "Self and Other: From Pure Ego to Co-Constituted We." *Continental Philosophy Review* 48: 143–60.

———. 2017a. *Husserl's Legacy: Phenomenology, Metaphysics, and Transcendental Philosophy*. New York: Oxford University Press.

———. 2017b. "Ownership, Memory, Attention: Commentary on Ganeri." *Australasian Philosophical Review* 1, no. 4: 406–15.

———. 2018. "Collective Intentionality and Plural Pre-Reflective Self-Awareness." *Journal of Social Philosophy* 49, no. 1: 61–75.

———. 2019a. "Consciousness and Minimal Selfhood: Getting Clearer on For-Me-Ness and Mineness." In *The Oxford Handbook of the Philosophy of Consciousness,* edited by Uriah Kriegel, 635–53. New York: Oxford University Press.

———. 2019b. "Second-Person Engagement, Self-Alienation, and Group-Identification." *Topoi* 38: 251–60.

———. 2021a. "Applied Phenomenology: Why It Is Safe to Ignore the Epoché." *Continental Philosophy Review* 54: 259–73.

———. 2021b. "Phenomenology as Metaphysics." In *The Routledge Handbook of Metametaphysics*, edited by Ricki Bliss and J. T. M. Miller, 339–49. London: Routledge.

———. 2021c. "We in Me or Me in We? Collective Intentionality and Selfhood." *Journal of Social Ontology* 7, no. 1: 1–20.

———. 2022. "Individuality and Community: The Limits of Social Constructivism." *Ethos: Journal of the Society for Psychological Anthropology* 50, no. 4: 392–409.

———. Forthcoming. "I, You, and We: Beyond Individualism and Collectivism." *Australasian Philosophical Review*. (1) I, you, and we - beyond individualism and collectivism | Dan Zahavi - Academia.edu.

Zahavi, Dan, and Philippe Rochat. 2015. "Empathy Does Not Equal Sharing: Perspectives from Phenomenology and Developmental Psychology." *Consciousness and Cognition* 36: 543–53.

Zahavi, Dan, and Odysseus Stone. 2021. "Phenomenology and Mindfulness." *Journal of Consciousness Studies* 28, no. 3–4: 158–85.

———. 2022. "Bare Attention, Dereification, and Meta-Awareness in Mindfulness: A Phenomenological Critique." In *Routledge Handbook on the Philosophy of Meditation*, edited by Rick Repetti, 341–53. New York: Routledge.

Zimmerman, Michael E. 1994. *Contesting Earth's Future: Radical Ecology and Postmodernity*. Berkeley: University of California Press.

Zubizarreta, Rosa. 2014. "Zuhören, um der Lebendigkeit Raum zu Geben." In *Dynamic Facilitation: Die erfolgreiche Moderationsmethode für schwierige und verfahrene Situationen*, edited by Matthias zur Bonsen and Rosa Zubizarreta, 182–200. Weinheim: Beltz Verlag. English translation at https://www.academia .edu/97289152/Listening_for_Aliveness.

Index

absorption, 146
action, attention and, 13; Arendt
on, 183, 186–87; body-
constituting and, 56
active attention, 3, 44–45, 183, 218n8;
attention deficit democracy and,
174–75; autonomy and, 145,
177–78; background for, 104;
definition of, 10, 139; in Eastern
religions, 105; experiments in,
106–7; as explicit self-awareness,
50, 93, 107; Heidegger on, 217n2;
in hermeneutical circle of attention
and, 41; Husserl on, 100–101, 106–7,
109, 118–19; immanent reflexivity
from, 122; indubitability of, 107–9;
integration enabled by, 140; intuition
and, 107; James on, 101, 218n9,
231n8; lived body-environment
and, 106, 142; neuroscience of,
87; passive attention compared to,
233n12; phenomenological reflective
attentiveness and, 104–5; placement
of attention and, 53–54; political
activity and, 149; primacy of, 44,
105; self-manifestation and, 94–95;
unification through, 104–9; Zahavi
on, 115–16, 169–70
actualization, 157

affection, self-manifestation and, 93
analytical metaphysics, 9
Anwesen. See being as presencing
apperception, 221n20, 228n9
appropriation, 211, 237n27
Arendt, Hannah, 6–7, 233nn9–10; on
action, 183, 186–87; on attention,
183–86; on citizen councils, 188;
on consent, 184–86; *The Human
Condition,* 181; on natality, 183,
192; on political engagement,
176; on power, 183–86; public
spaces for, 173, 181–83; speech as
ephemeral, 187
Aristotle, on attention, 217n3
articulation, hermeneutical truth
and, 65–66, *66*
attention: as abyssal ground, 170–72,
186–87; in academic literature,
11–16; Arendt on, 183–86; bare,
139; bottom-up, 81; circumspection
and, 218n4; in cognitive science,
1–2, 218n7; concreteness of, 42;
consciousness as distinct from, 24,
28; context for, 132; definitions of,
139; deployment of, 38, 118–19,
155–57, 212; direction of, 135;
in early philosophical discourses,
217n3; efforts of, 3; endogenous,

placement of attention, *54, 166,* 166–67,
168; active attention and, 53–54;
bodily understanding and, 55;
Focusing and, 55–56; harmonization
of the body in action, 52; Heidegger
on, 52–53; lived body-environment
and, 51, 53–55; passive attention
and, 54–55; reflection and, 52
political engagement: active attention
and, 149; Arendt on, 176; mindful,
174, 180–87, 190–91. *See also* public
engagement
political realities, formation of, 80
political science, attention as limited
capacity resource, 10
political thought, 9
power: Arendt on, 183–86; of consent,
184–86; hermeneutical truth and,
66–67; nature of, 191–92
pre-reflective experience, 115–16,
127, 130; background processes
as, 226n19
pre-reflective self-awareness, 90, 130;
minimal self and, 131
presence: engagement and, 219n18;
metaphysics of, 155, 234n3
presencing: being as presencing,
206–11; first foothold on the way
to being, 210. *See also* human
presencing
private engagement, mindfulness
in, 173–74
private spaces, 182
processing resources, 4
proprioception, 221n19, 229n12
protention, 230n16
protoconversations, 60, 63
public engagement, mindfulness
in, 173–74
public-private divide, attention and:
deliverances of attention, 80–81;
joint attention, 77–78; language in,
77; Merleau-Ponty on, 79; mutual
attention, 78; phenomenology and,

79; public accessibility and, 78;
relational holism and, 80
public spaces, 221n15; for Arendt, 173,
181–83; citizens in, 186; mindful
political engagement and, 181–83
pure ego, 92, 96, 108–9, 153, 162; self-
manifestation and, 95

quantum physics, 73–75
quarks, 77–78

radical ecology movement, 193
reality. *See* theory-reality divide
reasoning. *See* hermeneutical reasoning
reciprocal causation, 85
reflection, 30, 225n9; active attention
and, 122; through body, 31–32;
Herder on, 62; Husserl on, 113–14;
immanent, 122; intuition and, 125;
language and, 62; phenomenological,
98, 106–7, 112–14, 116, 121, 227n1;
placement of attention and, 52; pre-
reflective experience, 115–16, 127,
130; pre-reflective self-awareness,
90; self-awareness and, 113; Zahavi
on, 111–16
relational holism: enactivist thought
and, 9; limited conception of
nature and, 8; in neuroscience of
attention, 83–86; phenomenology
and, 9; physicalism and, 8;
public-private divide and, 80;
representationalism and, 8
relationality, in physics, 71–74
relational presencing, 189
relaxation, mindfulness and, 140
representationalism: Heidegger on limits
of, 203; relational holism and, 8
representationalist model, of
attention, 26
retention, 230n16
reversibility thesis, 31
Rousseau, Jean-Jacques, 176

Sartre, Jean-Paul, 112

About the Author

Lawrence Berger began writing on the philosophy of attention in 1982, and his first article was published in 1989 ("Economics and Hermeneutics," in *Economics and Philosophy*, Cambridge University Press). After receiving a PhD in applied economics from the Wharton School in 1985, he was a business school professor at the University of Iowa from 1985 to 1989, then went back to Wharton as a professor from 1989 to 1994. He then worked as a professional economist for a number of years while continuing his philosophical work on attention, eventually receiving a PhD in philosophy at the New School in 2016. His March 2015 article in the *New York Times*, "Being There: Heidegger on Why Our Presence Matters," was the most emailed article of the day on nyt.com and attracted more than five hundred comments. The present book is a full-length version of the article with an application to politics. He currently teaches philosophy at Marist College.

Printed in the USA
CPSIA information can be obtained
at www.ICGtesting.com
LVHW092042271223
767549LV00004B/68